Activist Citizenship in Southeast Europe

This volume explores recent episodes of progressive citizen-led mobilisation that have spread across Southeast Europe over the past decade. These protests have allowed citizens the opportunity to challenge prevailing notions of *citizenship* and provided the chance to redress what is perceived to be the unjust balance of power between elites and the masses. Each contribution debunks the myth of inherently passive post-socialist populations imitating West European forms of civil society activism. Rather, we gain a deeper sense of progressive and innovative forms of activist citizenship that display essentialist and particular forms of protest in combination with the antics of global protest networks. Through richly detailed case study research, the authors illustrate that whilst the catalysts for protest in Southeast Europe were invariably familiar (the expanse of private ownership into urban public spaces; the impact of austerity), the pathology of such protests were undoubtedly indigenous in origin, reflecting the particular post-socialist/post-authoritarian trajectories of these societies.

The chapters in this book were originally published as a special issue in *Europe-Asia Studies*.

Adam Fagan is Professor of European Politics at Queen Mary University of London, UK. His research interest is in civil society and social movements, with a particular focus on the post-authoritarian polities of Central and Eastern Europe and the Western Balkans. His most recent edited book is *The Routledge Handbook of East European Politics* (co-edited with Petr Kopecký). Fagan is also the co-editor in chief of *East European Politics*.

Indraneel Sircar is a Fellow at the London School of Economics and Political Science, UK. His research focuses primarily on Europeanisation and citizen-led mobilisation in the Western Balkans.

Routledge Europe-Asia Studies Series
A series edited by Terry Cox, University of Glasgow

The **Routledge Europe-Asia Studies Series** focuses on the history and current political, social and economic affairs of the countries of the former 'communist bloc' of the Soviet Union, Eastern Europe and Asia. As well as providing contemporary analyses, it explores the economic, political and social transformation of these countries and the changing character of their relationships with the rest of Europe and Asia.

Recent titles in this series include:

Self-Determination after Kosovo
Edited by Annemarie Peen Rodt and Stefan Wolff

State against Civil Society
Contentious Politics and the Non-Systemic Opposition in Russia
Edited by Cameron Ross

The State of Democracy in Central and Eastern Europe
A Comparative Perspective
Edited by Ramona Coman and Luca Tomini

The Ukraine Conflict
Security, Identity and Politics in the Wider Europe
Edited by Derek Averre and Kataryna Wolczuk

Russian Modernisation
Structures and Agencies
Edited by Markku Kivinen and Terry Cox

Authoritarian Powers
Russia and China Compared
Edited by Stephen White, Ian McAllister & Neil Munro

Activist Citizenship in Southeast Europe
Edited by Adam Fagan and Indraneel Sircar

Please find a full list of titles in this series at https://www.routledge.com/Routledge-Europe-Asia-Studies/book-series/REAS.

Activist Citizenship in Southeast Europe

Edited by
Adam Fagan and Indraneel Sircar

First published 2019
by Routledge
2 Park Square, Milton Park, Abingdon, Oxon, OX14 4RN, UK

and by Routledge
711 Third Avenue, New York, NY 10017, USA

Routledge is an imprint of the Taylor & Francis Group, an informa business

Introduction, Chapters 1, 3–5, 7 © 2017 University of Glasgow
Chapter 2 © 2017 Astrid Reinprecht. Originally published as Open Access.
Chapter 6 © 2017 Piotr Goldstein. Originally published as Open Access.

With the exception of Chapters 2 and 6, no part of this book may be reprinted or
reproduced or utilised in any form or by any electronic, mechanical, or other means,
now known or hereafter invented, including photocopying and recording, or in any
information storage or retrieval system, without permission in writing from the
publishers. For details on the rights for Chapter 2 and 6, please see the chapters' Open
Access footnotes.

Trademark notice: Product or corporate names may be trademarks or registered
trademarks, and are used only for identification and explanation without intent to
infringe.

British Library Cataloguing-in-Publication Data
A catalogue record for this book is available from the British Library

ISBN13: 978-1-138-60489-6

Typeset in Times New Roman
by codeMantra

Publisher's Note
The publisher accepts responsibility for any inconsistencies that may have arisen
during the conversion of this book from journal articles to book chapters, namely the
possible inclusion of journal terminology.

Disclaimer
Every effort has been made to contact copyright holders for their permission to reprint
material in this book. The publishers would be grateful to hear from any copyright
holder who is not here acknowledged and will undertake to rectify any errors or
omissions in future editions of this book.

Contents

Citation Information	vi
Notes on Contributors	viii

Introduction: Activist Citizenship in Southeast Europe   1
Adam Fagan & Indraneel Sircar

1   Reshaping Citizenship through Collective Action: Performative and
Prefigurative Practices in the 2013–2014 Cycle of Contention
in Bosnia & Hercegovina   10
Chiara Milan

2   Between Europe and the Past—Collective Identification and Diffusion of
Student Contention to and from Serbia   26
Astrid Reinprecht

3   From Protest to Party: Horizontality and Verticality on the Slovenian Left   47
Alen Toplišek & Lasse Thomassen

4   Contesting Neoliberal Urbanism on the European Semi-periphery: The
Right to the City Movement in Croatia   65
Danijela Dolenec, Karin Doolan & Tomislav Tomašević

5   'We Are All Beranselo': Political Subjectivation as an Unintended
Consequence of Activist Citizenship   94
Bojan Baća

6   Post-Yugoslav Everyday Activism(s): A Different Form of Activist Citizenship?   119
Piotr Goldstein

7   The Role of the Feminist Movement Participation during the Winter 2012
Mobilisations in Romania   137
Alexandra Ana

Index   163

Citation Information

The chapters in this book were originally published in the journal *Europe-Asia Studies*, volume 69, issue 9 (November 2017). When citing this material, please use the original page numbering for each article, as follows:

Introduction
Activist Citizenship in Southeast Europe
Adam Fagan & Indraneel Sircar
Europe-Asia Studies, volume 69, issue 9 (November 2017) pp. 1337–1345

Chapter 1
Reshaping Citizenship through Collective Action: Performative and Prefigurative Practices in the 2013–2014 Cycle of Contention in Bosnia & Hercegovina
Chiara Milan
Europe-Asia Studies, volume 69, issue 9 (November 2017) pp. 1346–1361

Chapter 2
Between Europe and the Past—Collective Identification and Diffusion of Student Contention to and from Serbia
Astrid Reinprecht
Europe-Asia Studies, volume 69, issue 9 (November 2017) pp. 1362–1382

Chapter 3
From Protest to Party: Horizontality and Verticality on the Slovenian Left
Alen Toplišek & Lasse Thomassen
Europe-Asia Studies, volume 69, issue 9 (November 2017) pp. 1383–1400

Chapter 4
Contesting Neoliberal Urbanism on the European Semi-periphery: The Right to the City Movement in Croatia
Danijela Dolenec, Karin Doolan & Tomislav Tomašević
Europe-Asia Studies, volume 69, issue 9 (November 2017) pp. 1401–1429

Chapter 5
'We Are All Beranselo': Political Subjectivation as an Unintended Consequence of Activist Citizenship
Bojan Baća
Europe-Asia Studies, volume 69, issue 9 (November 2017) pp. 1430–1454

CITATION INFORMATION

Chapter 6
Post-Yugoslav Everyday Activism(s): A Different Form of Activist Citizenship?
Piotr Goldstein
Europe-Asia Studies, volume 69, issue 9 (November 2017) pp. 1455–1472

Chapter 7
The Role of the Feminist Movement Participation during the Winter 2012 Mobilisations in Romania
Alexandra Ana
Europe-Asia Studies, volume 69, issue 9 (November 2017) pp. 1473–1498

For any permission-related enquiries please visit:
http://www.tandfonline.com/page/help/permissions

Notes on Contributors

Alexandra Ana is a PhD Candidate in Political Science and Sociology at the Italian Institute of Human Sciences at the Scuola Normale Superiore di Pisa, Italy. Her current research interests concentrate on social movements in comparative perspective, feminist movements, the political economy and cultural sociology of protests, the Europeanisation of social movements, post-transition and resistance in Central and Eastern Europe, feminist perspectives on power, cyber-protest and new media, global and local inequalities, and social justice.

Bojan Baća is a PhD candidate in Sociology and a Researcher in the Global Digital Citizenship Lab, both at York University, Toronto, Canada. His research focuses on the relationship between socio-economic/political transformation and civic engagement in post-socialist societies and, more broadly, on the role of activist citizenship and social movements in democratisation processes.

Danijela Dolenec is an Assistant Professor in the Faculty of Political Science at the University of Zagreb, Croatia. Her primary interest is in post-socialist democratisation. She received the 2013 National Science Award for her book *Democratic Institutions and Authoritarian Rule in Southeast Europe* (2013).

Karin Doolan is an Associate Professor in the Department of Sociology at the University of Zadar, Croatia. Her academic interests are social class inequalities; educational inequalities; and Bourdieu's theory of practice, higher education policies, and qualitative research methods.

Adam Fagan is Professor of European Politics at Queen Mary University of London, UK. His research interest is in civil society and social movements, with a particular focus on the post-authoritarian polities of Central and Eastern Europe and the Western Balkans. His most recent edited book is *The Routledge Handbook of East European Politics* (2017, co-edited with Petr Kopecký). Fagan is also the co-editor in chief of *East European Politics*.

Piotr Goldstein is a British Academy Postdoctoral Research Fellow in Russian and East European Studies at the University of Manchester, UK. His research interests include civil society and broadly understood activism in South-/Central-Eastern Europe, minority activism, the East-West paradigm in civil society and social movements/popular protest research, mixed methods research, and visual and sensory ethnography.

Chiara Milan is a Postdoctoral Research Fellow in Political Science and Sociology at the Institute of Humanities and Social Sciences at the Scuola Normale Superiore di Pisa,

NOTES ON CONTRIBUTORS

Italy. Her research interests are social movements and contentious politics in South-Eastern Europe, civil society development, civic participation, and post-Communist transition and European integration.

Astrid Reinprecht works at the Austrian Society for Environment and Technology. She was the Head of Media and Communication at the Kelman Institute, Vienna, Austria from January 2016 to December 2017. As a trained mediator, her special interests are in political, intercultural, societal, and transnational conflicts. She has published on human rights, democracy, participation, and mediation.

Indraneel Sircar is a Fellow at the London School of Economics and Political Science, UK. His research focuses primarily on Europeanisation and citizen-led mobilisation in the Western Balkans. Between 2013 and 2016, he worked as a Postdoctoral Researcher at Queen Mary University of London, UK for the EU FP7-funded project 'Maximizing the integration capacity of the European Union', examining the influence of EU strategies in transforming the rule of law in the Western Balkans.

Lasse Thomassen is a Reader at the School of Politics and International Relations at the Queen Mary University of London, UK. His current research focuses on three areas: debates within radical democratic theory and radical politics (autonomy vs hegemony, the indignados movements, Podemos, etc.); identity politics and the politics of inclusion, particularly in the context of the UK and Europe; and new approaches to the concept of representation.

Tomislav Tomašević is Programme Manager at the Institute for Political Ecology, Croatia. His research interests are related to commons, transformation of public services, critical urban theory, environmental justice, and social movements. He has received several awards and scholarships, including the Marshal Memorial Fellowship, Chevening Fellowship, and Cambridge Overseas Trust Fellowship.

Alen Toplišek is a Teaching Associate at the School of Politics and International Relations at Queen Mary University of London, UK. His research interests are: contemporary political theory; anti-politics; de-politicisation studies; social movements and populism studies; and critical political economy. His current research focuses on the de-politicisation of politics in neoliberal societies, left-wing populist political parties and social movements, and the emergence of resistance in times of crisis.

Introduction: Activist Citizenship in Southeast Europe

ADAM FAGAN & INDRANEEL SIRCAR

THE CONTRIBUTIONS TO THIS COLLECTION ON PROTEST AND ACTIVIST citizenship in Southeast Europe (SEE)[1] delve far beyond discussions about the efficacy and legitimacy of non-governmental organisations (NGOs) and social movement organisations that have dominated the study of civil society in post-communism. They focus instead on how certain types of citizenship—most notably 'activist citizenship'—are forged or not forged; how citizens are drawn into 'acts of citizenship' (Isin 2008, 2009) other than through joining or supporting established NGOs. The essays illustrate what political scientists find it difficult to uncover—non-institutionalised and non-formal modes of collective action, symbolic politics, cultural challenges, acts of citizenship, and participation that defy notions of 'weak civil society' (Rose 2001; Crotty 2003; Howard 2003) or the 'NGO-isation' of civil society spaces (Jacobsson & Saxonberg 2013).

They each critique the NGO-isation thesis—the dominance in post-communist states of externally funded, apolitical, and non-participatory professional organisations focused on policy and governance (Quigley 2000; Wedel 2001; Mandel 2002)—by illustrating the activism that takes place outside of NGOs or completely separate from them. They thus contest the assertion that NGOs have colonised the civil society space and interrogate the notion that a premature institutionalisation of civil society organisations has killed off political activism and any vestige of radicalism.

Each case study highlights the extent to which a rejection, or at least a suspicion, of the institutions of liberal democracy as the mechanisms for political participation underpins much of the activism. This in itself does not make the SEE states under scrutiny here particularly unusual. Cultural protest and non-institutionalised forms of activism have long been seen in established Western democracies (Melucci 1988) and have, as Dolenec *et al*. observe, become a global phenomenon since the financial crisis of 2008.

What, then, is surprising or specific about contemporary activism in these countries? First and foremost, it is that this level of civic engagement and activist citizenship is occurring in countries that we were told had 'weak' civil societies and very little civic participation (Petrova & Tarrow 2007). Citizens were apparently politically timid due to the lingering legacy of Soviet-style authoritarianism, because of their failure to fully grasp democratic politics, or

---

[1]In this special issue, Southeast Europe will be understood to mean Albania, Bulgaria, Romania, and the former Yugoslav territories (Bosnia & Hercegovina, Croatia, Kosovo, Macedonia, Montenegro, Serbia, and Slovenia).

© 2017 University of Glasgow

through the engendered passivity of liberal democratic institutions. There has been barely any dissent from the assertion that citizens of post-socialism have neither aptitude nor appetite for radicalism or protest.

Second, this collection of scholarship finally lays to rest the notion of post-socialist semi-peripheral Europe 'catching up' with the hinterland of mature liberal democracies in terms of civil society activism and social movement development. The implicit assumption in much of the extant literature of post-socialist states emulating a model of Western-inspired activism based on channelling participation through liberal institutions and deploying the strategies of conventional social movements as a primary stage prior to the likely emergence of more radical and 'progressive' forms of activism is a myth squarely debunked. The activism of SEE is clearly not a stage behind; an immature or amateur version of what we may find in the UK, France, Spain, or Greece. The countries and their activists studied herein are potentially trailblazing forms of activist citizenship that fundamentally challenge the core–periphery power relationship that has dominated post-socialist studies for three decades. What seemingly gives their activism poignancy and fervour is a disillusionment with the institutions of liberal democracy that stretches back much further than the financial crisis of a decade ago. The message from each contribution is loud and clear: these countries should not be considered as being a step behind the West, nor are they necessarily emulating Western patterns of activism: local contexts are giving rise to expressions of activist citizenship that are certainly similar to what has been seen across the rest of Europe, but some of the mobilisations appear to be genuinely innovative.

A third contribution made by these authors is to emphasise the significance of what James C. Scott (1990) refers to as 'infra-politics', forms of activism that are often dismissed as occurring 'below the parapet', as an elementary stage in the emergence of institutionalised civil society and as having little impact on the formal political sphere. What each of the contributions illustrates is that the cultural challenges or the incidents of symbolic 'everyday' activism that occur often on a very small scale—in the bookshop cafes of Serbia (see Goldstein in this collection) or the photographs and fabricated images on billboards in rural Montenegro (see Baća in this collection) are vital. This is not treated here as evidence of an immature or immanent civil society, but as the life-blood of a civil society that cannot be reduced to the number of registered NGOs.

All the contributions draw on Isin's notion of 'activist citizenship'. For Isin (2008, 2009), 'active' citizenship is when an individual performs her/his duties within the (democratic) polity, such as voting, taxpaying, and adhering to the legal order. On the other hand, 'activist' citizenship impels individuals to break with prevailing routines and practices in order to bring into being new political subjects making justice claims (Isin 2008, 2009). Activist citizens do this through 'acts of citizenship', which are acts that constitute what is meant by 'citizens' (insiders) as opposed to 'aliens' (outsiders) (Isin 2008).

In a nutshell, the focus in this collection is how citizens across SEE are, in the context of semi-authoritarian or partially democratic contexts, learning and developing their citizenship. Supporting a Western-funded NGO by making a donation or attending a meeting or demonstration is not an expression of activist citizenship; it may well be a valuable precursor, but it tells us relatively little about the substantive interaction between citizens and elites, between the powerful and the powerless. NGOs can be weak, poor, and ignored by swathes of citizens, but activist citizenship and political contestation may well be very developed and effective. Likewise, the NGO sector and formal civil society can be strong, established, and highly prominent without any challenge whatsoever to the power of capital or corrupt elites emerging from citizens or marginalised voices.

The overarching question that emerges from the collection—and the focus of future research, no doubt—is whether the emergence of this sort of activist citizenship in a small corner of Europe is best understood as a 'local' response to a much broader crisis of representative institutions of liberal democracy, or whether there is in fact something much more specific and noteworthy emerging that challenges our theoretical and empirical understanding of contemporary activism. What each contribution seems to conclude is that there is indeed something more that has been unearthed. For Dolenec *et al.*, the 'right to the city' movement in Zagreb is indeed 'part of a global phenomenon of resisting neoliberal transformations, [but] … its local configuration relates to the context of the post-socialist semi-periphery'. However, by highlighting the particularly aggressive reconfiguration of public spaces and the corrupt processes surrounding privatisation, she encourages us to directly question the idea that protest in the Balkans and activism in cities is best studied as merely a local manifestation of a global phenomenon. The intensity of the crisis and the response to it in SEE brings greater clarity regarding what types of activist citizenship have the most impact.

The imprint of the post-socialist, semi-peripheral European 'local' resonates through each of the contributions. To interpret SEE manifestations of activist citizenship simply as part of the 'global crisis' fails to acknowledge how the legacies of authoritarianism, combined with the two decades of post-socialist, post-conflict development, have led to a particular depoliticisation of these countries. This may well have been accentuated by the 2008 crisis and the austerity that followed, but in the case of SEE, the political disconnect between citizens and elites reaches back much further. For Montenegrin, Serbian, or Romanian activists, their democratic institutions have not suddenly started to degenerate or lose their capacity to channel societal interests to elites. Rather, electoral democracy and the formal structures of civil society have arguably never been perceived to fully exist or function. The protests in SEE may look the same as those which occur elsewhere, but the empirical cases we are introduced to in this special issue are less about liberal institutions in crisis and more about the myth of liberal institutions having been consolidated in countries where established elites have maintained a steadfast grip on power, through privatisation, 'democratisation' and Europeanisation.

Contributions to the special issue

A recurrent theme across the contributions in the special issue is the evolutionary and strategic nature of the acts of citizenship explored. Although these movements are supposedly 'leaderless' and horizontal, it is crucial to reveal the forms of authority and agency provided by (formal or informal) leaders which significantly affect trajectory and outcomes (Aidukaitė 2016). Hence, one must not assume 'spontaneity' (Dalakoglou 2012; Flesher Fominaya 2015) to explain the start of citizen-led movements, since this endorses the mythology of the protest which activists may want to portray (Polletta 1998).

A second feature of the contributions is the complementarity of the literatures of radical politics and social movements in exploring the post-2008 protest movements in SEE and in other parts of the world. Isin (2017) highlights that performative citizenship rests on rights-related claim-making that is central to the framing of social movements and episodes of contentious politics (Tilly 2008). However, these theories focus less on the structural conditions which allow certain moments of liminality (Turner 1969), conditioned by changes in political opportunity and resource mobilisation that enable the subjects to break habitus and bring the new actor into being. By contrast, social movement studies often closely explore the contextual factors which facilitate or impede the development of protest movements. There is also a focus on identifying who protests, and Della Porta (2015) identifies the citizen as the subject of anti-austerity protests. However, there is little theoretical focus on the acts that brought into being the '99%' (the citizen) in contrast to the '1%' (predatory elite), or the tensions between the claims to justice and the methods used to address them. It is here that the radical politics literature is crucial.

Chiara Milan investigates the 2013 and 2014 protest cycles in Bosnia & Hercegovina and illustrates how they differ, since both are instances of citizen-led mobilisation beyond the practices of 'active citizenship'. The author complements Isin's (2017) notion of performative citizenship with Leach's (2013) concept of 'prefigurative politics'. In other words, the means employed by social movements shape the ultimate objectives. For example, in the case of Bosnia & Hercegovina, the establishment of direct-democratic citizen-led assemblies in 2014 prefigured the aim of creating a more egalitarian society (in contrast to 2013 demonstrations). In 2013, participants protested the lack of a nationwide law on ID cards, which prevented a critically ill infant from seeking medical care abroad, by organising protest marches. One year later, violent protests in response to the closure of privatised factories in the eastern city of Tuzla soon gave way to the establishment of citizen-organised popular assemblies ('plenums') similar to those set up during the anti-austerity protests in Spain and in Greece. As in the cases of Croatia (see Dolenec *et al.* in this collection) and Montenegro (see Baća in this collection) examined in this special issue, participants in Bosnia & Hercegovina underwent a learning process by which they gradually used more radical and disruptive modes of dissent across waves of protest. However, unlike these other cases, the protests in Bosnia & Hercegovina did not trigger the constitution of a new type of de-ethnified citizen resting on a rights-based notion of citizenship.

Astrid Reinprecht looks at student protests in Serbia since 2005, which predated the other instances of citizen-led mobilisation studied in this special issue. Student protest movements in the former Yugoslavia were amongst the first in the region to recognise the connection between the adverse effects of neoliberalisation and the post-socialist transition (Baćević 2010). The trigger for student dissent was the signing of the declaration that marked Serbia's accession to the European Higher Education Area (commonly known as the 'Bologna Declaration'). At the end of 2005, activists from the University of Belgrade carried out a number of protest actions, including blockades, demonstrations in front of government buildings, and 'performances'. However, these activities did not result in significant public support or media coverage. In subsequent actions, student activists occupied the University of Belgrade's Faculty of Philosophy (2006) and Faculty of Arts (2007). By conducting interviews with activists, the author shows that the two dominant frames devised for the occupations were those of commercialisation and direct democracy. Critics of the Bologna Process across Europe claimed that the objective of creating unified standards for university degrees was at best unnecessary bureaucratisation and at worst the marketisation of higher education. However, activists could not invoke the 1968 Belgrade university occupations without accusations of 'Yugonostalgia', nor could they connect to the legacies of the anti-Milosevic

ACTIVIST CITIZENSHIP IN SOUTHEAST EUROPE

protests in 2000, carried out by liberal activists, whilst critiquing neoliberalism. Ultimately, the Belgrade activists drew on the frames (commercialisation) and repertoires (occupation, popular assemblies) of student activism in Western Europe, particularly the UK, France, and Greece. The occupations in Belgrade inspired similar actions in Zagreb (Ćulum & Doolan 2015) and other places in former Yugoslavia, and *via* direct contacts (for example, at the Subversive Festival) and indirect emulation, through which a new student manifestation of 'activist citizen' was constituted (Baća 2017).

Lasse Thomassen and Alen Toplišek critically assess the concept of horizontality (Sitrin 2012, 2014) underlying the direct-democratic frame highlighted by Reinprecht which was at the heart of the popular assemblies in SEE and elsewhere in the post-2008 period. The authors investigate the case of Slovenia, which stands out in SEE as the only case where an anti-austerity movement formed the basis for a political party (the United Left) that not only formed in the wake of the protests, but also garnered sufficient support to earn parliamentary representation. As such, it is the only example of a successful Podemos-like 'movement party' in SEE (Kitschelt 2006; Della Porta *et al.* 2017). The authors conclude that, contrary to prevailing views by Sitrin and other political philosophers, it is impossible to disentangle horizontality and verticality. This is because, despite the insistence on a leaderless movement, there are informal leaders who come to represent or embody the movement externally (see Ana in this collection for the Romanian case). Moreover, for horizontality to function in the protest committees, it was necessary for some verticality (for example, the authority of a chairperson) to guarantee the preservation of the horizontal guiding principle. Once elements of the movement formed into the United Left, the party sought to preserve hybridity between verticality and horizontality by having elected representatives in legislatures and leaders like other parties, yet also having more informal features such as working groups and local committees. It remains to be seen whether this delicate balance between horizontality and verticality can be preserved in the United Left.

Danijela Dolenec, Karin Doolan, and Tomislav Tomašević examine the trajectory of the Zagreb Right to the City Movement. In particular, the authors question the 'iron law of oligarchy' posited by Michels (1968) and empirically validated by Rucht (1999) and others. According to Michels, social movements that institutionalise into conventional forms of political participation (that is, parties) de-radicalise, become co-opted into the political system, and lose the potential to trigger fundamental social change. This resonates with Tarrow (2011), who differentiates between trajectories of institutionalisation (as Michels does) contrasted with radicalisation. Tarrow further argues that social movements who wish to stay true to their radical values eventually burn out as a result of the challenges of sustaining anti-establishment mobilisation without a strong bureaucratic structure. However, the authors show how the Right to the City in Zagreb problematises this 'iron law'. Using interviews with activists triangulated with primary and secondary materials, the authors show how the movement began as a constellation of NGOs willing to collaborate with city authorities ('active citizenship'), and gradually began to employ more 'illegal' actions when their efforts were thwarted ('activist citizenship'). The Right to the City crystallised around plans to build a shopping centre and luxury residences on one part of 'Flower Square' in Zagreb. In addition to occupying the space, activists devised performative and creative actions to highlight injustice, such as: affixing a fake street sign reading 'Victims of [Mayor] Milan Bandić Square' (parodying the 'Victims of Fascism Square' in Zagreb) and putting up yellow 'crime scene' tape around the

Ministry of Environment, Planning, and Construction to highlight the responsible minister's conflict of interests. The movement developed further in response to plans to build on one part of the square, on Varšavska Street. Activists again organised occupations of the disputed space, as well as creative actions, such as building a large Trojan Horse (to underline that elite pronouncements of 'public interest' were self-serving). Eventually, the fight was lost, but the movement did not burn out (*contra* Tarrow), but rather supported similar actions elsewhere in Croatia, as well as in Bosnia & Hercegovina, Macedonia, and Serbia.

Bojan Baća explores how acts of citizenship initiated by residents of Beranselo, a small settlement in northeast Montenegro, protesting the process determining the location of a regional landfill, unintentionally brought into being a new political subject of the *Beranselac* (that is, a resident of Beranselo, plural 'Beranselci'). Although the actions never took place under the banner of a unified social movement, the acts of citizenship in this rural setting were the first in a process of accretion whereby the political subjectivation of the 'Beranselac' became the actor ('we are all Beranselci') highlighting injustice by predatory and exploitative elites across the country. Using interviews with three of the most visible activists and supported by secondary sources, Baća shows how the Beranselo 'movement' can be understood using the stages of 'political subjectivation', developed by Rancière (1992, 1999, 2010), to performatively assert equality from an initial position of inequality: first, disagreeing with the existing modes for registering grievances; second, creating new scripts for political participation; and third, recognition by other exploited parties as symbolic of their own plight. As in the case of the Zagreb Right to the City movement (see Dolenec *et al.* in this collection), residents in Beranselo initially pursued existing scripts as 'active citizens' to highlight their grievance and only wrote new scripts when they felt unjustly impeded by authorities. Most interestingly, Baća concludes that the accretion of acts of citizenship was not purposeful (*contra* Isin), but rather a result of uncoordinated everyday acts of micro-resistance, such as the sharing of parody images about Beranselo on social media.

Focusing on instances of everyday activism also examined by Baća, Piotr Goldstein seeks to identify instances of activist citizenship that are largely hidden away from the public gaze by studying what the author calls 'discreet activisms' with a longer-term horizon and less radical perspective than the other cases presented in this special issue. The author conducts participant observation of independent café-bookshops, alongside interviews with the owners, in Novi Sad (capital of the autonomous Serbian province of Vojvodina) by using Lefebvre's (1991) notion of the 'counter-space' where citizens can resist the dominant metanarrative of the capitalist city at the micro-level and thus influence the 'everyday'. Goldstein finds that many of these bookshops do not prioritise profit-making, but rather focus on creating spaces for social engagement alongside more 'public' forms of activism. Moreover, the resulting spaces and scripts are not created solely by the proprietors of the bookshops but through a process of co-creation in which participants are actively involved. These 'everyday utopias' (Cooper 2014) may be ephemeral, but the alternative scripts created can accrete over time and provide a 'preamble' for more public activism.

Alexandra Ana disentangles the role of feminist activists during the 2012 Romanian protests in order to recover their voice during the mobilisation. The author conducted interviews with a number of feminist activists involved in the protest, as well as observing the 2012 protests, and investigated the process of (and impediments to) constituting a feminist citizen. To do this, Ana uses the concept of 'perspectival dualism' developed by Fraser and Honneth (2003) to argue that appeals to justice in social movements rest on claims related to recognition and redistribution, which are inter-linked. This perspectival dualism is complemented by Ferree's focus on the role of power relations exercised through structures understood both as the individual's autonomy to self-determine and the role of collective authority (Ferree & Gamson 2003). Since these forms of power are themselves interlinked with class and race, they are also connected to justice related to recognition and redistribution (Ferree & Martin 1995). The notion of citizenship (as a form of recognition) at the heart of this special issue was understood in two ways. On the one hand, the existing notions of citizenship allowed women to participate fully in the protest movements as 'active citizens'. However, a second group of feminists saw claims through prevailing ideas of Romanian citizenship as inadequate, since they did not question the *status quo* and thus did not have the potential to trigger a rupture and reconstitution of the political ('activist citizenship').

The authors thus position themselves at various points within the realm of infra-politics. For Thomassen and Toplišek, this is the juncture or interface between horizontal protest networks and the vertical manifestations of protest, including parties and more established formal iterations of civil society in Slovenia. For Dolenec *et al.*, it is the physical location of the city. Each vantage point offers insights into forms of activist citizenship that do not entirely reject parties and NGOs, but organise their activism separately from institutionalised civil society; deploy different tactics, logics, and strategies; and fundamentally challenge the tacit assertion that the only activism or politics that matters is that which takes place 'formally', within the contours of 'the system' and its institutions. From the realm of infra-politics and below the parapet of the formal political sphere, 'capacity-building' (training), the availability of material resources (project grants), and access to elites (policy consultations and round table negotiations) all become less relevant. Making demands on the state, challenging it, and seeking to influence political elites is not absent or lost, but the vertical interaction between activists and the state is merely one dimension of these forms of action.

The contributions are interested in how activist citizenship develops. Is there a temporal dimension in the sense that the movements or incidents of protest learn from previous examples? How important to this cumulative learning are the dissident movements that challenged socialism in the late 1980s and early 1990s? Do activists learn from what occurs in neighbouring (Balkan) states? If so, how and under what circumstances? If there is transnational or even global 'learning' and 'sharing' taking place, where do the activist movements of Southeast Europe sit within this? Are they somewhat passively copying or reflecting activism learnt elsewhere, or are they actually initiating and innovating?

ACTIVIST CITIZENSHIP IN SOUTHEAST EUROPE

References

Aidukaitė, J. (2016) 'The Role of Leaders in Shaping Urban Movements: A Study of Community Mobilisation in Lithuania', *East European Politics*, 32, 1.

Baća, B. (2017) 'The Student's Two Bodies: Civic Engagement and Political Becoming in the Post-Socialist Space', *Antipode*, 49, 5.

Baćević, J. (2010) 'Masters or Servants? Power and Discourse in Serbian Higher Education Reform', *Social Anthropology*, 18, 1.

Cooper, D. (2014) *Everyday Utopias: The Conceptual Life of Promising Spaces* (Durham, NC, & London, Duke University Press).

Crotty, J. (2003) 'Managing Civil Society: Democratisation and the Environmental Movement in a Russian Region', *Communist and Post-Communist Studies*, 36, 4.

Ćulum, B. & Doolan, K. (2015) '"A Truly Transformative Experience": The Biographical Legacy of Student Protest Participation', in Klemenčič, M., Bergan, S. & Primožič, R. (eds) *Student Engagement in Europe: Society, Higher Education and Student Governance* (Strasbourg, Council of Europe).

Dalakoglou, D. (2012) 'Beyond Spontaneity: Crisis, Violence and Collective Action in Athens', *City*, 16, 5.

Della Porta, D. (2015) *Social Movements in Times of Austerity: Bringing Capitalism Back into Protest Analysis* (Cambridge, Polity).

Della Porta, D., Fernandez, J., Kouki, H. & Mosca, L. (eds) (2017) *Movement Parties Against Austerity* (Cambridge, Polity).

Ferree, M. M. & Gamson, W. A. (2003) 'The Gendering of Governance and the Governance of Gender: Abortion Politics in Germany and the USA', in Hobson, B. (ed.) *Recognition Struggles and Social Movements* (Cambridge, Cambridge University Press).

Ferree, M. M. & Martin, P. Y. (1995) 'Doing the Work of the Feminist Movement: Feminist Organizations', in Ferree, M. M. & Martin, P. Y. (eds) *Feminist Organizations: Harvest of the New Women's Movement* (Philadelphia, PA, Temple University Press).

Flesher Fominaya, C. (2015) 'Debunking Spontaneity: Spain's 15-M/Indignados as Autonomous Movement', *Social Movement Studies*, 14, 2.

Fraser, N. & Honneth, A. (2003) *Redistribution or Recognition: A Political-Philosophical Exchange* (London, Verso).

Howard, M. M. (2003) *The Weakness of Civil Society in Post-Communist Europe* (Cambridge & New York, NY, Cambridge University Press).

Isin, E. F. (2008) 'Theorizing Acts of Citizenship', in Isin, E. F. & Nielsen, G. M. (eds) *Acts of Citizenship* (London, Palgrave Macmillan).

Isin, E. F. (2009) 'Citizenship in Flux: The Figure of the Activist Citizen', *Subjectivity*, 29, 1.

Isin, E. F. (2017) 'Performative Citizenship', in Shachar, A., Bauböck, R., Bloemraad, I. & Vink, M. (eds) *The Oxford Handbook of Citizenship* (Oxford, Oxford University Press).

Jacobsson, K. & Saxonberg, S. (eds) (2013) *Beyond NGO-ization: The Development of Social Movements in Central and Eastern Europe* (Farnham, Ashgate).

Kitschelt, H. (2006) 'Movement Parties', in Katz, R. S. & Crotty, W. (eds) *Handbook of Party Politics* (London, Sage).

Leach, D. K. (2013) 'Prefigurative Politics', in Snow, D. A., della Porta, D., Klandermans, B. & McAdam, D. (eds) *The Wiley-Blackwell Encyclopedia of Social and Political Movements* (Oxford, Wiley-Blackwell).

Lefebvre, H. (1991) *The Production of Space* (Oxford & Cambridge, MA, Blackwell).

Mandel, R. (2002) 'Seeding Civil Society', in Hann, C. M. (ed.) *Postsocialism: Ideals, Ideologies and Practices in Eurasia* (London, Routledge).

Melucci, A. (1988) 'Social Movements and the Democratization of Everyday Life', in Keane, J. (ed.) *Civil Society and the State: New European Perspectives* (London & New York, NY, Verso).

Michels, R. (1968) *Political Parties: A Sociological Study of the Oligarchial Tendencies of Modern Democracy* (New York, NY, Free Press).

Petrova, T. & Tarrow, S. (2007) 'Transactional and Participatory Activism in the Emerging European Polity', *Comparative Political Studies*, 40, 1.

Polletta, F. (1998) '"It Was Like a Fever …" Narrative and Identity in Social Protest', *Social Problems*, 45, 2.

Quigley, K. F. F. (2000) 'Lofty Goals, Modest Results: Assisting Civil Society in Eastern Europe', in Ottaway, M. & Carothers, T. (eds) *Funding Virtue: Civil Society Aid and Democracy Promotion* (Washington, DC, Carnegie Endowment for International Peace).

Rancière, J. (1992) 'Politics, Identification, and Subjectivization', *October*, 61.

Rancière, J. (1999) *Disagreement: Politics and Philosophy* (Minneapolis, MN, University of Minnesota Press).

Rancière, J. (2010) *Dissensus: On Politics and Aesthetics* (New York, NY, Continuum).

Rose, R. (2001) 'How People View Democracy: A Diverging Europe', *Journal of Democracy*, 12, 1.

Rucht, D. (1999) 'Linking Organization and Mobilization: Michels's Iron Law of Oligarchy Reconsidered', *Mobilization: An International Journal*, 4, 2.

Scott, J. C. (1990) 'The Infrapolitics of Subordinate Groups', in Scott, J. C. (ed.) *Domination and the Arts of Resistance: Hidden Transcripts* (New Haven, CT, & London, Yale University Press).

Sitrin, M. A. (2012) *Everyday Revolutions: Horizontalism and Autonomy in Argentina* (London, Zed Books).

Sitrin, M. A. (2014) 'Goals Without Demands: The New Movements for Real Democracy', *South Atlantic Quarterly*, 113, 2.

Tarrow, S. (2011) *Power in Movement: Social Movements and Contentious Politics* (Cambridge, Cambridge University Press).

Tilly, C. (2008) *Contentious Performances* (Cambridge, Cambridge University Press).

Turner, V. (1969) *The Ritual Process: Structure and Anti-Structure* (Chicago, IL, Aldine).

Wedel, J. R. (2001) *Collision and Collusion: The Strange Case of Western Aid to Eastern Europe, 1989–1998* (New York, NY, St. Martin's Press).

Reshaping Citizenship through Collective Action: Performative and Prefigurative Practices in the 2013–2014 Cycle of Contention in Bosnia & Hercegovina

CHIARA MILAN

Abstract

This essay analyses the strategic practices adopted by social movement actors during the 2013 and 2014 mobilisations in Bosnia & Hercegovina. By bridging critical citizenship studies with literature on social movements, it classifies them as belonging to the realm of activist citizenship, but also as having a performative and prefigurative dimension. While the strategies adopted during the 2013 wave had a performative dimension, as they disrupted routines and created opportunities for social change, the 2014 practices are to be considered prefigurative, as they developed modes of interaction embodying a new model of citizenship at odds with the existing one based on the institutionalisation of ethno-national categories.

IN THE LAST DECADE, THE COUNTRIES OF THE FORMER YUGOSLAVIA witnessed a resurgence of contentious collective action. Several street protests were undertaken with the purpose of opposing the privatisation of public and common goods such as parks, urban spaces, and public utility infrastructures (Arsenijević 2014; Bieber 2014; Jacobsson 2015). The citizens of Zagreb opposed the commercialisation of public space in Croatia in 2006 and 2014,[1] while in 2009 students protested the commodification of higher education through faculty occupations in Croatia, Serbia, Slovenia, and Bosnia & Hercegovina (Baćević 2015). In 2011 and 2012, demonstrations in Slovenia called capitalism and austerity policies into question (Razsa & Kurnik 2012; Kraft 2015; Thomassen & Toplišek in this collection). Throughout these mobilisations, movement actors 'began to formulate a profoundly anti-capitalist and radically democratic vision of their societies', bringing radical politics back to what Horvat and Štiks have termed 'the rebel peninsula' (Horvat & Štiks 2015, p. 2).

Notwithstanding a range of unfavourable conditions for inclusive civic collective action, mass protests broke out in Bosnia & Hercegovina in 2013 and 2014. During the first wave, known as the 'Baby Revolution' or by the acronym #JMBG,[2] demonstrators called for the

---

[1]See Dolenec *et al.* in this collection.
[2]After the 13-digit *Jedinstveni matični broj gradana* (Unique Master Citizens Number—JMBG).

This work was supported by European University Institute.

© 2017 University of Glasgow

resolution of problems with the allocation of citizen registration numbers by taking to the streets in the main urban centres of the country. The second wave that followed in 2014, the so-called 'Social Uprising', began in a violent way in the former industrial hub of Tuzla and soon spread to several cities and towns across the country. Given the novelty of popular mobilisations in Bosnia & Hercegovina, this upsurge of collective action calls for further investigation and some systematic analysis of events.

Based on a detailed exploration of protest dynamics, trajectories, and strategic practices, in this essay I take both protest waves into account as instances of activist citizenship according to Isin's (2009) classification. By bridging the debates about citizenship with the social movement literature, I argue that the 2013 protests had a performative character, meaning that they represented moments of rupture that created possibilities for social change. By contrast, the 2014 protests are noteworthy for their prefigurative orientation, as they embodied alternative social arrangements that prefigured a new model of citizenship at odds with the existing one based on the institutionalisation of ethno-national categories. Besides distinguishing between the performative and prefigurative dimension of the 2013–2014 protests, empirical analysis also reveals that the 2013 protests were a learning experience for movement actors that created the conditions for the emergence of the 2014 wave, and that the cycle of contention had an empowering effect on the participants.

The essay is organised as follows. The first section outlines the theoretical and methodological framework and the concepts on which I draw to analyse the dynamics of the two waves of protest. The second section examines the social and political background in which both waves of protests emerged and unfolded. The following section investigates the two case studies, exploring key features relevant to the analysis. In particular, this part scrutinises the repertoires of action, frames, and organisational models adopted by movement actors. The next section then presents the cases in a comparative perspective, discussing the differences among the two protest waves, along with the learning and empowering effects created throughout the cycle of contention. The final section summarises the main findings of the study.

Theoretical and methodological framework

Citizenship is acknowledged to profoundly shape individuals 'as social and political beings', because of 'the status it bestows upon them, and … the privileges and restrictions it can entail' (Štiks 2015, p. 2). According to Isin, historical actors constitute themselves as citizens by enacting 'acts or deeds by which and through which subjects become, and constitute themselves as, citizens' (Isin 2009, p. 377). However, the way in which citizenship is expressed and the practices through which 'subjects act to become citizens and claim citizenship' have considerably changed throughout the twentieth century (Isin 2009, p. 368). In analysing this evolution, Isin identifies a distinction between 'active citizenship' and 'activist citizenship'. The former, he claims, is a concept that emerged during the French Revolution and persisted for two centuries, according to which the citizen is defined as a legal subject with singular loyalty, identity, and belonging, whose acts consist of 'routinized social actions that are already instituted' (Isin 2009, p. 379). These include activities such as 'voting, taxpaying and enlisting' (Isin 2009, p. 381). By contrast, 'activist citizenship' involves acts that might break the law, as they 'are not necessarily founded on law and responsibility' (Isin 2009,

p. 382). These are collective or individual actions that make a difference, as they 'rupture socio-historical patterns' (Isin & Nielsen 2008, p. 2). According to Isin, the shift from active to activist citizenship occurs when a citizen behaves 'in a way that disrupts already defined orders, practices and statuses' (Isin 2009, p. 384). These actions include, for instance, the occupation of public spaces such as squares, universities, and parks. It follows that activist citizens produce acts of citizenship as innovative moments through which they act to assert their rights (Isin & Turner 2002).

Isin's perspective on citizenship, which entails 'making rights claims across multiple social groups and polities' (2017, p. 501), seems to disregard the prefigurative orientation of certain acts of citizenship. Appropriating the concept of 'prefigurative politics' would allow a proper understanding of the strategic practices adopted by movement actors throughout the 2013–2014 cycle of contention in Bosnia & Hercegovina. In particular, the concept of 'prefiguration' could contribute to understanding the attempts made by movement actors to transform the existing model of citizenship based on the institutionalisation of ethno-national categories by enacting an alternative one through prefigurative practices. Therefore, I draw upon Leach's definition of prefigurative politics, which he refers to as 'a political orientation based on the premise that the ends a social movement achieves are fundamentally shaped by the means it employs, and that movements should therefore do their best to choose means that embody or "prefigure" the kind of society they want to bring about' (Leach 2013, p. 1004). Essentially, continues Leach, 'a prefigurative approach seeks to create the new society "in the shell of the old" by developing counterhegemonic institutions and modes of interaction that embody the desired transformation' (Leach 2013, p. 1004). Simply put, prefigurative actions entail acts that at once envision and actualise radical change. By embodying an alternative social arrangement, these practices prefigure in themselves an alternative (Graeber 2002). Hence, prefiguration means that a movement directly implements the changes it seeks, 'rather than asking others to make the changes on one's behalf' (Leach 2013, p. 1004). Examples of prefigurative acts are, for instance, the enactment of egalitarian practices that provoke 'cracks' in the surface of capitalism (Holloway 2010). In these struggles, horizontal and direct-democratic participatory forms of decision-making are attempted and created at the same time. Thus, they can be considered as examples of prefigurative politics, as they create a different kind of society in the course of the actual struggles themselves. As Sitrin (2007) aptly noted in her analysis of the occupation and recuperation of factories by workers in Argentina, horizontalism constitutes both the end and the means to reach that end, as in prefigurative politics means and ends are aligned (Leach 2013).[3]

In this essay, the 2013–2014 protests in Bosnia & Hercegovina serve as a case in point to investigate the attempts undertaken by movement actors to reshape social reality, in particular, the existing model of citizenship, by means of concrete acts. To grasp the transformative potential of such actions, the analysis of the protest cycle is based on the in-depth analysis of three factors in particular: the repertoires of action used, meaning the 'arrays of contentious performances that are currently known and available within some set of political actors' (Tilly & Tarrow 2006, p. 11); collective action frames, 'schemata of interpretation' that movement organisers use in order to 'enable individuals to locate, perceive, identify and

---

[3]Recuperation is used here to refer to a process by which workers or worker cooperatives seize control and/or ownership of their factories, often in response to a bankruptcy. After occupying them, workers re-start production following the principles of self- and horizontal management, and equal employee ownership.

label events and occurrences' (Goffman 1974, p. 21); and the actors involved in the protests, as well as their model of organisation. The essay relies on in-depth interviews, participant observation, and analysis of media articles. In particular, it draws on two different data sources: over 30 semi-structured in-depth interviews, of which 28 were with activists and non-governmental organisation (NGO) practitioners,[4] and two with external observers;[5] and archival material, media articles, press releases, flyers, and the magazine of the 2014 Sarajevo plenum (discussed below), *Glas Slobode* (*The Voice of Freedom*), collected both from the websites of the initiatives and in person during field trips to the country. I have chosen not to report identifying information about interviewees, given the sensitivity of the topics treated and the potentially easy identification of the subjects in the small activist environment in Bosnia & Hercegovina.[6]

Social and political context of Bosnia & Hercegovina: difficult circumstances for civic action

Bosnia & Hercegovina represents a challenging environment for the undertaking and development of inclusive civic action. Several factors such as the legacy of socialism, a post-conflict background, and the consociational system of power-sharing discourage mobilisation. Large-scale citizen-led protests are a phenomenon that has only recently emerged in the country, as the socialist system provided little room for the active expression of opposition through confrontational means of action. Historically, Bosnia & Hercegovina does not have a solid tradition of grassroots movements, nor of mass street demonstrations. By and large, street protests are not a common occurrence, as citizens of Bosnia & Hercegovina have seldom stepped out *en masse* to oppose the authorities since the end of the 1992–1995 war. Owing to the legacy of war, the general attitude of people towards public demonstrations is commonly one of fear and distrust. In a society still scarred by recent wars, the fear that massive gatherings will turn violent continues to discourage the population from adopting protests and street actions as tools of contention.

Moreover, in Bosnia & Hercegovina society is deeply divided along ethno-national lines; national and institutional rules foster further division amongst the citizens, and members of the ruling class are perceived as detached from the citizenry. A low voter turnout reflects the mistrust towards institutional politics: in the most recent local elections, only approximately 50% of eligible voters cast a vote (Kapidžić 2016). The consociational institutional configuration of the country divides people into three different nations, specifically mentioned in the Constitution as 'constitutive people': Bosniaks (Bosnian Muslims), Serbs, and Croats. The constitutional setting of the country was laid down in 1995 with the signing of the General Framework Agreement for Peace (GFAP), commonly known as the Dayton Peace Agreement. The agreement established Bosnia & Hercegovina as a consociational democracy and a triple power-sharing system (Bieber 2005), following the model envisioned by the political scientist

---

[4]Given the overlapping role of movement activists and NGO practitioners, it is difficult to make a clear distinction amongst the two categories, as the boundaries between the two are often blurred.

[5]The interviews were conducted in Bosnia & Hercegovina in July and November 2013, and April and May 2014, in the cities of Sarajevo, Banja Luka, Mostar and Tuzla.

[6]The interviewees have been identified as among the key actors in both waves of protests by following the snowball procedure, a technique used for gathering research subjects through the identification of an initial subject who helps to provide contacts with other relevant informants.

ACTIVIST CITIZENSHIP IN SOUTHEAST EUROPE

Lijphart (1969), applied over the years as default mode of conflict regulation in other divided contexts such as, for instance, Lebanon and the Republic of Macedonia (Nagle & Clancy 2010). By ensuring an equal share of power to all contending ethno-national groups on a permanent basis, consociational political systems aim to achieve governmental stability and maintain democracy in societies divided along ethnic or religious lines (Lijphart 1969; Touquet & Vermeersch 2008). While, on the one hand, the signing of the GFAP put an end to a four-year conflict in Bosnia & Hercegovina, on the other hand it recognised the territorial gains that the principal hostile parties had acquired through violence (Gordy 2016), legitimising the ambitions of ethno-national contenders. Consequently, what had been initially intended as a provisional arrangement became eventually the Constitution (Majstorović *et al.* 2016, p. 1). The GFAP divided the country into two distinct and almost ethnically homogeneous areas, the entities, Republika Srpska (RS) and the Federation of Bosnia Hercegovina (FBiH), and a third administrative unit, the autonomous Brčko district. Following the partition of the country into two entities, the capital Sarajevo was divided in two parts, one belonging to FBiH and the other, called Eastern Sarajevo (*Istočno Sarajevo*), to RS.[7] The two entities differ in terms of internal organisation. While RS is a centralised sub-state divided into municipalities, FBiH is composed of ten administrative and largely autonomous units called cantons. As a result of the decentralisation of the country, the central institutions of the state weakened, while the regional entities (FBiH, the cantons, and RS) enjoyed wide powers (Touquet 2012). Each sub-state layer of government is endowed with its own constitution, government, and court. Similarly, every entity has its own president, parliament, government, and court, as well as jurisdiction in the areas of civil administration, education, health, police, environment, and others. In FBiH, responsibility in these matters rests with the individual cantons, which are in turn divided into municipalities. The competences of the loose Bosnian–Hercegovinian central state institutions are limited to foreign policy and trade, defence, immigration, international communications facilities, inter-entity cooperation with regard to transportation, air traffic control, and fiscal and monetary policies.

The Constitution also enshrines a three-headed presidency which collectively serves as head of state. In order to guarantee equal representation to each constituent group, every president represents his ethnic constituency in the tripartite presidency. Hence, the Presidency of Bosnia & Hercegovina includes a Serb, a Croat, and a Bosniak member. The chairmanship of the presidency rotates every eight months (Bieber 2005, p. 48). Among its provisions, the GFAP established the Office of the High Representative, and appointed to the role of the High Representative a civilian with oversight of peace operations. Since 1997, the High Representative has held so-called 'Bonn Powers', namely the authority to adopt binding decisions in case of disagreement among local parties and to remove elected or appointed officials from office if they violate the commitments envisaged in the GFAP. The High Representative is not accountable to the state parliament of Bosnia & Hercegovina, only to the Peace Implementation Council, an international body composed of 55 states and charged with overseeing the country's peace process and implementing the Dayton Agreement. The state is estimated to spend half of its GDP maintaining this overly bureaucratic structure. Concerning political representation, the Constitution does not foresee any path outside the framework of

---

[7]The part of Sarajevo in RS was initially called 'Serb Sarajevo' (*Srpsko Sarajevo*) in 1992, but was renamed Eastern Sarajevo (*Istočno Sarajevo*) in 2005 after a decision of the Bosnian Constitutional Court stated that the name of this 'Serb counterpart of Sarajevo' discriminated against non-Serb returnees (Armakolas 2007, p. 80).

the three constituent peoples (Gordy 2016). The individuals who do not fall into the Serb–Croat–Bosniak ethno-national grid (Hromadžić 2015), or refuse to self-identify with one of these groups, fall into the category of 'others' (*ostali*).[8] The 'others' are prevented from holding major state posts, as they cannot be appointed either to the House of Peoples (*Dom naroda*), the state parliament's upper chamber, or the presidency. The constitutional order reinforces even further ethnic representation by recognising veto rights for each constituent people in case a vital interest of the group is threatened or endangered (literally 'it is destructive of a vital interest of the Bosniak, Croat or Serb people'). At the state level, in entities and most cantons, each community has the right to veto Parliament decisions that may negatively affect the community (Bieber 2005). Although the Constitution recognises as vital interests issues related to, for example, constitutional amendments, identity, education, and religion, veto rights can be expanded to include virtually any issue (Bieber 2005).

If, on the one hand, the Constitution institutionalises ethnic categories, the demographic changes that occurred in the aftermath of the war affected and further reshaped the country's social fabric, reinforcing segregation based on ethnic identification. The majority of the war's internally displaced persons (IDPs) did not return to the homes they inhabited in the pre-war period, while other systemic transformations such as mass emigration from the country, and massive displacement and redistribution of people within the country after 1995 reordered the sense of local belonging (Bougarel *et al.* 2007). As a result, the majority of Bosnian Serbs are now settled in RS, while Bosniaks have moved to cantons inhabited mostly by their ethnic peers in FBiH. The Bosnian Croats followed a similar pattern and now populate the Hercegovinian region and the area along the Sava River in the north (Touquet & Vermeersch 2008). In FBiH only two cantons out of ten are significantly ethnically mixed (Murtagh 2016), while the others are considered almost ethnically homogeneous. There is thus little mixing between the different communities. The alleged cultural distinctiveness between the groups is reflected in several aspects of everyday life, such as media outlets, sporting affiliations and trade unions, public holidays, and the education system. From the beginning of the war, education has been divided along ethnic lines, taking the form of segregated schools and/or school programmes throughout the country, with specific curricula studied by children according to their ethno-national category of belonging.[9]

Following a constitutional arrangement that gives 'strong preference [to the] collective rights of ethnic groups to the detriment of individual citizens' (Mujkić 2008, p. 17), even the concept of citizenship commonly overlaps with that of ethno-national belonging (Džankic 2015). As a consequence, 'the identity dimension of citizenship is considered to be more relevant than the status or rights bestowed by citizenship' (Sarajlić 2010, p. 14). There is still much to do to mould the different ethnic communities into a new, supra-ethnic group of Bosnia & Hercegovina citizenry that transcends ethno-national partitions. Ethno-national belonging intended as the primary identification with either Bosniak, Serb, or Croat ethno-national community, remains more salient than the identification with Bosnia & Hercegovina as a state. Yet the country misses a 'truly shared sense of a Bosnian identity' (Touquet 2012, p. 27). However, the complex meaning of 'citizenship' and its overlap with ethno-national

---

[8] These 'others' were estimated to be around half a million in 2013, that is to say one eighth of the Bosnian population (Belloni 2013, p. 283).
[9] For an in-depth account of the effects of school segregation on youth and civil society in the divided society of Mostar, see Hromadžić (2015).

belonging must be read against the background of a country in which citizenship and national identity never corresponded in the past, since Bosnia & Hercegovina 'has never been a nation state, nor developed crucial nation-state properties' (Sarajlić 2010, p. 2). At present, a model of citizenship founded on the attribution of collective rights to ethnic groups, which I define as 'ethnic-based citizenship', dominates over an approach grounded on the predominance of individual rights, which I call 'rights-based citizenship'.

The 2013 Baby Revolution[10]

The 2013 citizen protests erupted in Sarajevo on 5 June, sparked by a seriously ill baby girl in need of urgent medical treatment abroad. She was prevented from leaving the country because the Ministry of the Interior was unable to allocate her the 13-digit *Jedinstveni matični broj građana* (Unique Master Citizens Number—JMBG) necessary to obtain identity cards and other personal documents. The stalemate originated from a disagreement among Bosnian MPs upon the amendments necessary to adopt a unified state law on identification numbers.[11]

In the evening of 5 June 2013, a group of activists and relatives of the baby organised a demonstration in the capital to raise awareness of the problem and pressure politicians to resolve the issue of registration numbers (Horvat & Štiks 2015). The demonstrators occupied the square in front of the National Parliament building, while thousands of people formed a human chain that surrounded the premises, inside which a meeting of MPs and businessmen was taking place. In the following days, protests spread from the capital to the major urban centres of FBiH. On the streets, demonstrators urged the adoption of a legal framework allowing the allocation of identification numbers at the state level, in order for newborn babies to obtain their IDs and therefore access to citizenship rights. Day and night, several thousand demonstrators peacefully occupied the square in front of the National Parliament for 25 consecutive days. During this period, demonstrators organised meetings and set up a playground for children, ironically named 'the terrorists' playground', in response to the allegations of some MPs who accused the demonstrators of constituting a threat to their safety. The movement organisers publicly declared 1 July 'Dismissal Day' (*otkaz* in the local language) and stated that all of their MPs were dismissed, since they were 'no longer credible representatives of the citizens of Bosnia & Hercegovina'.[12] The protestors eventually released a communiqué on behalf of the citizens of Bosnia & Hercegovina, encouraging the international community to 'withdraw all the previous invitations to the representatives of Bosnia & Hercegovina to meetings, conferences and other formal events' in order 'to clearly show the Bosnia & Hercegovina politicians that they finally have to take responsibility and do the job they were elected to do'.[13] The demonstrators disbanded later that day (Mujkić 2013).

---

[10]Throughout the essay I use the terms 'Baby Revolution', #JMBG, and *bebolucija* interchangeably to refer to the protests taking place all over the country between 6 June and 1 July 2013.

[11]'Thousands Protest over Bosnia Baby ID Row', *Al Jazeera Balkans*, 11 June 2013, available at: http://www.aljazeera.com/news/europe/2013/06/2013611152720320390.html, accessed 20 December 2016.

[12]Interview with a self-identified independent activist, Sarajevo, 19 April 2014.

[13]'#JMBG Manifesto', *JMBG.org*, 21 June 2013, available at: http://www.jmbg.org/jmbg-manifesto/, accessed 5 July 2013.

ACTIVIST CITIZENSHIP IN SOUTHEAST EUROPE

Action repertoires

Throughout the protests, the repertoire of action was intentionally kept peaceful as movement organisers opted for a non-confrontational, collaborative stance towards the authorities. They submitted their demands to MPs; negotiated through a delegation on the second day of protest; and bargained with the High Representative, the highest authority in the country, for the 'release' of MPs and businessmen trapped inside the Parliament premises. As a matter of fact, protest organisers had publicly called for the use of non-violent methods throughout the square occupation. In a statement, they announced that dissatisfied citizens (*nezadovoljni građani* in the local language)[14] would protest by means of disobedience and other non-violent methods, since according to movement organisers the fight for children and the law on ID numbers had to be conducted with dignity and by non-violent means. Besides the occupation of the square, movement organisers also went on marches, carrying humorous effigies of the politicians from both Bosnia & Hercegovina entities with the intention to ridicule them. The choice of a formal repertoire, which envisaged the organisation of a concert as the final event, provoked criticism from many activists, who blamed the movement organisers for having turned a protest into a cheerful event, depriving it of its political meaning and contentious character,[15] which, in their opinion, 'undermine[d] the spring of a genuine movement'.[16]

Collective action frames

With the purpose of keeping the protests independent from interference by political parties and other formal organisations, movement organisers strove to frame their actions giving them a civic meaning from the beginning. Through the occupation of the square and the organisation of non-violent demonstrations, protestors claimed their rights to citizenship as granted by the Constitution. In so doing, they tried to avoid any reference to ethno-nationalism and party politics in their discourse, conscious of the risk of being discredited for 'politicising the issue'.[17] Similarly, they did not tackle the topic of constitutional changes, or other subjects that could have been labelled as having a political dimension. The terms 'politics' and 'political' have negative connotations for ordinary citizens in Bosnia & Hercegovina, implying 'ethnically driven' and 'subject to party manipulation'. Similarly, the term 'apolitical' does not mean 'without political meaning', but rather free of the influence of any political party, NGOs, or other 'partisan' subjects considered as being involved in immoral political deal-making (Helms 2007) or being unresponsive to local constituents owing to their dependence on donor funding and priorities (Pickering 2006). Therefore, during the #JMBG mobilisation, claims remained focused on human rights and the issue of ID numbers framed in civic and 'apolitical terms'. The primacy of citizenship over ethno-nationality as a unifying identity was made clear on a placard carried through the streets of Sarajevo, which read: 'Neither Serbs, Croats nor Bosniaks. Citizens above all' (*'Ni Srbi, ni Hrvati, ni Bošnjaci: Ljudska bića prije svega'*).

---

[14]Three official languages are recognised in Bosnia & Hercegovina: Bosnian, Croatian, and Serbian. Since linguistically they differ only slightly among each other, throughout the essay I refer to them using the singular term 'local language'.

[15]Interview with an activist and academic, Tuzla, 26 April 2014.

[16]Interview with an NGO practitioner participant of the #JMBG car blockade, Sarajevo, 29 October 2013.

[17]Interview with a self-identified independent activist, Sarajevo, 19 April 2013.

Actors and organisational models

The network among the actors on the square appeared quite loose throughout the month of occupation. At the start of the demonstrations, a press release was circulated, inviting official organisations, such as labour unions and youth associations, to support the protesters by sharing their spaces and resources, but on the condition that they only join the demonstrations on an individual basis. Although officially not participating in the protests as representatives or spokespersons of their organisations, NGO members were present on the square, acting as intermediaries between the demonstrators and politicians and the media.[18] Many informants blamed these protest leaders, many of which were employed in local and international NGOs, for participating with the intent of trying to divert popular dissatisfaction to their own goals. Such behaviour is said to have prevented the development of horizontal networks and coalitions necessary to trigger broader solidarity and build new subjectivities, and the adoption of a more radical repertoire. According to some informants, no room was left for open and participatory debate during the protests, and young people were denied full participation in the assemblies, as the leadership-centred organisation model adopted by several actors lacked elements of horizontality.[19] This also indicates a generational gap existing between an older generation employed in the third sector since the end of the war, and younger people who, although seldom politically active, were pushing to gain more space and opportunities for involvement.

The 2014 'social uprising'

Eight months after the 'Baby Revolution', in February 2014, a workers' demonstration in the north-eastern city of Tuzla triggered a wave of mobilisation that some scholars defined as 'the most significant bottom-up challenge to ethnically constituted disorder, bypassing ethnic division in favour of a proto-civic sense of common citizenship and class solidarity' (Majstorović *et al.* 2016, p. 3).

The protests started when redundant workers of recently privatised factories in the industrial hub of Tuzla organised a demonstration in front of the cantonal government building. The disenfranchised workers demanded the revision of the privatisation process of their factories, as well as their wage arrears and the unpaid benefits to which they were entitled but unable to collect (Milan 2014b). In fact, the companies went bankrupt after the owners became heavily indebted with bank loans. As a consequence, the owners stopped paying wages and pension funds to the workers. On 5 February 2014, riot police violently cracked down on the demonstrations, which sparked solidarity rallies all over the country, and the protests soon spread nationwide (Milan 2014a). The workers' strike of Tuzla had a domino effect: their rage transformed into a general upheaval, known as the 'Social Uprising' (*Socijalni bunt*) or 'Bosnian Spring' (*Bosansko proljeće*). In spite of the violent turn that the rallies initially took in Sarajevo, Zenica, and Mostar, these riots ended three days later, while street actions and protests continued until mid-May 2014.

---

[18]Interview with an activist who participated in the #JMBG car blockade in 2013 and the plenum of Sarajevo in 2014, Sarajevo, 20 October 2013.

[19]Interviews with an activist who participated in the #JMBG car blockade in 2013 and the plenum of Sarajevo in 2014, Sarajevo, 20 October 2013; a student who participated in both waves of protests, Sarajevo, 15 April 2014; and a human right activist, Sarajevo, 23 April 2014.

ACTIVIST CITIZENSHIP IN SOUTHEAST EUROPE

Action repertoires

The repertoire of action changed dramatically from the previous wave. The demonstrators shifted from the adoption of a conventional type of action, such as peaceful street demonstrations and the occupation of city squares, to a more confrontational and disruptive one, which included violent tactics. At first, groups of individuals stormed institutional buildings associated with political authority, targeting in particular the premises of cantons and municipal governments, as well as the headquarters of political parties. Although it is not clear yet whether violence was planned or spontaneous, during the first days of violent protests it was mostly young high school students and football fans who were seen in the main urban centres storming public buildings and creating havoc in the city centres. The media referred to them as 'hooligans' thereby depriving the protestors of any political legitimacy. In Mostar the headquarters of both nationalist parties, Bosniak Party of Democratic Action (*Stranka demokratske akcije*—SDA) and the Croatian Democratic Union of Bosnia & Hercegovina (*Hrvatska demokratska zajednica BiH*—HDZ BIH) became the target of the enraged crowd, while in Tuzla and Sarajevo groups of people entered the offices of the municipal and canton authorities, throwing outside fittings and furnishings. They set fire to private cars parked near the premises and ransacked the main urban centres, burning kiosks and hurling eggs and stones. After almost three days of riots, the situation calmed down. Local activists gathered together and began to organise peaceful street marches on a regular basis. Rallies and sit-ins took place in front of buildings associated with political authority.

After the turmoil, hundreds of Bosnia & Hercegovina citizens gathered to constitute participatory, leaderless assemblies called 'plenums'. The first plenum was organised in Tuzla a few days after the protest began. In the plenums, citizens articulated demands and grievances in a coherent way, and their demands were sent to politicians (Arsenijević 2014). The plenum model drew on the occupation of the Faculty of Philosophy in Tuzla in 2009 (Eminagić & Vujović 2013), during which horizontal assemblies were organised in order to discuss the demands of the students. In turn, the students of Tuzla followed the repertoire adopted during the student protests in Croatia the same year. In Bosnia & Hercegovina, plenums were set up between February and March 2014 in more than 20 different places across the country—although most of them were concentrated in FBiH.

Confronted by internal divisions between the faction wishing plenums to be recognised as a sort of citizen council, and the group who stressed their emancipatory potential as places to exercise direct democracy (Marković 2015), and weakened by concrete issues such as the lack of free space available for gathering, the majority of the plenums ceased their activities in May 2014.[20] During the floods that affected Bosnia & Hercegovina (and other parts of Southeast Europe) in mid-May 2014, the plenums that had not ceased their activities were converted into cells which served to coordinate the volunteers providing assistance to the victims of the flood through food and primary supplies distribution. In practice, the people active in the plenums and the volunteers joining them after the flood arranged transportation to drive people and aid material from the main towns to the villages hit by the inundation.

---

[20]'Why Bosnia's Protest Movement Ran out of Steam', *Balkan Insight*, 18 April 2014, available at: http://www.balkaninsight.com/en/article/why-bosnia-s-protest-movement-ran-out-of-steam, accessed 8 August 2015.

Furthermore, they promoted financial donations in support of the victims, hence creating a network of solidarity.

Collective action frames

During the #JMBG in June 2013, movement organisers elaborated a discourse that maintained a narrow focus on rights-based citizenship, setting aside any other economic and political concern, as well as any attempt to elaborate a critique of the existing constitutional setting of the country. By contrast, on the occasion of the February 2014 uprising socio-economic issues assumed a central importance, becoming the binding force that held together different social groups. The demands of the demonstrators tackled different topics, from the reform of the educational system to the improvement of economic policies, as well as calls for transparency and to fight corruption. Activists on the streets and in the plenums framed their grievances as socio-economic ones and blamed the unaccountable and irresponsible political class. This triggered a sense of injustice among the population that sparked solidarity across ethnic lines, boosting mobilisation across the ethno-national divide. Hence, the socio-economic frame resonated with diverse social groups and the general populace.

Actors and organisational models

The 2014 protests appropriated, to a certain extent, the form of the Occupy movement. This international movement has spread throughout the world since 2011, gaining popularity as a model of direct action democracy (Razsa & Kurnik 2012) and for embracing a non-representational and non-hierarchical structure as a reaction to a perceived crisis of representative politics (Sitrin & Azzellini 2014; Della Porta 2015). The adoption of direct democratic forms of decision-making was the main novelty of the movement, as opposed to previous international movements that made use of different types of organisational forms, developing alliances with formal actors such as voluntary organisations and trade unions alongside grassroots groups.[21] Formal actors such as NGOs, trade unions, and political parties were not allowed in the plenums, which were conceived as arenas with neither leadership nor representation. Every individual had the right to express an opinion and to vote regardless of ethno-national belonging. Citizens participated in the plenums as 'normal people in a normal country'.[22] This call for normality recurred throughout the plenum activities. To give one example, a moderator addressed the audience in Tuzla as 'normal citizens in a normal country'.[23] The reform proposals elaborated by the thematic working groups—on the basis of the demands that emerged collectively during the plenary sessions—were voted on by plenum participants following a direct-democratic method of decision-making, 'one person, one vote'. Thus, participants voted as individuals, rather than as members of a certain ethno-national group. Many NGO practitioners and public figures from cultural and political life often acted as moderators during the discussions, which included people from different social backgrounds. The moderators, who rotated at every session, were chosen to perform this role at the end of each plenum meeting and by means of public vote. As one activist put it,

---

[21]See for instance the study of the Global Justice Movement of the early 2000s (Della Porta 2007).
[22]Skype interview with an activist participating to the Social Uprising in Bihać, 13 July 2015.
[23]Ninth plenum in Tuzla, 22 February 2014.

I am involved in an NGO, like others: most of us come from an academic and NGO background. But there are also students, the unemployed, workers, it is pretty diverse. It is a heterogeneous group of people participating, nothing really fixed and categorised. We are there as ourselves, not representing anybody.[24]

In the plenums, representation was rejected in favour of an alternative model of direct democracy. The assemblies were allegedly leaderless; nobody was entitled to represent anybody else, nor to speak on his/her behalf.

Performative and prefigurative practices of citizenship

In the light of the factors analysed above, both waves of protest can be classified as constituting instances of activist citizenship. The acts of the demonstrators during the 2013 and 2014 protests went in fact beyond routinised social actions, typical of active citizenship, to break routines and practices (Isin 2009). The #JMBG mobilisation corresponded to a moment of rupture in which individuals expressed and enacted citizenship by occupying public space and calling for the right of Bosnia & Hercegovina citizens, and in particular babies, to a normal life. The occupation of the square in front of the Parliament can be classified as an act moving beyond formally designated spaces for citizenship, which define 'active citizenship'. I classify these strategic actions as performative, as movement actors limited themselves to demanding that the ruling elite fulfil their duties, without creating or forming a new socio-political model of citizenship. Similarly, the claims of movement actors focused narrowly on the respect for human rights and the rights of citizenship as established by the Constitution, without prefiguring another type of system opposed to the existing one, which had made such a political stalemate possible. Furthermore, the protest lacked a horizontal orientation, as a small group of NGO practitioners and activists tended to prevail and lead the demonstrations to the detriment of wider participation.

By contrast, during the 2014 'Social Uprising', demonstrators at first adopted a more radical and violent repertoire, which physically defied the dominant order. Movement actors embraced strategic practices that at once challenged the traditional, hierarchal way of organising, typical of the previous wave of protest. Through the plenums, movement actors enacted a new socio-political model of citizenship based on direct democratic means of organisation and decision-making, which radically called into question the existing constitutional arrangement envisioning citizenship as grounded in ethnic partition. The plenums followed a more horizontal and participatory path, insofar as individuals took part and voted exclusively on an individual basis. The practices emerged throughout the 2014 mobilisation, and in particular the plenums, directly implemented the societal and institutional changes that movement actors sought. Thus, I qualify these strategic practices as prefigurative, because they aimed to transform the democratic politics of the country by enacting 'an alternative world in the present' (Yates 2015, p. 4). Specifically, the model of plenums reinforced a rights-based approach to citizenship, which to date still faces deep social and political challenges to establishing a foothold in the country owing to the salience of the ethnic-based model of citizenship. Furthermore, the demands elaborated in the plenums shifted the focus from the respect for and observance of human rights enshrined in the Constitution (as was the case in the 2013 protests) to a

---

[24]Interview with an activist, Tuzla, 26 April 2014.

radical change in the whole political system; a change that the citizens themselves enacted through the practice of plenums. Constituting new subjectivities, the plenums prefigured the creation of a different democratic model, based on participatory assemblies, working groups, and participation on an individual basis, regardless of ethno-national categorisation. Essentially, in the plenums movement actors did not limit themselves to submitting proposals that, if accepted by the ruling elite, would be implemented within the existing institutional and political framework in which citizens and the elite were embedded. Plenums did not only constitute acts of resistance that disrupted routines, as did the 2013 protests and the simultaneous occupation of the square in front of the National Parliament building, but also represented acts that prefigured a new socio-political paradigm that challenged the existing one established by the Dayton arrangement. In the words of Graeber, plenums performed a society 'as it has to be' (Graeber 2002), as the strategies and practices adopted by movement actors reflected their ends.

Learning and empowerment between 2013 and 2014

Besides prefiguring a new model of citizenship, the analysis also reveals that the 2013–2014 cycle of protests constituted a learning experience for movement actors. Several interviewees recount that the *bebolucija* represented an important occasion in which movement organisers 'learnt an important lesson'.[25] One informed observer claimed that the 2014 uprising would never have happened had the 2013 #JMBG protests not taken place,[26] as the 2013 events created the preconditions for the following wave to occur. Similarly, some demonstrators have suggested that the 2013 wave paved the way for further and more contentious mobilisations to occur since, by maintaining a peaceful mass protest and marginalising the violent fringes, movement actors contributed to normalising the practice of street demonstrations in a high-risk environment for contentious action.[27] From the interviews, it emerged that the #JMBG mobilisation had proved that civil disobedience and resistance could be accepted as conventional democratic tools of expressing citizenship in Bosnia & Hercegovina. In this regard, a movement leader commented that the 2013 *bebolucija* in Sarajevo broke 'the mental barricades of fear among the inhabitants of Sarajevo' which had so far prevented the citizens of the capital from taking to the streets (Arnautović 2013). Both activists and movement organisers stressed the significance of previous experience: they had learned from their participation in—and consequent reflection upon—the previous waves, and transferred this knowledge and experience from one to another.

This learning process that activists and movement organisers mentioned in the interviews seems to have begun earlier than 2013, though, and to not be limited to national experience. Protest leaders were inspired by similar events in the region and beyond. As mentioned above, the practice of the plenums drew on the model adopted during the student protests and occupations across the region, and also on the practices of the Occupy Wall Street protest movement that had begun in 2011 in the US, and the Spanish *indignados* the same year (Della Porta 2015). Additionally, the discourse identifying a cleavage opposing the majority of

[25]Interview with a self-identified independent activist, Sarajevo, 19 April 2013.
[26]Interview with a journalist who participated in both waves of protests, Sarajevo, 1 December 2014.
[27]Interviews with a student who participated in both waves of protests, Sarajevo, 15 April 2014; an activist of plenum Sarajevo, 20 April 2014; and a human right activist, Sarajevo, 23 April 2014.

citizens ('losers', ordinary people excluded from the decision-making process) to the 'winners' (corrupt politicians) invokes the slogan of those previous movements, 'We are the 99%'.

Amongst the interviewees, it emerged that participation in the cycle of mobilisation had empowered the demonstrators, some of whom perceived themselves as having gained political leverage over the ruling elite.[28] The resignation of multiple cantonal governments in the aftermath of the 2014 riots, as well as the (provisional) suppression of some benefits for state employees as demanded by the demonstrators, such as the abolition of the 'white bread' allowance,[29] contributed to fuelling this feeling of empowerment. As a young participant said: '[In 2014] power holders felt threatened even physically [by the violent turn the demonstrations took]. It is a fact, and it is the first time I saw the system was scared, that there was the possibility to change a bit the state of affairs'.[30] The protest wave also strengthened the activist network upon which the 2014 mobilisation was based. The oppositional front grew over the course of the protest cycle, as the networking process that had begun during the 2013 wave of mobilisation continued throughout and following the events of 2014.

Conclusions

By using the concept of 'prefigurative politics', this essay set out to demonstrate that acts of citizenship can have a performative orientation, breaking routines and challenging power relations, as well as a prefigurative dimension, aimed at transforming social reality by means of concrete acts. Specifically, analysis of the 2013–2014 cycle of protests in Bosnia & Hercegovina serves as a case in point to demonstrate the use of strategic actions to perform and embody a concept of citizenship at odds with the status quo. In both waves of protests, growing criticism of a model of citizenship grounded on ethnic divisions emerged and became evident in the practices and slogans voiced on the streets, which called for citizenship based on respect for individual rights. Reclaimed through street marches and the occupation of the square in front of the National Parliament during the 2013 protests, this civic model of citizenship was enacted in 2014 through the plenums, participatory assemblies that prefigured a transformed model of citizenship in which every person has the right to vote and can participate actively and in a horizontal way in the decision-making process. Instead of attempting to influence legislative and political decisions affecting their lives by urging the ruling elite to make the changes on their behalf, citizens enacted the change through the practice of plenums.

To conclude, this analysis has revealed that a prefigurative orientation of 'acts of citizenship' could help to grasp the transformative potential of the movements such as those that emerged in Bosnia & Hercegovina throughout the 2013–2014 cycle of protests. Moreover, it offers an alternative perspective on the development of such practices and the goals they envisioned and mirrored at the same time. Although one might claim that the 2013–2014 cycle of protests did not bring about any concrete change in terms of how citizenship is articulated at the institutional level, the transformative orientation embodied by the movement's strategic

---

[28]Interviews with a student who participated in both waves of protests, Sarajevo, 15 April 2014; an activist of plenum Tuzla, *via* Skype, 8 September 2014; and an activist of plenum Zenica, Zenica, 13 July 2015.

[29]According to the Law on Salaries and Allowances of FBiH, elected officials and holders of executive functions have the right to receive salaries for a whole year after their mandates end, of the same amount as they had while in office. Such an allowance is called 'white bread' (*bijeli hljeb*).

[30]Interview with a journalist, informed observer, who participated in both waves of protests, Sarajevo, 1 December 2014.

practices cannot be disregarded. Notwithstanding the presence of political and cultural hurdles to the affirmation of a rights-based citizenship in Bosnia & Hercegovina, citizens participated in the plenums as owners of certain rights rather than as members of a particular ethno-national group, prefiguring a new socio-political model that moves beyond the realm of activist citizenship and radically calls into question the existing constitutional arrangement based on ethnic partitions in practice.

ORCID

CHIARA MILAN ⓘ http://orcid.org/0000-0002-2604-3442

References

Armakolas, I. (2007) 'Sarajevo No More? Identity and the Sense of Place among Bosnian Serb Sarajevans in Republika Srpska', in Bougarel, X., Helms, E. & Duijzings, G. (eds).

Arnautović, A. (2013) 'JMBG.org. Dnevnik Aktiviste: Započeli Smo Nešto Veliko', 10 June, available at: http://www.media.ba/bs/magazin-mreze-i-web/dnevnik-aktiviste-2-zapoceli-smo-nesto-veliko, accessed 20 December 2016.

Arsenijević, D. (ed.) (2014) *Unbribable Bosnia. The Fight for the Commons* (Baden-Baden, Nomos Verlagsgesellschaft).

Baćević, J. (2015) '"They Had Sex, Drugs and Rock'n'Roll; We'll Have Mini-Jobs and Loans to Pay": Transition, Social Change and Student Movements in the Post-Yugoslav Region', in Horvat, S. & Štiks, I. (eds).

Belloni, R. (2013) 'Bosnia: Building States Without Societies? NGOs and Civil Society', in Chandler, D. & Sisk, T. D. (eds) *Routledge Handbook of International Statebuilding* (Abingdon, Routledge Handbooks).

Bieber, F. (2005) *Post-War Bosnia: Ethnicity, Inequality and Public Sector Governance* (New York, NY, Palgrave Macmillan).

Bieber, F. (2014) 'Is Change Coming Finally? Thought on the Bosnian Protests', 9 February, available at: http://florianbieber.org/2014/02/09/is-changecoming-finally-thoughts-on-the-bosnian-protests/, accessed 19 February 2015.

Bougarel, X., Helms, E. & Duijzings, G. (2007) *The New Bosnian Mosaic: Identities, Memories and Moral Claims in a Post-War Society* (Aldershot, Ashgate).

Della Porta, D. (ed.) (2007) *The Global Justice Movement: Cross-National and Transnational Perspectives* (Boulder, CO, Paradigm Publishers).

Della Porta, D. (2015) *Social Movements in Times of Austerity: Bringing Capitalism Back into Protest Analysis* (Cambridge, Polity Press).

Džankic, J. (2015) *Citizenship in Bosnia and Herzegovina, Macedonia and Montenegro: Effects of Statehood and Identity Challenges* (Farnham, Ashgate).

Eminagić, E. (2014) 'Yours, Mine, Ours? We Are All in This Together Now!', *Viewpoints from Southeast Europe—Rosa Luxemburg Stiftung Office for Southeastern Europe*, available at: http://www.rosalux.rs/userfiles/files/Emin%20Eminagic_Tuzla%20protests.pdf, accessed 20 December 2016.

Eminagić, E. & Vujović, P. (2013) 'Breaking the Silence—A Map of Protests in Bosnia and Herzegovina: Contexts, Methods and Ideas Towards a De-Ethnicized Politics', Paper Presented at the Conference *Rebellion and Protest from Maribor to Taksim. Social Movements in the Balkans*, Graz, 12–14 December.

Goffman, E. (1974) *Frame Analysis: An Essay on the Organization of Experience* (New York, NY, Harper and Row).

Gordy, E. (2016) 'Political Stalemate, Public Dissatisfaction and the Rebirth of Self-Organization', *Otvoreni-Magazin.net*, 18 February, available at: http://otvorenimagazin.net/en/18/02/2016/6-75ab/, accessed 19 December 2016.

Graeber, D. (2002) 'The New Anarchists', *New Left Review*, 13.

Helms, E. (2007) '"Politics Is a Whore": Women, Morality and Victimhood in Post-War Bosnia-Herzegovina', in Bougarel, X., Helms, E. & Duijzings, G. (eds).

Holloway, J. (2010) *Crack Capitalism* (London & New York, NY, Pluto Press).

Horvat, S. & Štiks, I. (eds) (2015) *Welcome to the Desert of Post-Socialism: Radical Politics After Yugoslavia* (Brooklyn, NY, Verso).

ACTIVIST CITIZENSHIP IN SOUTHEAST EUROPE

Hromadžić, A. (2015) *Citizens of an Empty Nation: Youth and State-Making in Postwar Bosnia-Herzegovina* (Philadelphia, PA, University of Pennsylvania Press).

Isin, E. F. (2009) 'Citizenship in Flux: The Figure of the Activist Citizen', *Subjectivity*, 29, 1.

Isin, E. F. (2017) 'Performative Citizenship', in Shachar, A., Bauböck, R., Bloemraad, I. & Vink, M. (eds) *The Oxford Handbook of Citizenship* (Oxford, Oxford University Press).

Isin, E. & Nielsen, G. M. (2008) *Acts of Citizenship* (London, Zed Books).

Isin, E. F. & Turner, B. S. (eds) (2002) *Handbook of Citizenship Studies* (London, Sage).

Jacobsson, K. (2015) *Urban Grassroots Movements in Central and Eastern Europe* (Farnham, Ashgate).

Kapidžić, D. (2016) 'Local Elections in Bosnia and Herzegovina', *Contemporary Southeastern Europe*, 3, 2.

Kraft, M. G. (2015) 'Insurrections in the Balkans: From Workers and Students to New Political Subjectivities', in Horvat, S. & Štiks, I. (eds).

Leach, D. K. (2013) 'Prefigurative Politics', in Snow, D. A., Della Porta, D., Klandermans, B. & McAdam, D. (eds) *The Wiley-Blackwell Encyclopedia of Social and Political Movements* (Malden, MA, Blackwell).

Lijphart, A. (1969) 'Consociational Democracy', *World Politics*, 21, 2.

Majstorović, D., Vučkovac, Z. & Pepić, A. (2016) 'From Dayton to Brussels *via* Tuzla: Post-2014 Economic Restructuring as Europeanization Discourse/Practice in Bosnia and Herzegovina', *Southeast European and Black Sea Studies*, 15, 4.

Marković, G. (2015) 'Goran Marković: Čemu Su Nas Naučili Protesti?', *Abrašmedia*, 7 February, available at: http://abrasmedia.info/goran-markovic-cemu-su-nas-naucili-protesti/, accessed 19 September 2017.

McCarthy, J. D. & Zald, M. N. (1977) 'Resource Mobilization and Social Movements: A Partial Theory', *American Journal of Sociology*, 82, 6.

Milan, C. (2014a) 'Sow Hunger, Reap Anger: Why Bosnia Is Burning', *ROAR Magazine*, 9 February, available at: http://roarmag.org/2014/02/bosnia-protests-tuzla-workers/, accessed 15 February 2014.

Milan, C. (2014b) 'Tuzla: The Workers' Revolt That Spawned a Bosnian Spring', *ROAR Magazine*, 1 May, available at: https://roarmag.org/essays/tuzla-workers-revolt-bosnia-protests/, accessed 2 May 2014.

Mujkić, A. (2008) *We, the Citizens of Ethnopolis* (Sarajevo, Centar za ljudska prava Univerziteta).

Mujkić, A. (2013) 'On the Way to the Bosnian Multitude. Review of the JMBG Protests of June 2013', Paper Presented at the Conference *Rebellion and Protest from Maribor to Taksim. Social Movements in the Balkans*, Graz, 12–14 December.

Murtagh, C. (2016) 'Civic Mobilization in Divided Societies and the Perils of Political Engagement: Bosnia and Herzegovina's Protest and Plenum Movement', *Nationalism and Ethnic Politics*, 22, 2.

Nagle, J. & Clancy, M. A. C. (2010) *Shared Society or Benign Apartheid?: Understanding Peace-Building in Divided Societies* (Basingstoke & New York, NY, Palgrave Macmillan).

Pickering, P. M. (2006) 'Generating Social Capital for Bridging Ethnic Divisions in the Balkans: the Case of two Bosniak Cities', *Ethnical and Racial Studies*, 29, 1.

Razsa, M. & Kurnik, A. (2012) 'The Occupy Movement in Žižek's Hometown: Direct Democracy and a Politics of Becoming', *American Ethnologist*, 39, 2.

Sarajlić, E. (2010) *A Citizenship Beyond the Nation-State: Dilemmas of the 'Europeanisation' of Bosnia and Herzegovina*, Working Paper 9 (Edinburgh, CITSEE University of Edinburgh).

Sitrin, M. (2007) 'Ruptures in Imagination: Horizontalism, Autogestion and Affective Politics in Argentina', *Policy & Practice-A Development Education Review*, 5, 4.

Sitrin, M. & Azzellini, D. (2014) *They Can't Represent Us!: Reinventing Democracy From Greece To Occupy* (Brooklyn, NY, Verso).

Štiks, I. (2015) *Nations and Citizens in Yugoslavia and the Post-Yugoslav States: One Hundred Years of Citizenship* (London, Bloomsbury).

Tilly, C. & Tarrow, S. G. (2006) *Contentious Politics* (Boulder, CO, Paradigm Publishers).

Touquet, H. (2012) *Escaping Ethnopolis: Postethnic Mobilization in Bosnia-Herzegovina*, PhD Dissertation, Leuven, Katholieke Universiteit Leuven.

Touquet, H. & Vermeersch, P. (2008) 'Bosnia and Herzegovina: Thinking Beyond Institution-Building', *Nationalism and Ethnic Politics*, 14, 2.

Yates, L. (2015) 'Rethinking Prefiguration: Alternatives, Micropolitics and Goals in Social Movements', *Social Movement Studies*, 14, 1.

Between Europe and the Past—Collective Identification and Diffusion of Student Contention to and from Serbia

ASTRID REINPRECHT

Abstract

This essay examines diffusion between student social movements against higher education reforms in the countries of the former Yugoslavia. It firstly explores how—despite a strong tradition of protest in socialist Yugoslavia and in Serbia under Milošević—activists involved in the 2006 Serbian student protests chose not to reclaim the past but rather drew on experiences from student movements in France, Germany, and Greece. Second, it uncovers how the wave of protest that started in Serbia evolved into a model for contention for the whole region of the former Yugoslavia, long before the 2011 anti-austerity protests could serve as inspiration.

STUDENTS AND YOUTH ARE OFTEN AT THE FOREFRONT OF SOCIAL movements (Lipset 1971; Gill & DeFronzo 2009, p. 204). Particularly since the waves of protest in 1968, academics have tried to explain why students are so frequently, and often intensely, mobilised. The region of the former Yugoslavia is no exception. During the 1980s, Yugoslavia had the highest number of protests in the communist world (Musić 2009, p. 161; Vladisavljević 2011, p. 143). Students, young academics, and urban youth played a crucial role in most of these protests: students occupied the University of Belgrade in 1968; students triggered the so-called Croatian Spring of 1973; students marched the streets of Kosovo in the early 1980s; students participated in anti-war activities in the early 1990s; and students spearheaded the anti-Milošević demonstrations of 1996–1997 that precipitated his fall in autumn 2000. It thus may come as no surprise that, after a few years of relative calm, the University of Belgrade again became the epicentre of a student occupation in November 2006. For six days, students blocked lectures and university facilities. There are no exact figures for the number of supporters and participants, but the booklet *Borba Za Znanje* (*Struggle for Knowledge*)—a compendium of documents, interviews, and articles published in early 2007 by a group of activists—states that roughly 17,000 students signed petitions in support of the occupation's demands (Borba Za Znanje 2007, p. 7). According to key figures of the occupation, the event heralded the 'arrival of a new generation' (Borba Za Znanje 2007, p. 7) of activists who,

---

This is an Open Access article distributed under the terms of the Creative Commons Attribution License (http://creativecommons.org/licenses/by/4.0/), which permits unrestricted use, distribution, and reproduction in any medium, provided the original work is properly cited.

for the first time, occupied university spaces through decision-making in direct democratic plenary assemblies.

But how new were these tactics, and how did these tactics come to be decided upon by the activists involved? The struggles of 2006 paved the way for what Štiks (2015) has labelled the 'new left' in the former Yugoslavia.[1] According to Štiks' analysis, the new left unites 'generally progressive political and social movements' which are characterised by their 'experiments or advocacy of direct, participatory, and horizontal democracy [and their] critique of the neoliberal capitalist transformation of the post-Yugoslav societies' (Štiks 2015, p. 137). Broadly in line with scholars such as Della Porta (2015), Štiks links the development of this emancipatory politics to the 2008 global economic crisis. This essay refines such findings in two important ways. First, it traces the beginnings of the new left back to the Serbian student occupation in 2006. In other words, the essay shows that the origins of contention in the former Yugoslavia predate the 2008 global economic crisis and the 2011 protest cycles in the Middle East (Sadiki 2015), the US, and Southern Europe (Prentoulis & Thomassen 2014). Serbian activists in 2006 created the contours of subsequent student mobilisation for the whole region of the former Yugoslavia.

Second, the essay refines Štiks' (2015) observation of the new left's 'internationalist approach'. It uncovers how students in 2006 oriented themselves towards student movements outside the post-Yugoslav region, rather than to past experiences with fringe politics under communism. The contention of 2006 arose from a perceived necessity to distinguish mobilisation from earlier incidents of student protests. This does not imply that past experiences with protests did not matter at all. However, my essay analyses the puzzle of why students downplayed links to the past while elevating references to student movements in France, Germany, Greece, and other European countries. The finding is that—faced with a broadly unquestioned pro-EU (even if often superficial) discourse by their adversaries as well as with participants' left orientation— Serbian activists deliberately referenced student movements at the margins of Western European societies to legitimise their own struggle. My analysis of Serbian activists' achievements in 2006 hence permits a rich appreciation of mobilisation in Southeast Europe.

In my exploration of the Serbian student contention, I draw from social movement scholarship on collective identity and discursive opportunity structures.[2] Cultural processes of collective identification and 'framing' are singled out as primary conceptual tools to enlighten us about movements' organisational forms, strategies, and tactics. In order to dissect the differences between historic forms of mobilisation in Yugoslavia and the occupation in 2006, I first provide a brief historical background of grassroots activism under communism and during the ensuing Yugoslav Wars between 1991 and 2001.[3] I then present the contours of mobilisation, focussing on frames and related tactics in 2005, 2006 and 2007. My insights derive from online and offline documents produced by student activists around the entire post-Yugoslav region (except Kosovo) from 2005 up until summer 2014, and from 30 semi-structured interviews with key informants conducted in 2012 and 2013 in Croatia and

---

[1] For the purpose of this essay I employ the terms 'successor states of Yugoslavia', also termed the 'former Yugoslavia', to designate the countries which once formed the Socialist Federal Republic of Yugoslavia (Croatia, Bosnia & Hercegovina, Kosovo, Serbia, Slovenia, Macedonia, and Montenegro).

[2] A discursive opportunity structure results from contests between various interpretive frames held by activists (Gamson 2011).

[3] The comprehensive label for the ten-day war in Slovenia (1991), the war in Croatia (1991–1995), the war in Bosnia (1992–1995), the Kosovo War and the NATO bombings against the Federal Republic of Yugoslavia (1998–1999), and the violent conflict in Macedonia (2001).

Serbia.[4] For the sake of clarity, I point to regional developments where necessary, but keep my overall focus on Serbia. I then move on to the core part of the essay, where I analyse the diffusion of certain frames and tactics from student movements in Europe to Serbia and explain the adoption of such elements by Serbian student activists as conditioned by the necessity to construct an inwardly and outwardly appealing collective identity. The empirical part concludes with a brief illustration of how Serbian innovations from 2006 inspired Croatians in 2009, and were then diffused back to Serbia in 2011, and on to the whole region. In my conclusion, I relate my discussion to broader debates around mobilisation and resistance in Southeast Europe.

Diffusion as a corollary of collective identification processes

The actions and narratives of social movements are rarely *sui generis* but draw on conflicts that have occurred at different times and/or in different places. In the following section, I summarise the meanings of fundamental terms such as 'repertoire', 'frame', 'identity', and 'diffusion'. These terms will serve as a basis for my argument, according to which the need to construct a sound collective identity may induce social movement actors to draw inspiration from elsewhere instead of inventing their own tactics and framing. For the purpose of this essay, I define student movements as a subcategory of social movements that unite a large portion of students in the 'relatively organized effort ... to either bring about or prevent change in any one of the following: policies, institutional personnel, social structure (institutions), or cultural aspects of society' (Gill & DeFronzo 2009, p. 208). As with social movements in general, the conflictive nature of student movements is crucial. It captures the movements' role in expressing (and acting upon) social conflicts. Social movements are orientated towards interrupting the social and/or cultural *status quo*: 'fostering or halting change is the *raison d'être* for all social movements' (Snow *et al.* 2011, p. 8).

However radical their orientation and framing, social movements commonly rely upon repertoires, or 'established ways in which pairs of actors make and receive claims bearing on each other's interests' (Tilly 1993, p. 265). Repertoires bundle diverse courses of action together. This may include a social movement's tactics and strategies, as well as less tangible behaviour such as ideas, slogans, and frames. Repertoires are bent on historicity; they 'are learned cultural creations ... they emerge from struggle' (Tilly 1993, p. 264). Various authors (Tilly 1978, 2004; Tarrow 1989; Traugott 1993; Beissinger 2002) have investigated how repertoires change over time. Coming from a tradition of political process theory, Tilly (2006) holds that repertoires shift incrementally in relation to underlying transformations of large-scale socio-economic and cultural opportunity structures. Tarrow (1997) proposes that short-lived and highly publicised 'moments of madness do not transform [repertoires] at once' (Tarrow 1997, p. 329), but that these peaks of larger protest cycles contribute to the evolution and—if proven successful—'modularisation' of innovative contentious practices (Tarrow 1997, p. 337). Modularisation occurs when innovations stabilise into routines, and thus enrich previously established repertoires.

---

[4]The interviews with 16 Serbian interviewees were conducted within the framework of my doctoral research in Zagreb (on 18 May 2012) and Belgrade (20–24 May 2013). The interviews with 14 Croatian interviewees took place in Zagreb (on 18 and 19 May 2012 and 15–19 May 2013). See the Appendix for an anonymised list of interviewees.

In contrast to political process approaches (Kriesi 2011), new social movement scholars concentrate on inner dynamics of mobilisation and insist on the structuring impact of frames and identification on mobilisation (Offe 1985; Della Porta & Diani 1999, pp. 24–33; Benford & Snow 2000). Most new social movement scholars agree that generating a sense of shared purpose and emotional belonging is essential for mobilisation. Identity fulfils several essential functions for social movements. First, identity might constitute an implicit or explicit goal for contention. Second, it may form the basis for collective claims and motivate potential adherents to act. Third, it may be used to legitimise activists' choices and tactics (Polletta & Jasper 2001, pp. 286–97). This last point is essential for our present discussion: the form of the movement itself (Melucci 1989, p. 60) and its organisation, tactics, and strategies do not merely flow from the availability of resources or environmental incentives, to give one example, but must also conform to the exigencies of identity. In other words, 'answers to the pragmatic question of "How do we organize?" reverberate inward to the shaping of collective identity and outward to link movements to institutions or opportunity structures' (Clemens 1996, p. 209).[5] Moreover, as Gamson and Meyer (1996) have pointed out, activists' readings of opportunities and the outcomes of their 'framing contests' (Gamson 2011, p. 249) determine how they are affected by such opportunities. The objective existence of opportunities is not enough to understand why social movements (and their repertoires) change. In the most extreme case, for instance, activists might misjudge or simply not perceive obvious opportunities. Repertoires change not only because social movements respond to seemingly given circumstances, but because they conform to inner logics of collective identity construction. Adoptions and/or innovations do not only take place because of unstable environments or because old ways have proven ineffective. Social activists might be looking out for new ways to wage their struggle if they feel that the existing repertoire fails to represent them adequately.

The above definition of repertoires includes the term 'established'. This implies that, once tested and adopted, repertoires remain fairly consistent over time: 'the distinctive features that set the repertoire apart are the considerable stability it exhibits … and the constraining influence it exercises over participants in collective action' (Traugott 1993, p. 310). It is rare that social movement actors radically overhaul previous practices; they prefer to adopt rather than invent (Biggs 2013, pp. 408–9). It may be more efficient to learn from other examples of mobilisation and adapt what has been achieved elsewhere to one's own situation. This is where the notion of diffusion—defined as a 'flow of innovations' (Soule 1997, p. 860) within or between contending social actors—comes in. Diffusion occurs when an innovation (frames, stories, claims, tactics, strategies, practices, or organisational forms) spreads from the innovating social movement to the adopting social movement (Givan *et al.* 2010, p. 1; Soule 2011). Contrary to what might be assumed, diffusion involves a substantial degree of activity either by the innovating and/or the adopting movement.[6] 'Diffusion implies that outsiders make a conscious decision to copy what happens in another state' (Bunce & Wolchik 2006, p. 286).

Three factors simplify the diffusion of innovative practices. First, diffusion is easier the more practices are condensed into ready-made modules that 'can easily be transferred from setting to setting, by groups of social actors who are not engaged in face-to-face discussion'

---

[5]See also Taylor and Van Dyke (2011).
[6]Types of diffusion are discussed further in Benford and Snow (2002, pp. 27–37).

(Soule 1997, p. 859). Second, previous success (or at least the perception of success) increases the likelihood that another social movement adopts a new practice (Tilly 1993, p. 266). Aligning oneself with successful movements elsewhere might help to establish legitimacy with the audience, that is, a movement's constituency (adherents, potential participants, sympathisers) and adversaries. Third, objective and/or perceived commonalities underpin diffusion (Givan *et al*. 2010, p. 6). Similarities are not just 'out there', they must be attributed and constructed. Hence, diffusion comes to depend on processes of attributing and constructing similarities (Benford & Snow 2002). Thus, it is closely intertwined with processes of identification and framing.

Framing can be defined as a process through which activists build cognitive schemes (frames) to explain and interpret certain aspects of the world (Snow *et al*. 1986). Frames serve to simplify and condense (Benford & Snow 2000, p. 614) reality through defining and diagnosing a problem, articulating possible solutions, and motivating activists (Benford & Snow 2000, pp. 614–18). With regard to diffusion, activists thus need to frame (interpret) their own reality as comparable to the reality of the other movement. Only when the adopting activists understand and articulate who they are (or are not) and what the surrounding context is (not) like, will they be able to comprehend whether another movement is similar enough to serve as a role model. What other social movements have done will only be perceived as feasible, legitimate, or effective if activists frame their situation as comparable. Framing thus underpins diffusion, which is much more than instrumental learning: 'Through the construction of new meanings, identities, and issue frames ... actors alter their conception of what is politically feasible or desirable. Diffusion, in short, often entails a transformation of political consciousness' (Tilly 1993, p. 9).

Student mobilisation in Serbia: from the past to the present?

Before proceeding with the analysis of the 2006 student protests, it is instructive to briefly outline previous student-led mobilisations in the former Yugoslavia.[7] Such an endeavour serves to clarify the precedent from which Serbian student activists in 2006 sought to differentiate themselves. Compared to the Soviet Union, mobilisation was not uncommon in communist Yugoslavia. The main reasons for this were malleable state–society relations and the peculiar location of the Yugoslav Federation 'between East and West' (Kanzleiter 2011).

After his break with Stalin in 1948, Yugoslavia's ideological mastermind and leader Josip Broz Tito created a separate version of socialism (Calic 2010, p. 192). Its main elements included non-alignment in foreign-policy matters, a transnational identity scheme ('brotherhood and unity'), federalised political structures, and self-management of workers at the company level (Allcock 2000; Ramet 2006). The gradual devolution of decision-making to the Republics of Bosnia, Croatia, Macedonia, Serbia, and Slovenia culminated in the new constitution of 1974. What had been devised as a means to (re)gain legitimacy and reduce centrifugal tendencies eventually weakened the central state: 'insofar as this regional pluralization operated within a federal structure founded on differences of a-nationality, it was apt, in conditions of political illegitimacy and economic deterioration, to reinforce nationalism'

---

[7]Some notable pieces of research include Bieber (2003, 2011), Steinberg (2004), Kanzleiter (2008), Nadjivan (2008), Mujkić (2010) Djokić and Ker-Lindsay (2011).

(Ramet 2006, p. 379). Conversely, as state power declined, the power of society grew (Irvine 1997, p. 9). Opportunities for social assembly, cultural expression, and voicing 'grass roots expression[s] of discontent' (Vladisavljević 2002, p. 10) increased as points of access to the system multiplied. For young, mostly urban people from the mid-1960s and 1970s, cultural associations, critical magazines and journals, and music clubs became more open to alternative ideas and practices rooted in anarchism, feminism, ecology, and pacifism (Figa 1997, pp. 168–73; Dvornik 2009, p. 141).

A turning point in the history of Yugoslav grassroots activism occurred in 1968. On 3 June 1968, students occupied the University of Belgrade and established 'the Red University of Karl Marx' (Kanzleiter 2011, p. 84). The following day, protests quickly spread to other universities around the federation. For the first time since World War II, students 'destroyed the illusion of a conflict-free society' in communist Yugoslavia (Kanzleiter 2008, p. 100). They called into question the regime's claim to be the sole interpreter of society's interests (Beslin 2009, p. 61). Authorities at first condoned the events as legitimate self-management. Eventually, however, repression increased, and many of the activists were imprisoned (Spehnjak & Cipek 2007, p 278). The events of 1968 transgressed the established boundaries of grassroots activism, as students publicly claimed the right and the capacity to reinterpret Yugoslav communism. However, this claim was not contentious in the sense of challenging Yugoslav communism as a system of political power *per se*. As time passed and student protests developed in other republics, the nature of these movements shifted. Thus, during the so-called Croatian Spring between 1971 and 1973, proponents of an explicit federalisation of Yugoslavia co-opted student protest. Backed by proto-nationalist intellectuals, especially from within the *Matica Hrvatska* (Croatian Academy of Sciences and Arts), nationalist (that is, anti-Yugoslav) ideas gained ground (Ramet 2006, pp. 285–323).

From the 1980s, other segments of society outside urban and intellectual epicentres were involved as well. In the industrial complexes of northern Kosovo, miners and rural youth were drawn into strikes that were motivated first by social but then increasingly nationalist demands. Nationalism was an 'unintended consequence of the high levels of mobilization and spiralling of various conflicts in a highly decentralized, authoritarian multi-nation-state' (Vladisavljević 2011, p. 156). It remains disputed in the literature as to how much nationalist mobilisation was authentic (Vladisavljević 2002, p. 2) or manipulated (Magaš 1993, p. 206; Musić 2009, p. 161) by politicians in their quest to enlarge their 'extra-institutional power base' (Mujkić 2010, p. 17). However, it is predominantly accepted that Kosovo and its future status became a focal point for nationalist mobilisation. In the end, Slobodan Milošević's 'anti-bureaucratic revolution', starting in 1987, contributed to the destabilisation of the Yugoslav Federation (Mønnesland 1997, pp. 318–20). Whatever the precise trigger, content, and nature of mobilisations, the Yugoslav Federation offered space for ordinary people to become active, and this space grew markedly while federal institutions (such as the League of Communists, the cult of the leader Josip Broz Tito) withered away (Irvine 1997; Vladisavljević 2011, pp. 145–46).

After the first democratic breakthrough in Slovenia and Croatia in the early 1990s, the Yugoslav Wars resulted in ethno-nationalism, war, genocide, and increasing authoritarianism (Ramet 2005). In Serbia, Slobodan Milošević established a 'hybrid regime' (Bieber 2003, p. 74) with tight control over the media, administration, and security sectors. Though elections took place, they were not necessarily free or fair. Yet, despite widespread censorship

(Kurspahic 2003, pp. 3–26), war-induced economic hardship and clientelism, the space for dissent never fully closed, as Bieber (2003) argues. Even if mobilisation[8] remained restricted to Belgrade for a long time, the 'Other Serbia' (*Druga Srbija*)[9] 'fulfilled an important symbolic function in challenging the seeming homogeneity in intellectual and popular support for extreme nationalist policies' (Bieber 2003, p. 83). During the early years of the war, anti-war demonstrations (Bilić 2011, 2012; Stubbs 2012) gathered activists from pre-existing networks of students, feminists, pacifists, and ecologists in Serbia, Croatia, Bosnia, and Slovenia. Rock music (Steinberg 2004) and alternative media (such as the Belgrade radio station B92) (Collin 2001; Kurspahic 2003) were important means of information, motivation, and diffusion. For example, B92 was 'much more than a little student radio station playing noisy rock records. It was now the centre of a social movement: anti-war, anti-nationalism; pro-democracy, pro-human rights' (Collin 2001, p. 56). The winter protests of 1996 relied upon student networks but also included some opposition parties and platforms (Bieber 2011). Because public assemblies were forbidden, activists strolled around the streets, dancing, singing, and banging their drums. Thus, 'the crowds occupied space and thereby claimed it, physically and politically, with their bodies, their noise, their banners and so on' (Jansen 2001, p. 40). From the mid-1990s, recruitment was slightly adapted as activists for the first time actively sought to unite different strands of society (including, for example, churches and rural youth) in one movement, which was called *Otpor!* (Resistance!). The focus shifted from attacking the cultural hegemony of nationalism to an overt critique of political leadership. The street as primary locus of contention became ever more crucial, both as a space of appearance and media-staging (Nadjivan 2008, pp. 139–76). After 2000, *Otpor!* and other social movements around the post-Yugoslav region reorganised as non-governmental organisations (NGOs) or political parties, partly as a consequence of the increased interest from outside. In a 2009 article, Vetta lays out how NGOs in Serbia increasingly lost their grassroots character due to foreign funding: 'the donors promoted the "NGO model" as the ideal type of civic engagement to create a new political culture and in doing so, encouraged the emergence of a new urban local elite and fostered "technocratic capital"' (Vetta 2009, p. 30). Many Serbians perceived this as a loss of authenticity (Grødeland 2006).

This brief overview summarises the recurrent waves of protest and a related increase of contentious experiences and knowledge within activists' networks. Students and young people readily participated in and contributed to popular dissent. Most significantly, however, a repertoire of contention slowly evolved. In the early period of grassroots activism, during the 1960s and 1970s, Yugoslav citizens were already creatively experimenting with diverse tactics such as covert cultural events and concerts, mobilisation through magazine and media production, street protests and marches, strikes, and occupation. From the 1980s, public demonstrations became more prevalent, with Milošević mobilising masses of ordinary people in the streets (Nadjivan 2008, pp. 90–1). During the mobilisation of 1996–1997 and 2000, the tactics of street protests, marches, and public demonstrations crystallised into a regional repertoire.

---

[8]Bieber (2003, p. 83) counts six waves of protest in Serbia between 1991 and 2000.
[9]*Druga Srbija* was a term used to denote groups and individuals, who were critical of Milošević and to the principles he stood for (nationalism, authoritarianism, war), as well as supportive of protests against his regime.

ACTIVIST CITIZENSHIP IN SOUTHEAST EUROPE

Contours of the 2006 Serbian occupation

On 22 November 2006, students occupied the Faculty of Philosophy at the University of Belgrade for six days. During the subsequent spring, two more occupations occurred at the Faculty of Arts in Belgrade (19 March–1 April 2007 and 8–15 May 2007). These occupations arose from experiments in contentious action in winter 2005, during which student activists from the University of Belgrade had blocked streets and bridges, assembled in front of government buildings, staged theatre performances, and started a hunger strike (Pantić 2005).[10] However, activists subsequently acknowledged that these efforts were neither successful in spurring participation, nor did they garner substantive public (or media) attention and support: 'we realised that we did not have traditional organisations and networks we could count on to mobilise people'.[11] Thus, activists had to re-orient themselves and think of alternatives. I will analyse why students chose to learn from instances of student mobilisation in Europe rather than from previous Yugoslav examples of citizen activism. In the section below, I outline how students discursively substantiated their purpose through the frames of commercialisation and direct democracy.

The occupations of autumn 2006 followed the introduction of the new Law on Higher Education of August 2005 with which Serbia sought to carry forward the so-called Bologna Process.[12] Serbia, along with almost all other countries of the former Yugoslavia, had signed the Declaration on the European Higher Education Area in 2003 as part of its EU ambitions. The Bologna Process—even if at the outset legally not an EU policy—had become part of the broad push to Europeanise Southeast Europe. This 'generate[d] a battle between the forces of reform and reaction' (Anastasakis 2005, p. 77). Higher education reforms in the name of the Bologna Process brought more autonomy for universities. As a result, rules about tuition, studying conditions, and criteria for grants were altered. For Serbian student activists, the (more or less stringent) application of reforms following Serbia's joining the Bologna Process symbolised a political consensus to commercialise higher education. This understanding formed the core of the movement's framings, as I outline in the subsequent section.

The Serbian student mobilisation of 2006 combined the frame of commercialisation and the frame of direct democracy. In accordance with Benford and Snow (2000, pp. 615–18) I argue that the frame of commercialisation identifies the problem, the aims, and adversaries of mobilisation. The frame of direct democracy, building upon the interpretation presented through the first frame, invalidates the use of various tactics and courses of action. Namely, Serbian activists expressed a local problem (remodelling higher education after communism and war following European standards) according to an internationalised vocabulary.[13]

The commercialisation frame connects higher education reforms with an unjustified move towards global capitalism. The introduction of the Law on Higher Education—of which the

---

[10]'Blokadom do Uslova', 2005, *Novosti Online*, 7 December 2005, available at: http://www.novosti.rs/vesti/naslovna/aktuelno.69.html:177040-Blokadom-do-uslova, accessed 29 September 2017.

[11]Interviewee RS-B, male student, aged 27, Zagreb, 18 May 2012.

[12]The 'Bologna Declaration on the European Higher Education Area' started out as a series of multilateral meetings and agreements to harmonise university education across Europe in the late 1990s. The declaration brought a unified structure for studying, a new system of credits, more autonomy to universities, and intensified international collaboration. With the exception of Slovenia, which signed the treaty in 1999, all other countries in the region became members of the Bologna Process as of 2003. It is important to note that joining the Bologna Process was part of the conditions for preparing EU membership.

[13]For more on transnational activism see Tarrow (2005, pp. 59–76).

rise in tuition fees was one of the most contested elements—symbolised the transformation of public education into a private commodity. Students regarded this as a flagrant injustice, since, according to their interpretation, the education acquired by students had a broader social benefit for the whole society.[14] Following this line of argumentation, the localities of this production (universities) acquired a public value in a double sense. First, knowledge acquired at universities was seen as relevant to all. As one student expressed in an online posting, 'education should be completely free of charge, because it is, first and foremost, a public good' (Borba Za Znanje 2007, p. 175). Second, because universities were funded by the state and the state was financed through taxes, all taxpayers were identified as having a stake in higher education. The introduction of higher education reforms 'ha[d] broader consequences for students ... and the whole of society'.[15] In short, this frame constructs citizens as the ultimate constituency for student mobilisation. The identified adversaries are— interchangeably—the markets and the institutions incorporating 'market logic' such as the EU, the International Monetary Fund (IMF), and the Organisation for Economic Co-operation and Development (OECD). Members of the political elite were framed as the 'henchmen' of these international culprits, and placed in opposition to the aggrieved students, academics, and citizens generally. The slogan 'We study, while they profit' (Borba Za Znanje 2007, p. 113) displayed during a demonstration on 16 November 2006 in Belgrade and the poster posing the question 'Whose are our faculties?' illustrate this line of reasoning. As other scholars have pointed out (Kraft 2013), 'neoliberalism has been almost completely absent from the post-Yugoslav public sphere. The student movements were the first to make the connection between this concept and the ongoing processes of transformation in the societies of the former Yugoslavia' (Baćević 2015, p. 235).

Whereas the commercialisation frame diagnoses the sell-out of universities as the core problem, the direct democracy frame contains the rationale for appropriate action. This frame blames capitalism for hollowing out democratic representativeness and proposes to remedy this misrepresentation of the (silenced) majority through direct democratic methods. In *Borba Za Znanje* (2007, p. 265), one student writes: 'direct democracy [was thought to be the] solution to the manifold limitations of parliamentary democracy .... For this reason, activists rightfully saw parliamentary democracy, in its form of students' parliaments at university, as something, which in reality bears non-democratic traits'. Student activists were constructed as 'standing up for', as opposed to 'standing in for' (that is, representing), the majority. They were considered to be defending democracy at a substantial and procedural level: at a substantial level through criticising the commercialisation of higher education; procedurally because they demanded direct democratic deliberation based on inclusivity and equality.

The Serbian activists aspired to restore a true sense of participation; participation that appeared nullified by representative democracy: 'if we define democracy as having free elections, it exists [in Serbia]. Nobody steals elections [in Serbia]. But if we define that people would participate in the real sense of making a difference ... then [there is no democracy]'.[16] Deliberation and decision-making in an equal, inclusive, and non-dominant fashion were considered the only legitimate ways to outbalance the perceived failure to represent students through student parliaments at universities and citizens through national parliamentary elections. In this frame, occupation is constructed as a logical—but not necessarily

[14]Compare also Baćević (2010).
[15]Interviewee RS-F, male student, 29, Belgrade, 22 May 2013.
[16]Interviewee RS-F, male student, 29, Belgrade, 22 May 2013.

ACTIVIST CITIZENSHIP IN SOUTHEAST EUROPE

temporal—prerequisite for direct democratic decision-making: without free spaces, no truly 'free' decisions for all could be achieved. As one respondent noted, 'occupation as a [space] apart from everything else is a nice way of building something completely different from everything else. When you start experiencing freedom ... you have people who start to think without restraints, without pressures from outside. They start to depend on themselves and on each other'.[17] By rejecting conventional political representation, the activists endorsed a radical understanding of democracy (Little & Lloyd 2009). Moreover, Serbian activists' claims about the defects of representative democracy at universities, as well as in Serbian society at large, expose 'the fact that a particular regime ... has captured and hegemonised the term democracy and presents both the term and itself [the regime] as its unrivalled and impeccable realisation' (Machart 2002, p. 306).

Beginning in 2005 and continuing through 2006, Serbian student activists introduced the frames of commercialisation and direct democracy, as well as the combination of occupation with direct democratic decision-making. These twin tactics of occupation plus direct democracy amounted to a structural disruption of higher education facilities (Gonzalez-Vaillant & Schwartz 2012, p. 1). By experimenting with unorthodox democratic decision-making methods, the activists introduced a moment of rupture in the *status quo* of representative democracy and brought into being new 'forms ... of being political' (Isin 2009, p. 383). Serbian student contention introduced new strategies to the existing repertoire which—as I have described above—at the time encapsulated street protests under hierarchical leadership and re-positioned students as equal actors on the 'community stage' (Rancière 1999, p. 109). The occupation of 2006 functioned as a 'moment of madness' (Tarrow 1993) through which the twin tactics of occupation and direct democratic decision-making were forged into a model fit for use elsewhere in the post-Yugoslav region.

Learning from abroad and collective identification

Why did Serbian students decide in November 2006 to occupy the Faculty of Philosophy? Why did they not adopt the previously described repertoire of social contention—street protests, marches, and public demonstrations—that had evolved through communism until the end of Milošević's regime? Why did they insist on principles of equal, inclusive, and non-hierarchical decision-making in direct democratic plenary assemblies instead of opting for clear leadership structures? The following section attempts to answer this puzzle.

After having unsuccessfully experimented with various contentious strategies over the second half of 2005, Serbian student activists in 2006 had two options: turn to previous examples of social mobilisation in communist Yugoslavia and/or during the authoritarian regime of Slobodan Milošević; or, look further afield. Interestingly, activists chose the second option. Serbian activists' inclination to learn from Europe,[18] rather than from the past,[19] can be explained by collective identification. The hegemonic discourses in Serbia influenced how

---

[17]Interviewee RS-J, male student and translator, 26, Belgrade, 20 May 2013.

[18]With the notion of Europe I do not seek to reify a binary between an ostensible civilisational Western sphere and the Balkans as its 'dark Alter Ego' (Todorova 1999, p. 267). I appeal to a malleable reference point for alternative understandings of European marginalities. This notion transcends both Europe as a geographic marker as well as the EU as a hegemonic political project (Horvat & Štiks 2015, p. 8).

[19]With 'the past' I hark back to the socialist legacy as continuity (Todorova 2015, p. 94), present throughout the region but denied by the forceful pro-EU orientation of elites (Džihić & Wieser 2008, p. 5).

ACTIVIST CITIZENSHIP IN SOUTHEAST EUROPE

activists positioned themselves. At the same time, the need to remain attractive in the eyes of current and potential participants meant that not too many compromises could be struck in terms of identity. According to one of the activists, 'Greece and France were crucial. ... We were inspired from outside to try something, to pose those questions, to put them on the table for public discussion'.[20] The reason for this was that Serbian student activists hoped their frames would resonate with the Serbian public while still harmonising with their own basic self-identification as an anti-capitalist force (Borba Za Znanje 2007, p. 240). In the subsequent paragraphs, I demonstrate how Serbian student activists framed their movements as being similar to other instances of student mobilisation in Europe and dissimilar to earlier mobilisation in Yugoslavia in the 1990s.

Europe and us

During the 1990s, resistance to Milošević not only comprised resistance against nationalism (Bieber 2003) but also an orientation towards liberalism. The intellectuals associated with *Druga Srbija* advocated European democracy and a market economy (Collin 2001). During the demonstrations that led to Milošević's overthrow, the people, groups, and initiatives associated with *Druga Srbija* filled the ranks of *Otpor!* After 2000, members of *Otpor!* comprised the economic, political, and intellectual elites of post-Milošević Serbia (Bieber 2003, p. 87; Nadjivan 2008). For this elite, the EU represented the only way forward (Džihić *et al.* 2006). Many of the policies endorsed in the early 2000s stemmed directly from EU conditionality or were rationalised by reference to the EU. In other words, '"Europe" developed to be the ultimate instrument in advocating one's own politics and dismiss [*sic*] arguments of others' (Džihić & Wieser 2008, p. 87). For student activists in 2006, the resistance of the 1990s was opportunistic and politicised (Borba Za Znanje 2007, pp. 218, 269, 275), because it carried with it an affirmation of political liberalism and economic neoliberalism (Borba Za Znanje 2007, p. 214) and cooperated with political parties from the opposition. By adopting direct democratic strategies, student activists of 2006 signalled that they were independent from political parties and thus from the protests of the 1990s. As well as criticising the overtly pro-EU stance of their leaders, Serbian student activists questioned the teleology of transition towards EU membership. As interviewee RS-B said,

> we have this strong culture of de-politicisation in Serbia that occurred after the revolution of October 5, 2000. Because on one hand, on the level of mainstream politics you had more or less a consensus that we are a pro-EU country that we want to get integrated into the whole EU concept. So the mainstream politics became reduced to the level of policies.[21]

Yet student activists not only re-politicised higher education policies (Baćević 2015, p. 236) but contested what they argued was a neoliberal logic behind reforms undertaken with reference to European integration. For instance, interviewee RS-J explained: 'when Slovenia entered the EU it became a huge shopping mall. ... Standards increased but it's an empty kind of living. Everything got globalised'.[22] Higher education reforms undertaken in the name of the Bologna Process in this way became associated with other neoliberal

---

[20]Interviewee RS-B, male student, 27, Zagreb, 18 May 2012.
[21]Interviewee RS-B, male student, 27, Zagreb, 18 May 2012.
[22]Interviewee RS-J, male student and translator, 26, Belgrade, 20 May 2013. At the time of the interview in 2013, Slovenia still was the first and only former Yugoslav country to have joined the EU.

reforms and processes. Student activists regarded them as hegemonic, because they observed that all the parties from the political establishment (regardless of their ideological stance) implemented pro-European policies (Dzihić *et al.* 2006). In order to position themselves as a political alternative within Serbia, student activists of 2006 hence refused to align with the EU and all that it represented for them.

At the same time, students framed their struggle as part of other European struggles against higher education reforms. As laid out in the theoretical discussions above, movements adopt other movements' frames if and when the adopters regard themselves as similar to the innovators. The student activists saw Serbia as the semi-periphery of a larger process of change that affected all European countries.[23] Since Serbian student activists believed that students around Europe suffered the same fate as them, struggling against the Bologna Process induced them to learn from those who were already embroiled in the struggle. This self-identification as a European semi-periphery was rooted in an attempt at re-appropriating a discourse that degrades the region (and its people) as less developed, less civilised, and less Western (Bakić-Hayden 1995; Todorova 1999). Identification with European student contention thus facilitated the diffusion of mobilisation against Bologna from European countries at large to Serbia.

At a conference of the UK National Union of Students (NUS) in April 2005, students established a campaign for free and accessible education.[24] They framed the problem as one of commercialisation. After three years, the NUS abandoned the campaign 'Education is Not for Sale' due to internal factions about the effectiveness and generalness of the campaign.[25] Meanwhile, student activists in Germany, France, and Greece had already picked up on this critique of neoliberalist restructuring of universities and interlaced it with a critique of representative democracy, arguing that the 'tyranny of the majority'[26] benefitted neoliberal elites and that direct democracy was more genuine and just. In early March 2006, French students occupied the Sorbonne University in Paris. Their anti-capitalist frame invited activists to consider occupation as viable and necessary: 'the insurrectionist collectivity must also constitute a blocking collectivity, physically blocking all circulation of goods'.[27]

Serbian students were directly inspired by events at the Sorbonne. One activist (Interviewee RS-B), who had studied in Paris, organised an event, 'Sorbonne in Flames', at the University of Belgrade on 18 April 2006. This event was the first opportunity in Serbia to hear first-hand about best practices from France and elsewhere. In addition, it was designed to identify people who were interested and—potentially—ready to become involved (Borba Za Znanje 2007, pp. 131–36). Debates evolved over the summer in the framework of a group called

---

[23]See the essay 'Attack on Neo-liberalism' in Borba Za Znanje (2007, pp. 8–23); for similar reasoning see Horvat and Štiks (2013).

[24]See the post by Daniel Randall, member of the Education is Not for Sale Network, elected into the Union as a representative in April 2005, available at: http://www.guardian.co.uk/education/mortarboard/2006/mar/24/danielrandalleducationnotf, accessed 24 February 2012.

[25]'NUS Drops Free Education Doctrine', *Guardian*, 2 April 2008, available at: http://www.guardian.co.uk/education/2008/apr/02/highereducation.uk2, accessed 24 February 2012.

[26]'Il appartient à notre lutte de limiter autant que possible la tyrannie du vote majoritaire'. Communiqué by the direct democratic general assembly of the Sorbonne in Exile from 17 March 2006, available at: https://lignesdeforce.wordpress.com/tag/anti-cpe/, accessed 28 March 2015.

[27]'Dans un monde de flux, le parti de l'insurrection ne peut être que parti du blocage, du blocage physique de toute la circulation marchande ....', in 'Ultime communiqué du comité d'occupation de la Sorbonne en exil', *Étudiants pas Contents*, June 2006, available at: http://etudiantspascontents84.viabloga.com/news/archives-cpe-ultime-communique-du-comite-d-occupation-de-la-sorbonne-en-exil, accessed 25 August 2015.

Socijalni Front.[28] According to these early gatherings, the occupations in France and Greece had yielded some success, albeit discursive rather than material: these student movements had won (media) attention and, through this attention, been able to shape public debate. By adopting their tactics, Serbian students hoped to gain more visibility and thus discursive power. They also hoped to motivate more people to join their activities. In the *Borba Za Znanje* booklet (2007), the imperative of direct democracy is explained in terms of the inability of the newly established student parliaments at Serbian universities to safeguard students' interests and the overall failure of representative democracy in Serbia. As mentioned above, this line of argumentation echoes criticism of representative democracy in France and other European countries by local student movements.

We are not the past

A second reason to learn from abroad rather than from the Yugoslav past, lay in the attempt to maintain legitimacy with regards to the general Serbian public (that is, the potential constituency) and local elites (adversaries). The discursive opportunity structure after the collapse of the communist regime in Serbia stigmatises positive allusions to left/social—or seemingly socialist—ideas. All around the region, the majority of (and the most powerful) politicians and media routinely condemned the commemoration of Titoist Yugoslavia (Todorova 2010, p. 4). Anyone who publicly identified as left ran the risk of being ridiculed as 'Yugonostalgic' (Lindstrom 2005). This made it difficult for Serbian activists in 2006 to frame the communist past constructively, for instance, by making reference to models of direct democracy used during the occupation of the University of Belgrade in 1968 or to workers' self-management: 'any kind of social struggle … is totally demonised. … When we come out with [social] demands, it looks like a thing of the past'.[29] Attributes of the Left were downplayed in communications with potential participants and sympathisers:

> in 2006 our idea was to … well, as a left-wing group we are aware that we cannot mobilise all the students …. We were also aware that if you are a small movement, trying to ignite a larger movement, you won't share left wing ideas as dominant, and the left-wing will not be leading the movement.[30]

Confronted with this context, student activists rejected the historical example of 1968 and emphasised dissimilarities between the communist higher education system in Yugoslavia and the higher education system in postwar Serbia. The perception of Serbian universities as embedded within European—and global capitalist—relations of power formed a crucial reason for differentiation from the past. According to their commercialisation frame (as laid out above), the overall aim of activists in 2006 was to reverse commercialisation in higher education. If Serbian student activists wanted to build a collective identity that appealed to current and potential participants, they could not entirely abandon their anti-capitalist orientation but had to re-inscribe claims for social justice into the public sphere. This explains their eagerness not to be associated with the mobilisations of 1996–1997 and 2000.

The ineffectiveness of the previous repertoire of contention and the apparent success of students in European countries is one part of the explanation for the particular shape of

---

[28]The *Socijalni Front* was at the heart of the occupation of the Faculty of Philosophy in Belgrade the following autumn, but had disbanded by mid-2007.
[29]Interviewee RS-C, male student, 23, Belgrade, 21 May 2013.
[30]Interviewee RS-B, male student, 27, Zagreb, 18 May 2012.

ACTIVIST CITIZENSHIP IN SOUTHEAST EUROPE

Serbian student contention in 2006. The main reason for looking outside the region lies in the need to construct a collective identity that would appeal to current and potential participants while remaining acceptable to the Serbian general public. By turning to anti-Bologna Process student movements, they reduced the possibility of the pro-EU members of the elite (their identified adversaries) de-legitimising them as regressive 'Yugonostalgics'. Through turning to marginalised rather than mainstream actors in Europe, Serbian activists avoided being dismissed as inauthentic. This engendered a highly complex process of constructing differences and similarities. 'Europe' as a synonym for the EU was staunchly rejected as a reference point: the EU stood for exactly those neoliberal policies—propagated by the Serbian elites—which student activists sought to stop. By highlighting similarities with social movement activists at the margins of Western European societies, Serbian student activists signalled they were not alone in their fight but firmly located on the map of contention in Europe. This appeared more promising in gaining wider public acceptance than an orientation towards de-legitimised models of mobilisation from communist Yugoslavia or Milošević's Serbia.

Regional diffusion: from Serbia to Croatia and back

The 2006 occupation in Serbia constituted a transformative contentious event. A contentious event is transformative if it shifts 'the very cultural categories that shape and constrain human action' (Sewell 1996, p. 263). In the case examined here, the Serbian actors inspired activists in Croatia in 2009. The latter adopted and partly enhanced the Serbian experience and, again, served as an example for Serbian student occupiers in 2011. Diffusion happened both directly and indirectly: aided by the reciprocal intelligibility of the Serbian and Croatian languages, many activists developed personal friendships across borders. The Figure below gives an overview over occupation events in Croatia and Serbia and illustrates paths of diffusion (see Figure 1).

Theoretical debates and exchanges intensified as personal encounters revolved around the Subversive Festival. The festival was founded by Croatian activist Srećko Horvat in Zagreb in 2008 and had evolved from a film-oriented festival to an event to discuss an alternative politico–philosophical agenda. Over time, the festival became 'a much-needed gathering of Balkan progressive forces and an urgent development of their cooperation as well as of a common vision of another Balkans built on true democratic foundations, social equality and international solidarity'.[31] This relational diffusion (Givan *et al.* 2010, p. 2) through personal communication and mutual visits was complemented by non-relational diffusion.

After their first occupations in 2006, Serbian activists put together a booklet of documents (reprints of posters, leaflets, and photos), reprinted interviews and commentaries, entitled *Borba Za Znanje* (*Fight for Knowledge*). All the Croatian interviewees who had participated in the first occupation in spring 2009 admitted to having read *Borba Za Znanje*: 'at the time, this information gave us confidence'.[32] Between the first and second Croatian occupation in 2009, Croatian activists themselves published lessons learned in the booklet *Blokadna Kuharica* (*Occupation Cookbook*).[33] Again, the mutually intelligible languages simplified

---

[31] Available at: http://www.subversivefestival.com/txtl/1/185/en/conference#sthash.j5rmJPNe.dpuf, accessed 25 November 2015.

[32] Interview HR-E, male student, unemployed, 28, Zagreb, 19 May 2013.

[33] The Croatian version is available at: http://www.mediafire.com/file/mn2kny3uqu1/Blokadna+kuharica+fin.pdf, accessed 29 September 2017; the English version is available at: http://marcbousquet.net/pubs/The-Occupation-Cookbook.pdf, accessed 29 September 2017.

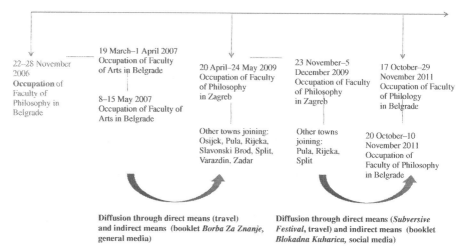

FIGURE 1. DIFFUSION OF CONTENTION BETWEEN SERBIA AND CROATIA.
Source: Created by the author.

the reception of these texts across the borders, and beyond Croatia and Serbia in the whole post-Yugoslav region. Croatian students also maintained the website *Slobodni Filozofski* (Free Faculty of Philosophy). For some years, this website provided a hub for contentious action and thinking, and even operated in English for some time.[34]

As proposed in the introduction, the Serb model of contention diffused to Croatia, from whence it travelled on to other countries in the region. In 2009, student contention erupted in Macedonia when students established the initiative *Slobodni Indeks* (Free Index) at the Faculty of Philosophy of the SS Cyril and Methodius University in Skopje.[35] This initiative ended around 2012 but provided resources in terms of people and knowledge when a law aimed at changing examination procedures at Macedonian universities was introduced when plans about a law aimed at changing examination procedures at Macedonian universities became public in late 2014. Thus, in late 2014, students from the same university formed a new initiative dubbed *Studentski Plenum* (Student Plenum).[36] The *Studentski Plenum* was the guiding force behind mobilisations that occupied various parts of faculties in Macedonia. The plenum espoused direct democratic strategies and a staunch critique of market-oriented reforms in higher education. Over time, this mobilisation focused on higher education merged with larger social unrest, which was triggered by scandals surrounding corruption, espionage, and the abuse of political power (Petkovsky 2014). In addition to the university occupations in Serbia, Croatia, and Macedonia (in 2015), Slovenian activists also occupied faculties at the University of Ljubljana. Slovenian students raised their stakes in May 2010 when around 8,000 activists gathered to protest against an education bill. The bill was contentious because it put a cap on the maximum wage students could earn through part-time work while still being funded

---

[34] The Croatian version of the website is available at: http://www.slobodnifilozofski.com/; English version is available at: http://slobodnifilozofski.org/, last accessed 25 January 2012—the English version has been removed, but the Croat version was still accessible as of 29 September 2017.
[35] Available at: https://slobodenindeks.noblogs.org/, accessed 28 February 2016.
[36] Available at: http://www.studentskiplenum.org, accessed 28 February 2016.

by public scholarships.[37] Roughly a year later, in spring 2011, a new initiative was founded under the name *Mi Smo Univerza* (We Are the University).[38] *Mi Smo Univerza*, together with the initiative *Pokreta 15.0*, blocked the Faculty of Arts in Ljubljana for two months, until January 2012. In its resolution from 27 November 2011, students clearly associated themselves with the strategies and principles laid out by Serbian and Croatian social movements by claiming to provide a forum for 'democratic, inclusive and well-founded debate[s]'[39] on higher education, employment, and social policy. Thus, in many countries around the region, activists emancipated themselves from existing representative fora of decision-making and developed something new: different frames (commercialisation and anti-representative democracy), and a different strategy (occupation plus direct democratic assemblies).

As demonstrated throughout this essay, their activities were rooted in an attractive model of contention that was first formulated in Serbia in 2006. The modularisation of Serbian tactics permanently widened the historical repertoire of contention, which had been developing since communist times and finally stabilised under the post-communist authoritarian regimes. This is not to say that students in the region of the successor states of Yugoslavia could not learn independently from other European student movements as well. However, Serbian tactical and framing innovations were more easily adopted because of the contextual similarities and the direct and indirect links between activists as described above.

Conclusion

This essay has investigated the question of why Serbian students in 2006 looked to student movements in other European countries for inspiration, rather than to past cases of mobilisation in communist Yugoslavia or Milošević's Serbia. The main finding was that the particular cultural environment as well as the expectations of participants and potentially interested supporters induced Serbian student activists to carefully design their collective identity: caught between the taboo on positive alignment with anything remotely reminiscent of the Socialist Federal Republic of Yugoslavia and the ideological inappropriateness of anti-Milošević mobilisation, they integrated elements of student movements in European countries into their own frames of commercialisation and direct democracy. The two-pronged Serb strategy of occupation plus direct democracy was used to distinguish the activists from, first, the 1968 occupation of the University of Belgrade, and second, the anti-Milošević protests in Serbia during the 1990s. In contrast to 1968, Serbian student activists in 2006 identified themselves as essentially pro-democratic, even if they were staunchly critical of the current form of democracy. Furthermore, in contrast to the 1990s anti-Milošević protests, they adhered to a pronounced left ideology which was in opposition to the former's neoliberal orientation. The choice of direct democratic decision-making flowed from the attempt to forge a collective identity in tune with the anti-Yugoslav discursive context, while the choice of occupation as a tactic demonstrates the students' self-identification as (anti-EU) anti-capitalists. Diffusion not only occurred for reasons of efficiency and feasibility—though these had some relevance—but

[37]'Student Protest in Slovenia', *No Comment TV*, 20 May 2010, available at: https://www.youtube.com/watch?v=CN8ZevN6yYw, accessed 28 February 2016.
[38]Available at: https://www.facebook.com/mismouniverza/, accessed 28 February 2016.
[39]'Želimo vzpostaviti demokratično, vključujočo in poglobljeno razpravo', *Mi Smo Univerza*, 27 November 2011, available at: http://mismouniverza.blogspot.co.at/2011/11/kaj-je-zasedba-zasedba-je-zacasna.html, accessed 28 February 2016.

for reasons of attractiveness and legitimacy in the eyes of adversaries, participants and potential supporters, and potential participants. Only by embedding their own struggles within the larger processes of Europeanisation and globalisation could Serbian student activists in 2006 define themselves as a social and anti-capitalist force.

Serbian student activists portrayed themselves as outside of, or rather beyond, corrupt and non-accountable representative politics: 'people, especially young people have no faith in politics. Politics is something that politicians do, and we all know politicians are scum. So we don't want to have anything to do with politics'.[40] At the same time, their choice of direct democratic organisation implied that Serbian students explored the role of 'activist citizens' (Isin 2009), and 'citizens as rebel' (Balibar 2013). Thus they 'engaged in [re]writing scripts' (Isin 2009, p. 381) of how democracy was being enacted in Serbia. Even if politicians did not endorse all of their demands and activities dissipated over the course of 2007, I do not dismiss the events of 2006 as only partially successful.

For the first time, Serbian activists elaborated a comprehensive critique of neoliberalism in the public sphere of postwar Serbia. Their objections to perceived social injustices resulting from higher education reforms questioned the very essential 'existing inscriptions of equality' (Rancière 1999, p. 100) in Serbian society. Thus, Serbian students not only redefined the procedure of democracy through creating new subject positions (roles) for citizens, but they also disputed the substantive distribution of social rights and brought issues of class cleavage back into Serbian debates. They heralded the trend of protests against austerity, which returned with force in the aftermath of the 2008 economic crisis. At the juncture of 2006, core European countries influenced Serbia-as-a-periphery more than its own past or current situation, and this well before the anti-austerity movements made their way back from the periphery to the core of Europe and the United States (Della Porta 2015).

However, Serbian student activists in 2006 did more than just inject new meanings into Serbian politics (Baćević 2010). They re-invented and tested forms of direct democratic action, which had fallen into oblivion (or rather, into disgrace) in the whole region since the fall of communist Yugoslavia and the de-legitimisation of any kind of left or seemingly left politics. In his seminal work on the 'end of post-communism', Boris Buden postulates that transition in Southeast Europe corresponds to a process of educating post-communist societies into infantility (Buden 2009, pp. 40–51). According to Buden, the only means of escape is through resistance, to put an end to this childlike state of powerlessness. Student mobilisation in Serbia 2006 was the starting point for recurrent waves of protest through which 'radical politics was reborn in the rebel peninsula' (Horvat & Štiks 2015, p. 2; Kraft 2013). Through the diffusion of Serbian frames and tactics to Croatia, this kernel of a new democratic practice was refined and modularised into a repertoire for the whole region.

---

[40]Interviewee RS-B, male student, 27, Zagreb, 18 May 2012.

ACTIVIST CITIZENSHIP IN SOUTHEAST EUROPE

References

Allcock, J. B. (2000) *Explaining Yugoslavia* (New York, NY, Columbia University Press).

Anastasakis, O. (2005) 'The Europeanization of the Balkans', *Brown Journal of World Affairs*, XII, 1.

Baćević, J. (2010) 'Masters or Servants? Power and Discourse in Serbian Higher Education Reform', *Social Anthropology*, 18, 1.

Baćević, J. (2015) 'They had Sex, Drugs and Rock 'n' Roll; We'll Have Mini-Jobs and Loans to Pay': Transition, Social Change and Student Movements in the Post-Yugoslav Region', in Horvat, S. & Štiks, I. (eds) *Welcome to the Desert of Post-Socialism. Radical Politics After Yugoslavia* (London, Verso).

Bakić-Hayden, M. (1995) 'Nesting Orientalisms: The Case of Former Yugoslavia', *Slavic Review*, 54, 4.

Balibar, E. (2013) 'Demokratie durch Widerstand: Der Staatsbürger als Rebell', *Blätter für deutsche und internationale Politik*, 3.

Beissinger, M. (2002) *Nationalist Mobilization and the Collapse of the Soviet State* (Cambridge, Cambridge University Press).

Benford, R. & Snow, D. (2000) 'Framing Process and Social Movements: An Overview and Assessment', *Annual Review of Sociology*, 26.

Benford, R. & Snow, D. (2002) 'Alternative Types of Cross-national Diffusion in the Social Movement Arena', in Della Porta, D., Rucht, D. & Kriesi, H. (eds) *Social Movements in a Globalizing World* (Basingstoke, Palgrave Macmillan).

Beslin, M. (2009) 'Uticaj "Juna" 68 na političku situaciju u Jugoslaviji', in Tomić, D. & Atanacković, P. (eds) *Novi društveni pokreti u Jugoslaviji od 1968. do danas* (Novi Sad, Rosa Luxemburg Stiftung).

Bieber, F. (2003) 'The Serbian Opposition and Civil Society: Roots of the Delayed Transition in Serbia', *International Journal of Politics, Culture, and Society*, 17, 1.

Bieber, F. (2011) 'Popular Mobilization in the 1990s: Nationalism, Democracy and the Slow Decline of the Milošević Regime', in Djokić, D. & Ker-Lindsay, J. (eds).

Biggs, M. (2013) 'How Repertoires Evolve: The Diffusion of Suicide Protest in the Twentieth Century', *Mobilization: An International Quarterly*, 18, 4.

Bilić, B. (2011) 'A Concept that is Everything and Nothing: Why Not to Study (Post-) Yugoslav Anti-War and Pacifist Contention from a Civil Society Perspective', *Sociologija*, LIII, 3.

Bilić, B. (2012) *We Were Gasping for Air. (Post-)Yugoslav Anti-War Activism and Its Legacy* (Nomos, Baden-Baden).

Borba Za Znanje (2007) *Borba Za Znanje: Studentski Protest 2006* (Belgrade, CAD).

Buden, B. (2009) *Zone des Übergangs: Vom Ende des Postkommunismus* (Frankfurt am Main, Suhrkamp).

Bunce, V. & Wolchik, S. (2006) 'International Diffusion and Post-communist Electoral Revolutions', *Communist and Post-Communist Studies*, 39, 3.

Calic, M. (2010) *Geschichte Jugoslawiens im 20. Jahrhundert* (Munich, C.H. Beck).

Clemens, E. (1996) 'Organizational Form as Frame: Collective Identity and Political Strategy in the American Labor Movement, 1880–1920', in McAdam, D., McCarthy, J. D. & Zald, M. (eds) *Comparative Perspectives on Social Movements. Political Opportunities, Mobilizing Structures, and Cultural Framings* (Cambridge, Cambridge University Press).

Collin, M. (2001) *This is Serbia Calling: Rock 'n' Roll Radio and Belgrade's Underground Resistance* (London, Serpent's Tail).

Della Porta, D. (2015) *Social Movements in Times of Austerity: Bringing Capitalism back into Protest Analysis* (Cambridge, Polity Press).

Della Porta, D. & Diani, M. (1999) *Social Movements. An Introduction* (Oxford, Blackwell).

Djokić, D. & Ker-Lindsay, J. (eds) (2011) *New Perspectives on Yugoslavia: Key Issues and Controversies* (London, Routledge).

Dvornik, S. (2009) 'Actors Without Society. The Role of Civil Actors in the Post-communist Transformation', *Heinrich Böll Stiftung: Publication Series on Democracy*, 15.

Džihić, V., Nadjivan, S. & Paić, H. (2006) *Europa—verflucht begehrt. Europavorstellungen in Bosnien-Herzegowina, Kroatien und Serbien* (Vienna, Braumüller).

Džihić, V. & Wieser, A. (2008) 'The Crisis of Expectations—Europeanisation as "Acquis Démocratique" and Its Limits: The Case of Bosnia-Herzegovina and Serbia', *L'Europe en formation*, N° 349–350, Autumn–Winter.

Figa, J. (1997) 'Socializing the State: Civil Society and Democratization from Below in Slovenia', in Bokovoy, M., Irvine, J. & Lilly, C. (eds) *State–Society Relations in Yugoslavia, 1945–1992* (London, Macmillan).

Fouéré, E. (2014) 'Macedonian Student's Plenum—A Cry for Respect', *Balkans in Europe Policy Blog*, 15 December, available at: http://www.suedosteuropa.uni-graz.at/biepag/node/129, accessed 23 February 2015.

ACTIVIST CITIZENSHIP IN SOUTHEAST EUROPE

Gamson, W. & Meyer, D. (1996) 'Framing Political Opportunity', in McAdam, D., McCarthy, J. D. & Zald, M. (eds) *Comparative Perspectives on Social Movements. Political Opportunities, Mobilizing Structures, and Cultural Framings* (Cambridge, Cambridge University Press).

Gamson, W. (2011) 'Bystanders, Public Opinion, and the Media', in Snow, D., Kriesi, H. & Soule, S. (eds) *The Blackwell Companion to Social Movements* (Malden, Blackwell).

Gill, J. & DeFronzo, J. (2009) 'A Comparative Framework for the Analysis of International Student Movements', *Social Movement Studies: Journal of Social, Cultural and Political Protest*, 8, 3.

Givan, R. K., Roberts, K. & Soule, S. (eds) (2010) *The Diffusion of Social Movements. Actors, Mechanisms, and Political Effects* (Cambridge, Cambridge University Press).

Gonzalez-Viallant, G. & Schwartz, M. (2012) 'Student Movements and the Power of Disruption', *Mobilizing Ideas*, 2 May, available at: http://mobilizingideas.wordpress.com, accessed 13 June 2013.

Grødeland, A. B. (2006) 'Public Perceptions of Non-governmental Organisations in Serbia, Bosnia and Herzegovina, and Macedonia', *Communist and Post-Communist Studies*, 39, 2.

Horvat, S. & Štiks, I. (2013) 'Willkommen in der Wüste der Transformation! Postsozialismus, die Europäische Union und eine neue Linke am Balkan', in Kraft, M. G. (ed.).

Horvat, S. & Štiks, I. (2015) 'Radical Politics in the Desert of Transition', in Horvat, S. & Štiks, I. (eds) *Welcome to the Desert of Post-Socialism. Radical Politics After Yugoslavia* (London, Verso).

Irvine, J. (1997) 'Introduction: State–Society Relations in Yugoslavia, 1945–1992', in Bokovoy, M., Irvine, J. & Lilly, C. (eds) *State–Society Relations in Yugoslavia, 1945–1992* (London, Macmillan).

Isin, E. (2009) 'Citizenship in Flux: The Figure of the Activist Citizen', *Subjectivity*, 29.

Jansen, S. (2001) 'The Streets of Beograd. Urban Space and Protest Identities in Serbia', *Political Geography*, 20.

Kanzleiter, B. (2008) 'Die affirmative Revolte: 1968 in der Sozialistischen Föderation Jugoslawien (SFRJ)', in Kastner, J. & Mayer, D. (eds) *Weltwende 1968? Ein Jahr aus globalgeschichtlicher Perspektive* (Vienna, Mandelbaumverlag).

Kanzleiter, B. (2011) '1968 in Yugoslavia: Student Revolt between East and West', in Klimke, M., Pekelder, J. & Scharloth, J. (eds) *Between Prague Spring and French May. Opposition and Revolt in Europe 1960–1980* (New York, NY, Berghahn Books).

Kraft, M. G. (ed.) (2013) *Soziale Kämpfe in Ex-Jugoslawien* (Vienna, Mandelbaumverlag).

Kriesi, H. (2011) 'Social Movements', in Caramani, D. (ed.) *Comparative Politics* (Oxford, Oxford University Press).

Kurspahic, K. (2003) *Prime Time Crime: Balkan Media in War and Peace* (Washington, DC, US Institute of Peace).

Lassen, T. & Prentoulis, M. (2014) 'Autonomy and Hegemony in the Squares: The 2011 Protests in Greece and Spain', in Kioupkiolis, A. & Katsambekis, G. (eds) *Radical Democracy and Collective Movements Today: The Biopolitics of the Multitude versus the Hegemony of the People* (Farnham, Ashgate).

Lindstrom, N. (2005) 'Yugonostalgia: Restorative and Reflective Nostalgia in Former Yugoslavia', *East Central Europe*, 32, 1–2.

Lipset, S. M. (1971) *Rebellion in the University* (Boston, MA, Little Brown & Company).

Little, A. & Lloyd, M. (eds) (2009) *The Politics of Radical Democracy* (Edinburgh, Edinburgh University Press).

Machart, O. (2002) 'Demonstrationes des Unvollendbaren: Politische Theorie und radikaldemokratischer Aktivismus', in Basualdo, C., Enwezor, O. & Bauer, U. M. (eds) *Demokratie als unvollendeter Prozess. Documenta 11_Plattform 1* (Kassel, Hatje Cantz Verlag).

Magaš, B. (1993) *The Destruction of Yugoslavia: Tracking the Break-up 1980–1992* (New York, NY, Verso).

McAdam, D., Tarrow, S. & Tilly, C. (2001) *Dynamics of Contention* (Cambridge, Cambridge University Press).

McFaul, M. (2005) 'Transitions from Postcommunism', *Journal of Democracy*, 16, 3.

Melucci, A. (1989) *Nomads of the Present: Social Movements and Individual Needs in Contemporary Society* (London, Hutchinson).

Mønnesland, S. (1997) *Land ohne Wiederkehr. Ex-Jugoslawien: Die Wurzeln des Krieges* (Klagenfurt, Wieser Verlag).

Mujkić, A. (2010) 'Ethnic Mobilization in the Former Yugoslavia as a Kind of Structural Setting and Framing', *Southeastern Europe*, 34.

Musić, G. (2009) 'Jugoslovenski radnički protest, 1981–1991', in Tomić, D. & Atanacković, P. (eds) *Novi društveni pokreti u Jugoslaviji od 1968. do danas* (Novi Sad, Rosa Luxemburg Stiftung).

Nadjivan, S. (2008) *Wohl geplante Spontaneität: Der Sturz des Milošević-Regimes als politisch inszenierte Massendemonstration in Serbien* (Frankfurt am Main, Peter Lang).

Naumović, S. (2006) 'Otpor! kao postmoderni Faust: društveni pokret novog tipa, tradicija i prosvećenog reformizma i "izborna revolucija" u Srbiji', *Filozofija i Društvo*, 3.

Offe, C. (1985) 'New Social Movements: Challenging the Boundaries of Institutional Politics', *Social Research*, 52, 4.

Pantić, D. T. (2005) 'Protest studenata na Filozofskom—Opravdan štrajk', *Glas Javnosti*, 5 December, available at: http://arhiva.glas-javnosti.rs/arhiva/2005/12/05/pisma/srpski/pisma.shtml, accessed 29 September 2017.

Petričušić, A. (2011) 'Ethno-Mobilisation and its Consequences in Croatia', *Southeastern Europe*, 35.

Petkovsky, L. (2014) 'From Student Protests to Movement—The (Un)Expected Reinvention of Politics in Macedonia', *Balkans in Europe Policy Blog*, 16 December, available at: http://www.suedosteuropa.uni-graz.at/biepag/node/131, accessed 23 February 2015.

Polletta, F. & Jasper, J. (2001) 'Collective Identity and Social Movements', *Annual Review of Sociology*, 27.

Prentoulis, M. & Thomassen, L. (2014) 'Autonomy and Hegemony in the Squares: The 2011 Protests in Greece and Spain', in Kioupkiolis, A. & Katsambekis, G. (eds) *Radical Democracy and Collective Movements Today: The Biopolitics of the Multitude versus the Hegemony of the People* (Farnham, Ashgate).

Ramet, S. P. (2005) *Thinking about Yugoslavia. Scholarly Debates about the Yugoslav Breakup and the Wars in Bosnia and Kosovo* (Cambridge, Cambridge University Press).

Ramet, S. P. (2006) *The Three Yugoslavias: State-building and Legitimation, 1918–2005* (Washington, DC, Woodrow Wilson Center Press).

Rancière, J. (1999) *Disagreement. Politics and Philosophy* (Minneapolis, MN, University of Minnesota Press).

Sadiki, L. (ed.) (2015) *Routledge Handbook of the Arab Spring: Rethinking Democratization* (New York, NY, Routledge).

Schmitter, P. C. (2010) 'Twenty-five Years, Fifteen Findings', *Journal of Democracy*, 21, 1.

Sewell, W. (1996) 'Three Temporalities: Toward an Eventful Society', in McDonald, T. (ed.) *The Historic Turn in the Human Sciences* (Ann Arbor, MI, University of Michigan Press).

Snow, D. (2011) 'Framing Processes, Ideology, and Discursive Fields', in Snow, D., Kriesi, H. & Soule, S. (eds) *The Blackwell Companion to Social Movements* (Malden, Blackwell).

Snow, D., Kriesi, H. & Soule, S. (2011) 'Mapping the Terrain', in Snow, D., Kriesi, H. & Soule, S. (eds) *The Blackwell Companion to Social Movements* (Malden, Blackwell).

Snow, D. A., Rochford Jr, E. B., Worden, S. K. & Benford, R. D. (1986) 'Frame Alignment Processes, Micromobilization, and Movement Participation', *American Sociological Review*, 51, 4.

Soule, S. (1997) 'The Student Divestment Movements in the United States and Tactical Diffusion: The Shantytown Protest', *Social Forces*, 75, 3.

Soule, S. (2011) 'Diffusion Processes Within and Across Movements', in Snow, D., Kriesi, H. & Soule, S. (eds) *The Blackwell Companion to Social Movements* (Malden, Blackwell).

Spehnjak, K. & Cipek, T. (2007) 'Disidenti, opozicija i otpor—Hrvatska i Jugoslavija 1945–1990', paper presented at the conference *Opposition und Dissidenz in den staatssozialistischen Staaten Mitteleuropas*, Frankfurt an der Oder, 2 November.

Steinberg, M. (2004) 'When Politics Goes Pop: On the Intersections of Popular and Political Culture and the Case of Serbian Student Protests', *Social Movement Studies*, 3, 1.

Štiks, I. (2015) '"New Left" in the Post-Yugoslav Space: Issues, Sites, and Forms', *Socialism and Democracy*, 29, 3.

Stubbs, P. (2012) 'Networks, Organisations, Movements: Narratives and Shapes of Three Waves of Activism in Croatia', *Polemos*, 15.

Tarrow, S. (1989) *Democracy and Disorder: Social Conflict, Political Protest and Democracy in Italy, 1965–1975* (New York, NY, Oxford University Press).

Tarrow, S. (1993) 'Cycles of Collective Action. Between Moments of Madness and the Repertoire of Contention', *Social Science History*, 17, 2.

Tarrow, S. (1997) 'Cycles of Collective Action: Between Moments of Madness and the Repertoire of Contention', in McAdam, D. & Snow, D. (eds) *Social Movements: Readings on Their Emergence, Mobilization, and Dynamics* (Los Angeles, CA, Roxbury).

Tarrow, S. (2005) *The New Transnational Activism* (Cambridge, Cambridge University Press).

Taylor, V. & Van Dyke, N. (2011) '"Get Up, Stand Up": Tactical Repertoires of Social Movements', in Snow, D., Kriesi, H. & Soule, S. (eds) *The Blackwell Companion to Social Movements* (Malden, Blackwell).

Tilly, C. (1978) *From Mobilization to Revolution* (Reading, Addison-Wesley).

Tilly, C. (1993) 'Contentious Repertoires in Great Britain, 1758–1834', *Social Science History*, 17, 2.

Tilly, C. (2004) *Contention and Democracy in Europe, 1650–2000* (Cambridge, Cambridge University Press).

Tilly, C. (2006) *Regimes and Repertoires* (Chicago, IL, University of Chicago Press).

Todorova, M. (1999) *Die Erfindung des Balkans. Europas bequemes Vorurteil* (Darmstadt, Primus Verlag).

Todorova, M. (2010) 'Introduction: From Utopia to Propaganda and Back', in Todorova, M. & Gille, Z. (eds) *Post-communist Nostalgia* (London, Berghan Books).

Todorova, M. (2015) 'Re-Imagining the Balkans', in Horvat, S. & Štiks, I. (eds) *Welcome to the Desert of Post-Socialism. Radical Politics After Yugoslavia* (London, Verso).

Traugott, M. (1993) 'Barricades as Repertoire: Continuities and Discontinuities in the History of French Contention', *Social Science History*, 17, 2.

ACTIVIST CITIZENSHIP IN SOUTHEAST EUROPE

Vetta, T. (2009) '"Democracy Building" in Serbia: The NGO Effect', *Southeastern Europe*, 33.

Vladisavljević, N. (2002) 'States, Political Opportunities and Mobilization: The Case of Socialist Yugoslavia', paper presented at the 52nd Annual Conference of the Political Studies Association, University of Aberdeen, 5–7 April.

Vladisavljević, N. (2011) 'The Break-up of Yugoslavia: The Role of Popular Politics', in Djokić, D. & Ker-Lindsay, J. (eds).

Appendix

The following is an anonymised list of the 30 interviewees from Croatia and Serbia. It includes the basic information that interviewees provided in writing before the interview took place.

Interviewees from Croatia

Interviewee	Age	Gender	Occupation	Start of activism	Date of interview	Location of interview
HR-A	30	f	Freelance journalist, active at Subversive Festival	2007	18 May 2012	Zagreb
HR-B	29	m	Theoretician, active at Subversive Festival	2008	19 May 2012	Zagreb
HR-C	35	m	Journalist	2008	18 May 2013	Zagreb
HR-D	31	m	University professor	2008	17 May 2013	Zagreb
HR-E	28	m	Student, unemployed	2007	19 May 2013	Zagreb
HR-F	26	m	Student	2009	17 May 2013	Zagreb
HR-G	38	m	Activist, student	2002	16 May 2013	Zagreb
HR-H	38	m	Ph.D. in chemistry, assistant professor	1995	17 May 2013	Zagreb
HR-I	23	f	Student	2009	18 May 2013	Zagreb
HR-J	27	m	Student	2009	15 May 2013	Zagreb
HR-K	25	m	Student	2010	16 May 2013	Zagreb
HR-L	29	m	Ph.D. in civil engineering, assistant professor	2009	17 May 2013	Zagreb
HR-M	24	f	Student	2012	18 May 2013	Zagreb
HR-N	23	f	Student	2008	19 May 2013	Zagreb

Interviewees from Serbia

Interviewee	Age	Gender	Occupation	Start of activism	Date of interview	Location of interview
RS-A	29	f	Student, NGO-employee	2005	18 May 2012	Zagreb
RS-B	27	m	Student	2006	18 May 2012	Zagreb
RS-C	23	m	Student	2010	21 May 2013	Belgrade
RS-D	23	m	Student	2009	30 May 2013	Belgrade
RS-E	22	m	Student	2009	21 May 2013	Belgrade
RS-F	29	m	Student	2005	22 May 2013	Belgrade
RS-G	23	f	Student	2011	21 May 2013	Belgrade
RS-H	25	m	Student	2007	22 May 2013	Belgrade
RS-I	26	f	Student	2008	22 May 2013	Belgrade
RS-J	26	m	Student, translator	2006	20 May 2013	Belgrade
RS-K	24	m	Student	2008	22 May 2013	Belgrade
RS-L	21	f	Student	2011	22 May 2013	Belgrade
RS-M	25	m	Student	2006	23 May 2013	Belgrade
RS-N	22	m	Student	2010	24 May 2013	Belgrade
RS-O	24	m	Student	2009	24 May 2013	Belgrade
RS-P	23	f	Student	2011	24 May 2013	Belgrade

From Protest to Party: Horizontality and Verticality on the Slovenian Left

ALEN TOPLIŠEK & LASSE THOMASSEN

Abstract

This essay analyses the politics of horizontality—a key characteristic of recent forms of protest and activist citizenship—through the case of the 2012–2013 protests in Slovenia. The Slovenian case is illustrative because we can trace the emergence of the Initiative for Democratic Socialism and, subsequently, the United Left from protest through movement to party. Since we believe that horizontality and verticality are present in both movements and parties, we argue against a simple opposition between movements and parties. In particular, we focus on the reasons for the move from horizontalist ways of political organising to vertical structures.

THE LAST TWO DECADES HAVE SEEN A SURGE OF INTEREST IN activist citizenship (Isin 2009) and new forms of protest (Day 2005; Maeckelbergh 2009; Gilbert 2014; Sitrin & Azzellini 2014; Tormey 2015; Della Porta *et al*. 2017). This should be understood in light of the crisis of traditional forms of politics and representative institutions, including political parties. Across the world, and also in Europe, activists have opposed the vertical politics of institutions and parties in the name of horizontalist forms of organising. This was the case in the alter-globalisation movements and, from about 2011 onwards, in movements such as the Spanish *Indignados* and Greek *Aganaktismenoi*, Occupy, and the Gezi protests in Turkey. Activists claim that the crisis of representative democracy is a result of the way in which institutions and vertical forms of politics silence the voices of large parts of the population. The solution is to do politics differently. Although horizontality is only one among many concepts and practices, it is key (Maeckelbergh 2009; Sitrin & Azzellini 2014; Tormey 2015). This debate has a long history—think, for instance, of debates among communists and socialists at the beginning of the twentieth century about the roles of movements and parties; or the way new social movements challenged the political system from the 1960s onwards. Echoing earlier debates, the protest movements of the last two decades have often been met with the critique that, without 'going vertical', the protests will have no lasting effect (Errejón & Mouffe 2016). In some cases, political parties on the radical left have sought to channel the demands of the activists into the political system, most famously in the case of Syriza in Greece and Podemos in Spain.

Activists and commentators tend to oppose horizontality and verticality, with protests and movements on the side of horizontality and parties on the side of verticality. Here 'verticality' refers both to hierarchical relations within the movement and to the relations between the

© 2017 University of Glasgow

movement or the party and state institutions. This opposition is not simply analytical in character, for it is also suggested that the horizontal structure sets a normative standard (Day 2005; Sitrin & Azzellini 2014; Tormey 2015).[1] In this essay, we analyse the case of Slovenia to argue two things. We make the analytical argument that there is always both horizontality and verticality, and that the two are intrinsically linked (see also Kioupkiolis 2010; Lorey 2013; Prentoulis & Thomassen 2013, 2014). The question is then how horizontality and verticality are negotiated across protests, movements, and parties. This also serves as a counterpoint to any simple opposition between movements and parties. Additionally, we make the normative argument that the entwining of horizontality and verticality is not a bad thing, and that a form of 'movement party' is the best response to the crisis of representative politics.

The case of Slovenia is interesting because it has received less attention among academic commentators despite similarities with bigger countries such as Greece and Spain.[2] What justifies a closer examination of the Slovenian case is, above all, the pattern of the movement from protest through movement to party. The responses to the developments in Slovenia were the well-known complaints of the organised left that protests and movements are ineffective, and the reverse complaints by protesters about the 'verticalisation' of the movement when its demands were taken up by a political party. Our analysis is chronological and follows the movement from protest through movement to party, but we challenge the way this movement is usually understood as a simple move from horizontality to verticality.

The Slovenian protests that took place between 2012 and 2013 were first spurred by corruption charges against the mayor of Maribor,[3] the second biggest city in Slovenia, and later intensified by the release of an anti-corruption commission report accusing the then prime minister, Janez Janša, of having failed to report assets (Transparency International 2013).[4] One of the protest groups eventually resulted in the creation of the Initiative for Democratic Socialism (*Iniciativa za demokratični socializem*—IDS), which later became part of *Združena levica*, the newly created United Left political party.

The 2012–2013 Slovenian protests could easily be grouped together with other similar popular reactions that took place in Europe after the financial crisis, for example, the 2011 anti-austerity movements in Spain and Greece, the 2012–2015 Romanian and the 2013–2015 Bulgarian protests, and the 2014 protests and occupations in Bosnia (Horvat & Štiks 2015; Štiks 2015). They all share an anti-establishment orientation, with the movements made up of diverse groups of individuals, indignant that the political and economic elites have been unable to provide decent living standards following the 2008 financial crisis. Another

---

[1]See Fisher (2013), Mouffe (2013), Gilbert (2014), Srnicek and Williams (2015), Errejón and Mouffe (2016).

[2]On Slovenia and neighbouring countries, see Razsa and Kurnik (2012), Krašovec (2013), Musić (2013), Kirn (2014), Horvat and Stiks (2015), Kraft (2015), Štiks (2015).

[3]The corruption charges were made by opposition politicians in Maribor municipality after widespread public outcry at speed cameras that had recently been erected around the city of Maribor. The speed cameras were introduced as part of a public–private partnership, with 92% of the fines collected going towards covering the costs of the provided service. The charges were later also reviewed by the anti-corruption commission and the Court of Audit. See, 'Mariborska opozicija zahteva, da župan pokaže dokumentacijo', *RTVSLO*, 2 November 2012, available at: http://www.rtvslo.si/lokalne-novice/mariborska-opozicija-zahteva-da-zupan-pokaze-dokumentacijo/294924, accessed 9 September 2017.

[4]*Zaključno poročilo o nadzoru nad premoženjskim stanjem predsednikov parlamentarnih strank*, The Commission for the Prevention of Corruption of the Republic of Slovenia, 2013, available at: https://www.scribd.com/document/156703186/Ugotovitve-Nadzora-Nad-PS-Predsednikov-Parlamentarnih-Strank, accessed 9 September 2017.

feature unites all six countries in their political experience: the elite-led transition from an authoritarian regime to representative democracy. With their own idiosyncratic nuances, the protests challenge the official narrative of a successful transition and interrogate the role of the national political class in skewing the transition in favour of vested interests (Krašovec 2013; Musić 2013; Kraft 2015, pp. 201–5).

In order to analyse the ways in which horizontality and verticality were interlinked and negotiated, we first develop our theoretical and analytical framework. We do so through a critical analysis of the work of Marina Sitrin (Sitrin 2006, 2012, 2014; Sitrin & Azzellini 2012, 2014) who has written extensively about horizontality in new protest movements.

Politics between horizontality and verticality

The term 'horizontality' has become popular among political theorists and activists as a way to describe and make sense of new forms of activist citizenship and the ways in which new political and social movements organise themselves. It is used, for instance, to characterise the alter-globalisation movements of the 1990s and 2000s, the Occupy movements of 2011, and many locally based movements. Many activists in the Slovenian movements we analyse here also represented themselves as engaged in horizontal politics, at least initially. In brief, horizontality refers to relationships organised non-vertically, without leaders and without a privileged centre. In the words of Marina Sitrin and Dario Azzellini, horizontality 'is a dynamic social relationship that represents a break with the logic of representation and vertical ways of organizing. This does not mean that structures do not emerge, as they do with mass assemblies and autonomous governance, but the structures that emerge are non-representational and non-hierarchical' (Sitrin & Azzellini 2014, p. 17).[5] Our argument is two-fold: first, that there is no horizontality without verticality, that is, there are no purely horizontal relations; and, second, that it is possible to understand this sort of movement as caught in a tension between horizontality and verticality, which is negotiated differently in different contexts and by different agents.

Arguably the most developed account of, and argument for, horizontality is that of Marina Sitrin, who connects the concept of horizontality to contemporary movements such as Occupy and the *Indignados* in Spain and *Aganaktismenoi* in Greece (Sitrin 2006, 2012, 2014; Sitrin & Azzellini 2012, 2014). Sitrin is squarely on the side of horizontality as opposed to verticality. Our intention here is not to reverse this oppositional hierarchy between horizontality and verticality, but to subvert it. Engaging critically with Sitrin's work helps us develop the theoretical and analytical lens through which we will analyse the Slovenian case. We use Sitrin's work as a stepping stone for developing a theoretical framework, and, as we will show, her account of horizontality presents certain tensions that are also evident in the discourses of the political activists.

Sitrin opposes horizontality to verticality. Horizontality is a way to characterise the relationships between individuals and groups within a movement. A horizontalist movement is one that is horizontally organised without leaders and without a centre. Building on Sitrin's use of spatial metaphors, one might think of such a movement as a flat network structure where individuals or groups form the nodes in the network.

---

[5]See Srnicek and Williams (2015, pp. 26–9) for an alternative definition.

Sitrin connects horizontality to other concepts used to characterise these movements. Autonomy is one such concept, referring to the relationship of the movement *vis-à-vis* the state. Rather than making demands of the state, and rather than seeking to take over the state, which would assume the legitimacy of the state as an agent of social change, horizontalist movements withdraw from the state in order to safeguard the horizontality of the movement. Engaging directly with the state involves the danger of co-optation, but even when co-optation is avoided, the hierarchy and language of the state tend to be reproduced within a movement when it accepts funding from the state (Sitrin 2012, pp. 192–98; Sitrin & Azzellini 2014, p. 33).[6] Sitrin also connects horizontality to self-organisation: only a movement where members self-organise can be horizontal. Together horizontality, autonomy, and self-organisation imply a rejection of representative structures and of the state. The alternative to these forms of 'power-over' is the 'power-with' of movements that organise horizontally, withdraw from the state, and self-organise (Sitrin 2012, pp. 102–5). Only then is it possible for people to speak for themselves and for their voices to be heard.

Rather than opposing horizontality in the name of the (alleged) efficacy of vertical forms of politics, we propose that a more fruitful critique starts by asking about the conditions that make the creation of horizontal relations possible. We will thus try to identify the places in Sitrin's text—and, later, in the discourse of the Slovenian protesters and movements—where verticality is not simply opposed to horizontality, but becomes the condition that makes it possible for horizontality to exist.

The first thing to note is that horizontality is a relationship that has to be created and sustained. Sitrin's question is precisely how horizontality can be made possible and made to last; this is what she calls the question of success (Sitrin 2012, p. 3). We are not dealing with some form of spontaneism—'horizontal spaces do not just occur spontaneously' (Sitrin 2012, p. 79)—nor can we take horizontality as a given once it has been established. The horizontality of the movements has to be created out of a social and political space that is at least in part vertically structured, and it has to be made so by subjects who have been shaped by that vertical space. Those subjects have been shaped by more or less vertical relationships in the family, the workplace, political and social movements, and so on. They must learn horizontality; only then is it possible to explain how they create horizontal relationships and sustain them (Sitrin 2012, pp. 34–5, 73, ch. 4; Sitrin & Azzellini 2014, p. 18).

In Sitrin's words, a crisis of the formal structures of power in a society opens the social space for people 'to come together, look to one another, and create new supportive relationships'— that is, to self-organise in horizontal ways (Sitrin 2012, p. 3). This is what happened in Slovenia where the general perception of corruption surrounding the introduction of speed cameras in Maribor set off a series of localised protests (Bezjak 2016), which then morphed into a wider political crisis at the national level. The protesters gathered in public squares to call political representatives to account, and their coming together created a space for thinking and organising alternative ways of doing politics. The crisis opens up a space where horizontality can emerge. At the same time, for Sitrin (2012, p. 61), horizontal space makes possible the creation of new subjectivities. There is, thus, a mutual dependence between the structure (horizontal spaces) and the agents (subjects capable of creating horizontal spaces).

If horizontality is something to be created and defended by individuals, those individuals must agree on what horizontality means and the means to create and defend it. There will be

---

[6]See also Day (2005).

disputes about what horizontality is, and how to realise it; 'declaring something horizontal does not make it so' (Sitrin 2012, p. 75). If that is the case, then horizontality will be, as Sitrin (2012, p. 74) argues, a process. All we have are different representations or practices of horizontality, not horizontality as such, and never as an objective state of affairs where we can say that this is horizontality.

Finally, horizontality must be defended, above all against vertical forms of power. For instance, it must be defended against disruption by state agents and organisations of the old left (Sitrin 2012, pp. 67, 77). Horizontality cannot be all-inclusive as it necessarily relies on the exclusion of those who are against horizontality; without this exclusion, there can be no horizontality, at least not in the long run (Sitrin 2012, pp. 81–2). Here we cannot ignore the difficulty of defending horizontality when differences exist over the meaning of it. To defend horizontality is always to defend a particular meaning of horizontality, and so there is no horizontality without some closure and exclusion—the latter are the very conditions of possibility of horizontality.

What should be clear by now is that horizontality and verticality cannot be disentangled. Horizontal movements cannot not relate to the rest of society and its vertical structures. The horizontalist movements have numerous points of contact with vertical structures of power, whether the institutions of the state or other organisations and movements within civil society. As Sitrin herself acknowledges: 'it would be an illusion to think that a "happy island of horizontalism" could be created in the middle of the sea of capitalism' (Sitrin & Azzellini 2014, p. 17).[7] If we think of horizontality and verticality in terms of spaces of horizontal and vertical relations respectively, the point is that those spaces are necessarily entangled with one another.

This is not only a matter of the relations between a movement and the rest of society. It is also the case that vertical relations remain within the movements; think, for instance, of the emergence of informal leaders despite a movement's horizontal norms (Sitrin 2012, p. 78). In the case of the 2012–2013 Slovenian protests, the movement made a public point of not selecting a leader, and, in their press releases, the undersigned were always the protest groups, never individual leaders. Yet, the most visible representative of the movement was the organiser of the All-Slovenian People's Uprising protest group, Uroš Lubej. In this case, the relationship between the hierarchies within the movement (leaders) and the vertical structures of the external environment is closely connected because the movement's internal and external communication is channelled by media that are often vertical in their structure. Whether the protesters liked it or not, the media networks themselves identified the speakers of/for the movement and invited them to give interviews and appear on panel discussions. From within the movement, the same process of selection took place through the division of tasks and the role of speakers at public assemblies.

Horizontality is also entangled with verticality because the individuals who engage in horizontalist movements have lives outside those movements, lives in which they engage in non-horizontal relations, for instance, in the workplace.

We are not arguing that we should give up on horizontalist, autonomist or self-organising movements; on the contrary, these have a very important role to play in any democracy worth the name. Rather, for the activists and movements, the central question becomes one of how

---

[7]See also Sitrin and Azzellini (2012, p. 40).

horizontality and verticality are articulated together, and here there is no blueprint for how activists and movements should proceed. That is something they must figure out themselves, constantly adapting to dynamic circumstances.

As we will show in the case of Slovenia, the different articulations of horizontality and verticality will be particularly evident when moving from protest and other forms of non-institutional activism to more formal organisation, especially party politics. Having said that, one should avoid a simple opposition between protest and parties, because horizontality and verticality are present in both. In the following, we let the activists speak for themselves, but we frame this through the relationship between horizontality and verticality. This dynamic is partly imposed on the material we analyse, but it emerges from engaging with the activist discourses and is itself articulated by the activists themselves.[8] In a process where the self-representations of the activists as well as our representations of them are open to contestation, we hope to make possible a critical engagement with the movements without unilaterally imposing an external yardstick. This approach also brings out the heterogeneity of the movements.

A brief history of Slovenian activism

In order to understand how the relationship between horizontality and verticality played out during the 2012–2013 protests and during the emergence of the IDS and the United Left, we need to acknowledge the history of horizontalist practices preceding the protests. The following brief history of Slovenian activism and radical politics is merely a snippet taken out of a longer and more extended context reaching back to the days of civic activism in the former Yugoslavia.[9] We can situate the beginnings of organised and more coherent activism a decade after the independence of Slovenia, which at the time was still undergoing the transition to becoming a European liberal democracy. Rasza and Kurnik identify the alter-globalisation movement of the late 1990s and early 2000s as a key period when 'some activists in Ljubljana were first politicized' (Razsa & Kurnik 2012, p. 245). The alter-globalisation campaigns were quickly followed by protests against the US invasion of Iraq (March 2003) and Slovenia's bid to become a member of NATO (May 2004) (Kuzmanić 2002; Zadnikar 2002; Gregorčič 2005; Zdravković 2014). More generally, the mid-2000s in Ljubljana were characterised by a 'changing landscape of the city and its outskirts, the loss of the public realm through privatisation, the authoritarian management of populations and practices and the reduction of diversity all for the logic of profit' (Kurnik & Beznec 2009, p. 45). In response to this elite-led neoliberal transformation of the Slovenian capital, activists occupied an abandoned bicycle factory, Rog, in order to create a space for mobilising collective resistance and disrupting the corporatist vision of Ljubljana (Kurnik & Beznec 2009, p. 47). The occupied space served as a platform for the production of alternative ways of life and localised resistance through

---

[8]We have relied on the following news outlets for protesters' discourses, facts, and background information: *Žurnal24, RTVSLO, Delo, Mladina, Siol.net,* and *24ur.com*. Additionally, we have analysed the manifestos and press releases of the main protest committees, which have been disseminated through various independent media (*Čuvar.si, A-Infoshop*), forums (*Starševski ček and Slovenski anarhistični portal*), and social media (Facebook groups, 'Franc Kangler naj odstopi kot župan Maribora', 'Janez Janša naj odstopi kot premier Republike Slovenije' and 'VLV—Vseslovenska Ljudska Vstaja').

[9]For more on civil society and activism in the former Yugoslavia, see Lukšič (1990), Figa (1997), Jelušič (2006), Vodovnik (2014), Fink-Hafner (2015).

organised assemblies and the active participation of its users (Kurnik & Beznec 2009, p. 52). Struggles over citizenship and belonging came to dominate the Slovenian activist scene in the second part of the 2000s, with the horizontalist practices of direct action and decision-making informing the main organisational structure (Razsa & Kurnik 2012, p. 245). However, these protest actions were small in scale and did not have a demonstrable effect beyond activist and academic circles.

The financial crisis of 2008 and the worsening of socio-economic conditions provided fertile ground for protest movements around the globe on mass-scale. Inspired by the Arab Spring, the 15-M movement in Spain, and Occupy Wall Street, the Global Day of Action on 15 October 2011 kicked off protests and occupations in Slovenia. Activists in Slovenia gathered in Koper, Maribor, and Ljubljana, where a group of participants occupied the square in front of the Ljubljana Stock Exchange. The 15O Movement, or Occupy Slovenia, provided a common public space for the critique of financial capitalism and for the 'collective capacity to manage our own lives and reconstruct society from below' (Razsa & Kurnik 2012, p. 252). It represented an autonomist moment of horizontal direct democracy. Gathered behind the rallying cry 'No one represents us!', the aim of the 15O movement was to establish a new balance of forces with established structures of power on the basis of horizontal practices of direct democracy and action.[10]

The protests were thus clearly framed within the crisis of representation, arguing that the solution to this crisis was to think of democracy in terms of direct and horizontally organised action. Already here we find a tension between horizontality and verticality that we will analyse in more depth below in relation to the 2012–2013 protests. Take, for instance, the question of how to relate to the state. In their analysis, Razsa and Kurnik (2012, pp. 249–50) describe the dilemma faced by activists: on the one hand, making demands of the state and making rights-based demands of the state risks reproducing the very oppressive structures that the activists are struggling against; on the other hand, the activists must work with the situation as it currently stands. Razsa and Kurnik and their informants describe this in terms of 'contradictions' that cannot be resolved, and their conclusion is that horizontality can be neither counterfactually assumed nor be taken as an absolute goal. In that case, we are dealing with a continuous and never-ending negotiation between horizontality and verticality. Another and less obvious example is the activists' description of what they are doing as the 'creation of spaces', or frameworks, of encounter (Razsa & Kurnik 2012). These are spaces where, because they are autonomous and horizontalist, individuals and groups can come together and act in common. Yet, it is also clear that these are spaces that have to be carved out of a larger society composed of more vertical relations, and that these spaces have to be defended against co-optation and centrifugal forces by creating some common ground, thus introducing an element of verticality into them.

While the 15O occupation mainly took place in front of the Ljubljana Stock Exchange, the activists also helped mobilise students at the Faculty of Arts, University of Ljubljana, where the occupation lasted for three months, from the end of November 2011 to January 2012. As Anej Korsika and Luka Mesec (2014, pp. 85–6) recount, the occupation of the faculty was successful in bringing together a wealth of experience through its different participants, yet

---

[10] 'Tu smo zaradi vzpostavitve razmerja sil s sistemom in skupne blaginje', *Siol*, 19 October 2011, available at: http://siol.net/novice/slovenija/tu-smo-zaradi-vzpostavitve-razmerja-sil-s-sistemom-in-skupne-blaginje-58223, accessed 10 September 2017.

none of the demands put forward to the management were realised. The same fate hit Occupy Slovenia three months later. Due to internal conflicts and protest fatigue, the occupation in front of the Ljubljana Stock Exchange ended in April 2012. However, these short-term setbacks had longer-term benefits: when protests broke out later, from November 2012, many activists had already some experience with horizontality through these prior actions.

The 2012–2013 waves of protest in Slovenia

Without this 'rather long prehistory to the Initiative (IDS)', where most of its 'active members were already active in the student movement, various student organizations, newspapers, fights against plans to implement tuitions [tuition fees]' (Korsika & Mesec 2014, p. 85), we cannot comprehend the role that past experience in horizontal practices of organising played in the 2012–2013 Slovenian protests. Yet, as the case study will gradually reveal, horizontal practices of protests and movements themselves rely on vertical relations, both internally and in relation to the rest of society. Our observation goes against the common stance in much of the horizontalist and autonomist literature on the radical left in Slovenia, where the vertical conditions of active citizenship are often neglected by privileging horizontalism and associated ideas such as autonomy, spontaneity, prefiguration, and non-domination (Kuzmanić 2002; Gregorčič 2005; Razsa & Kurnik 2012; Kurnik 2013).

The first in the series of Slovenian protests and popular uprisings took place on 2 November 2012 in the second biggest city, Maribor, in front of the city hall.[11] The protest was organised spontaneously by citizens themselves as a result of their mounting frustration with newly installed speed cameras, managed through a public–private partnership (Bezjak 2016). The 'All-Slovenian People's Uprisings', as they were called in the media and by the protesters themselves, were organised through the use of horizontal networks of communication, mostly Facebook, blogs, and Twitter. Four weeks later, the protest movement grew to 20,000 people, calling for the mayor of Maribor, Franc Kangler, to step down. The protesters devised a resonant slogan that was taken on by the movement as a whole and quickly spread to other parts of the country: '*Gotof je!/Gotovi so!*' ('He's finished!/They're finished!').

While the first protests in Maribor were organised through social media by individuals rather than by any established organisation, as the protests reached the capital of Ljubljana and grew into a more sustained movement, existing civil initiatives and other organisations joined the movement. The protest movement became more and more heterogeneous in composition: from students, lecturers, and trade unionists to workers with insecure employment, pensioners, anarchists, ecologists, and socialists (Gračner 2013). Thus, the growing protest movement came to be seen as an opportunity for already existing social groups to join newly formed protest groups and contribute to setting the agenda. The coordination of activities and protests took place through the movement's General Assembly, which was supported by smaller coordination groups, such as the All-Slovenian People's Uprising Committee (*Odbor Vseslovenske ljudske vstaje*), the Committee for Social Justice and Solidarity (*Odbor za pravično in solidarno družbo*), the Coordination Committee of Slovenian Culture (*Koordinarcijski odbor kulture Slovenije*), the Committee for Direct Democracy (*Odbor za neposredno demokracijo*), a group

---

[11]For more on the material conditions for the emergence of protests in Slovenia and the socio-economic consequences of governmental neoliberal policies, see Močnik (2003), Musić (2013), Slameršak (2013), Kirn (2014), Korsika and Mesec (2014).

of young digital savvy students and academics called Today Is A New Day (*Danes je nov dan*), Direct Democracy Now! (*Neposredna demokracija zdaj!*), and the IDS (Gračner 2013).

The first protest in Ljubljana took place on 27 November 2012. The second was held only three days later. The organisers helped mobilise around 10,000 people. Five more waves of protests took place between December 2012 and March 2013, with the biggest, on Slovenian Culture Day, 8 February 2013, gathering more than 20,000 people. Between December and January, calls by the media and other vertical structures to put forward demands and establish a political party became hard to ignore. As one protester described the situation: in December no-one knew what demands to put forward; in January different committees were already busy drafting programmes; and in February, the protest groups were in the fragmentary phase of forging alliances (anonymous participant quoted in Zdravković 2014, p. 61). Discussions among protesters during this time revolved around the purpose, future, and organisation of the movement, including whether there was a need for a united position and leaders, whether the movement should bypass the vertical structures of representative politics, and, if so, what its relationship should be with the new political parties that might emerge from the movement (Zdravković 2014, pp. 59–61). The tension between horizontality and verticality was therefore very much at the centre of protesters' deliberations during this time.

By February 2013, the protesters compiled a list of demands to be debated and voted upon through online discussion groups, which included a key demand for Janez Janša's government to step down, the establishment of a transitional government, and new elections within six months (Čuvar 2013). Among the more substantial demands for the transitional government, the protesters listed the following: a public debate on the necessary changes to the legal and economic order; an end to austerity and structural reforms; reform of the judiciary; equalising the status of parliamentary and extra-parliamentary movements; the introduction of recall elections; and more direct democracy.[12] As can be noted, some demands were much more anti-systemic than others. Although the final draft represents a unified and common position of various groups participating in the protests, it is an amalgamation of the differing and, at times, ideologically conflicting interests of the participating groups. The different positions within the protest movement could be categorised into the following strands: the moralist strand, which sought ethical purity through rule of law and going beyond ideological divisions; the centre-left liberal defence of the diminishing social democratic consensus; the radical left strand extending the critique to the whole political and economic system; and the strand calling to deepen the existing system of representative democracy through enhanced deliberation and participation by active citizens. These different strands took different views of the need for vertical structures and the need to engage directly with state institutions.[13]

At the beginning of the protests, the main goal was to put pressure on the political elites to change the direction of Slovenian politics, which were mired in corruption, especially at the level of local government. According to the movements' communiqués, the protests were not merely anti-government, aimed solely at the then Prime Minister Janez Janša or his political party, but against 'the whole Slovenian political caste' (Čuvar 2013). The protest organisers took this position of externality in order to defend the spontaneous nature of the protests and

---

[12] 'VIDEO: Manifest Vseslovenske ljudske vstaje', *Radio Krka*, 4 January 2013, available at: http://www.radiokrka.com/poglej_clanek.asp?ID_clanka=174580, accessed 4 April 2016.
[13] Similar observations on the classification of protesters' demands were also made by Krašovec (2013, pp. 314–15), Kirn (2014, pp. 120–1).

to emphasise the fact that they were not orchestrated by oppositional political parties. This was crucial at the time in order to effectively counter accusations that the protests were organised by the opposition left-wing parties.[14] Moreover, the movement's refusal to be aligned with either the right or the left was similar to that of the *Indignados* in Spain: the left and the right were seen as equally corrupt, so the protest movement portrayed itself as above established politics and as neither left nor right.

The rapid succession of events between February and April 2013 had important consequences for the maintenance of this united position among the different protest committees. A key mobilising factor was the publication of an anti-corruption commission report in January (Transparency International 2013), accusing the prime minister, Janez Janša, of failing to report his assets properly to the commission. As the protests intensified in numbers, so did the pressure on Janša's coalitional partners to leave the government. On 27 February, Janša was ousted, following a parliamentary vote of no confidence. The toppling of the government was seen as a key success for the movement, yet at the same time it also marked the beginning of its end.

The united position of the movement started to break down after Janša was forced to step down as prime minister, and when it became clear that other established political parties, even the centre-left Social Democrats (*Socialni demokrati*) and Positive Slovenia (*Pozitivna Slovenija*), were not going to call for early elections. This is when the differences between the various groups about the way forward for the protest movement started to become starker. There was a clear division over the most appropriate political strategy and the aims of different protest committees. The two main responses that formed across the protest movement were: staying active in local communities and civil society (horizontally), but not taking part in party politics; or, establishing a hybrid political movement that would act on the ground in civil society (horizontally) and through new political parties (vertically) at different levels of governance (local, national, and EU level). The performative group of artists, musicians, and other creative individuals, Protestival, was premised solely on horizontal ways of organising; the same applies to the City Assembly Initiative (*Iniciativa mestni zbor*) in Maribor, which has acted as a local neighbourhood platform for the self-organisation of Maribor's citizens in tackling common local issues (Nemac 2014). On the other hand, the All-Slovenian People's Uprising Committee, and the Committee for Direct Democracy chose to adopt more vertical ways of organising in order to be able to compete with established political parties in the formal institutions of representative politics. So did the IDS, but because of its clear ideological orientation and the radical aims in its political manifesto (including an end to austerity, workers' management of state-owned corporations, an active role for the state in industrial policy and economic coordination (IDS 2015, pp. 30–5)), other main protest groups were reluctant to form a wider coalition with it.

Splits also occurred within protest committees themselves. This division is well exemplified by the split in the All-Slovenian People's Uprising Committee between two of the committee organisers, Uroš Lubej and Peter Petrovčič. In an interview for the Slovenian daily *Primorske novice* (*Littoral News*) a year after the protests, Petrovčič admitted that the main reason behind the failure to form a united front against all established political parties was that they could not come to an agreement on how to proceed (Vidrih 2014). Some committee organisers, like

---

[14]'Na protestu zombiji?', *Radio Krka*, 22 December 2012, available at: http://www.radiokrka.com/poglej_clanek.asp?ID_clanka=174186, accessed 10 September 2017.

Petrovčič, believed that the protest movement should demand the removal of all political elites, whereas others, together with Lubej, were satisfied with toppling Prime Minister Janša's right-wing government. The first group took the position that all politicians and political parties bear responsibility for corruption and for the state of the economy in Slovenia, regardless of whether they are on the right or the left. While the second group agreed with this stance, its members believed that the protest committee should focus on creating links with other protest committees and use the momentum to build a new force in the Slovenian political space (Golob 2013). This division between continuing with horizontal forms of activism or adopting vertical ways of organising was characteristic of the whole protest movement by summer 2013, which resulted in the loss of its momentum. Some of that energy was channelled into, or rather multiplied by, the decision of some parts of the movement to adopt more vertical structures of organisation.

Uroš Lubej and the majority of protestors from the All-Slovenian People's Uprising Committee joined the Committee for Social Justice and Solidarity and the Network for Direct Democracy, and together formed a new political party, Solidarity (*Solidarnost*).[15] In the campaign for the early parliamentary elections, *Solidarnost* formed a coalition with the Social Democrats, who, ironically, had been one of the targets of the protest movement. Solidarity failed to get any seats, however. Meanwhile, the IDS adopted a more hybrid structure based on both vertical and horizontal ways of organising. In the following, we will use the IDS to illustrate the tension between horizontality and verticality in the quest to construct an alternative to neoliberal and representative politics.

The emergence of the IDS and the United Left

The Initiative for Democratic Socialism (IDS) was formed as a more coherent grouping of some of the movement's protesters and activists around a clear political-ideological project of a democratic and ecological socialism. Their base drew intellectual energy largely from academic and student Marxist thinkers of different hues working within the Workers' and Punks' University (*Delavsko-punkerska univerza*), an educational project run as part of the Peace Institute in Ljubljana, and the activist group Direct Democracy Now![16] The valuable collective experience gained by some of the activists in previous horizontalist radical actions provided the basis for 'a clear understanding ... that different and most importantly much stronger organizational forms are necessary' (Korsika & Mesec 2014, p. 86). This did not mean that they were ready to abandon their roots—instead, the move was seen as a politically strategic multiplication and broadening of their impact. They still considered themselves primarily as a social movement, engaged in horizontalist practices and resistance, but with an added set of formal and vertical structures which could engage with and participate in the existing structures of established power, including political institutions (IDS 2016).

The IDS was first presented at a press conference in Ljubljana on 30 April 2013. In a critique of the moralist technocratic and liberal centre-left stances prevalent in the protest movement, the founding members made it clear that 'the current crisis is not a moral crisis

---

[15]'Kdo smo', *Solidarnost*, 2016, available at: http://solidarnost.si/kdo-smo/, accessed 11 January 2016.
[16]Since 2014, the Workers' and Punks' University has been continuing its activities within the framework of the newly established Institute for Labour Studies. See, 'Inštitut za delavske študije', 2017, available at: http://www.delavske-studije.si/, accessed 12 September 2017.

or the crisis of the rule of law, but a crisis of capitalism'. They added that Maribor should not be viewed as the cause of the protesters' movement, but as its trigger. What provided the conditions for the uprising, as in other similar uprisings around the world, were wider structural reasons, such as 'increasing unemployment and precarious jobs, cutting of social services and transfers, decreasing of wages and manifest corruption'.[17] This demonstrates the two ways in which the IDS articulated its critique. On the one hand, using Marxist class analysis, the problem was framed not in relation to individual corrupt politicians but, rather, to the system that conditioned this type of behaviour. On the other hand, the struggle of Slovenian protesters was not an isolated incident, but connected to other similar protests taking place around the world, giving the protest group a unique internationalist perspective. Thus, when the All-Slovenian People's Uprising Committee and the Committee for Social Justice and Solidarity were calling for the replacement of the current political class with experts who were not morally corrupt, IDS rejected this by arguing that capitalism as the dominant political economic system itself needed to be challenged. Moreover, the IDS managed not only to develop an effective critique of the system, but also an alternative, namely democratic socialism:

> Capitalism ... needs to be replaced by a more rational system, which will be based on cooperation, social ownership of the means of production, democratic planning of production and aimed towards fulfilling the social needs of all, hence socialism.[18]

The key message of the IDS was therefore that only by addressing the underlying class divide in society would the protest movement be able to solve the problems of widespread corruption in the Slovenian political system. With regard to the organisation of the initiative, the first step was to build a wider movement around these aims, which would possibly lead to the emergence of a new political party. As Korsika and Mesec explain in their article on the developments within the IDS, 'protests as such have definitely caused history to speed-up [sic] and processes that would otherwise demand much more time have unravelled rather quickly' (Korsika & Mesec 2014, pp. 85–6). Less than a year later, and just a few months before the 2014 European Parliament and early National Assembly elections, the IDS was ready to begin 'the long march through the institutions' (IDS 2016). The activists viewed this step as a way to fundamentally democratise the representative institutions, so that 'they would serve the working people and not the interests of capital' (IDS 2016).

On 8 March 2014, the IDS formally established itself as a political party. At the same time, it joined two other smaller and ideologically related parties, which led to the establishment of the United Left political party. The rationale behind this move to more vertical ways of organising is provided in the following justification from the IDS website:

> On the basis of our achievements, and especially our failures and the limitations to our activist operations, we have increasingly come to the realisation that we need a more stable and organised

---

[17]'Slovenija ima dobra izhodišča za demokratični socializem', *RTVSLO*, 30 April 2013, available at: http://www.rtvslo.si/slovenija/slovenija-ima-dobra-izhodisca-za-demokraticni-socializem/307815, accessed 7 April 2016.
[18]'Slovenija ima dobra izhodišča za demokratični socializem', *RTVSLO*, 30 April 2013, available at: http://www.rtvslo.si/slovenija/slovenija-ima-dobra-izhodisca-za-demokraticni-socializem/307815, accessed 7 April 2016.

form of operating. A decision was reached which acknowledged the need for operating within the centres of political power as well. We see the establishment of our party and our candidacy at the European elections in May 2014 as the next steps on the path of a broader and more organised movement. (IDS 2015)

This was viewed as a strategic move to combine horizontal ways of organising with vertical structures rather than as a rejection of the horizontal ways of organising, which was the predominant form of the IDS's operations during the 2012–2013 wave of protests. In its manifesto, the IDS explicitly underscored the need to establish local networks and working groups around the country, the purpose of which would not be to rubberstamp the decisions of the party structures, but to provide a framework for self-organisation, participation, and activism by local people (IDS 2015, 2016). Moreover, this strategic move was the result of a conscious decision on the part of the activists to expand the social impact of their activities, while acknowledging the dangers that vertical organisational structures entail:

[W]e perceive this as a political problem, [a] party must not be a goal in itself but only [the] means for achieving higher political goals. We do not want to build a classical bourgeois party that will be just one among many. Instead, we want to build a proper workers [sic] party that will be only an instrument of a wider and deeply rooted movement. (Korsika & Mesec 2014, p. 87)

One might expect a party programme that argued for democratic socialism, 'social ownership of the means of production', and 'democratic planning of production' to be connected to vertical forms of organisation. Indeed, this is how traditional parties on the left have approached the matter, in terms of both the organisation of the struggle for these goals and the organisation of a new society. In the case of the IDS, however, democratic socialism is articulated with a different and less vertical form of party organisation. The relationship between horizontality and verticality is thus understood more in terms of a mutually supportive relationship rather than a simple opposition. The hybridity of such a relationship can only be maintained through an ongoing process of activist dedication and pragmatism, while avoiding falling into either the 'fetishism of the party' or the 'fetishism of spontaneity'.[19] The active members of the IDS use the terms 'organisation' and 'spontaneity' to characterise this relationship: 'only an appropriate organisation can guarantee the political effectiveness of spontaneous impulses and thus prevent the dominant system from co-opting it, and only by maintaining a connection with spontaneous impulses, can we prevent the ossification of the organisation and ensure its adaption to changing circumstances'.[20]

Although there is a tension between them, organisation and spontaneity, or verticality and horizontality, are thus not opposed, but two different aspects of the same whole. The organisation of IDS goes beyond the relationship of horizontality to the party structure and to the structure of the political system, because the IDS are seeking to create a hegemony over not only the political system, but the wider network of social relations and structures. Thus, for instance, Korsika and Mesec write of the need to 'establish all kinds of workers

[19]'Prihodnost je demokratični socializem', Workers and Punks' University, 2013, p. 38 (Ljubljana, Institute for Labour Studies), available at: http://www.delavske-studije.si/wp-content/uploads/2013/03/Prihodnost_je_demokraticni_socializem.pdf, accessed 1 December 2015.
[20]'Prihodnost je demokratični socializem', Workers and Punks' University, 2013, p. 39 (Ljubljana, Institute for Labour Studies), available at: http://www.delavske-studije.si/wp-content/uploads/2013/03/Prihodnost_je_demokraticni_socializem.pdf, accessed 1 December 2015.

[sic] institutions' in order 'to contribute to building socialist hegemony' (Korsika & Mesec 2014, p. 88). Here, hegemony is understood as leadership through the creation of consent. This clearly implies a vertical relationship, but the consent cannot simply be manufactured from above; it must be rooted in horizontal and vertical relations within civil society.

When it comes to the need for leadership and the more professionalised organisation of a popular movement, a compelling question is the seemingly irreconcilable tension behind the hybrid nature of the new political force that the United Left represents in the Slovenian political landscape. The way the United Left represents itself and wants to be perceived by ordinary people is not only in terms of offering an alternative set of policy proposals and a new ideological direction in politics. The organisation also manifests an alternative form of organised politics in which operating through a political party (at the national level through parliamentary assemblies, and also at the local level) is just one form of political organising. The United Left differs from the established mainstream parties in its hybridity and its interpenetration with its grassroots base. Despite the United Left having representatives elected at different levels of established governance structures, its internal structures are partly composed of less formalised processes of political deliberation and organisation, such as working groups, regional committees, general assemblies, street protests, and consultations with the wider movement membership. Key policies, positions, and press releases are all deliberated and decided upon collectively by the IDS membership, mainly through working groups and regional committees. This work is facilitated by online applications, such as Google Groups and Documents, where members can sign up and contribute to shaping the United Left's internal documents.

What remains to be seen is how long this delicate relationship of hybridity will stay intact. By establishing a political party and gaining parliamentary representation, the IDS and the United Left have widened the ideological spectrum of Slovenian politics and gained valuable media access for the dissemination of otherwise marginalised ideas and initiatives that arise from civil society (for example, marriage equality, animal welfare legislation, legalisation of marijuana, a universal basic income). However, the dynamics of parliamentary work, which tends towards centralisation and the systematisation of internal decision-making, can clash with the more open and horizontal practices of civil society groups and social movements. This growing tension was the key reason for the stalemate at the second annual congress of the IDS in April 2016, where a fraction of the members successfully blocked plans to transform the coalition of the United Left into a single political party, but was ultimately defeated after members voted in an email correspondence session following the congress. This leaves open the question of whether the hybrid relationship between the United Left as a party and social movements is only a temporary stage in the maturation of their political project or a sustainable structural solution to the crisis of representative politics. Together with other radical left parties in Europe, with Syriza and Podemos being the two most notable cases, the question of 'governing' and the inevitability of making compromises along the way pose further challenges to the 'movement party model' of radical left politics (Mouffe 2014; Kriesi 2015; Della Porta *et al*. 2017).

Conclusion: from horizontal struggles to movement parties

New forms of protest and activist citizenship have challenged the vertical structures of existing parties, unions, and institutions, thereby opening up new ways of thinking and acting. A key part of this is the privileging of horizontality against the hierarchies of representative institutions and traditional organisations, including political parties. Rather than conceptualising the structures of protests, movements, and parties in terms of a mutually exclusive opposition between horizontal and vertical ways of organising, we have proposed viewing the different instances of political action as mutually reinforcing, yet still in a relationship of tension. We have tried to show this through critical analyses of, first, Marina Sitrin's extensive work on horizontality, and, second, the case of Slovenia. We found that while there was a greater degree of horizontality during the initial stages of protest and, conversely, a greater degree of verticality once the Initiative for Democratic Socialism and the United Left had been created, activists were struggling with the tension between horizontality and verticality from the very beginning. At the end of the more horizontal protests in 2012–2013, the strategy of the main protest committees was to maintain and multiply the effects of the horizontalist discourses and practices through the conscious use of vertical structures. This move was seen as key in bypassing the ephemerality of direct protest actions and harvesting the mobilising power of the protest movement. At the same time, the initial distancing of the protesters from established vertical practices and the structures of representative politics was necessary for the autonomous development of the movement and its legitimation in the eyes of the wider public. Only in this way could the protesters draw a line between the old ways of doing politics and the potential for a new politics.

Our conclusion resonates with recent work on social movements and parties where some scholars have also started to pay more attention to the interaction between movements and parties. If we no longer think of movements and parties as two different entities or political spaces, it then becomes necessary to reconceptualise the relationship between them. This is particularly important for contemporary politics on the European left, with Syriza in Greece, Podemos in Spain, and Corbyn and Labour/Momentum in the United Kingdom as the most obvious examples of what Donatella della Porta calls 'movement parties' (Della Porta *et al.* 2017).[21]

In her recent work on political movements, Chantal Mouffe has also pursued this line of argument, and we would suggest that her work is fruitful as a starting point for rethinking the relationship between movements and parties. Although at some points in her argument, Mouffe (2014) repeats the functionalist dichotomy between social movements and political parties that has dominated the social movement literature, in her recent work on left-wing populism, she provides the theoretical stepping stones for establishing a synergy between electoral competition and social struggles. Noting the inadequacy of traditional hierarchical parties to absorb the plurality of democratic demands in our society, Chantal Mouffe proposes a new form of political organisation is needed which can articulate both horizontality and verticality:

> We need a synergy between electoral competition and the wide range of struggles that take place in the social arena. It's clear that the democratic demands that exist in our societies cannot find an expression solely through the vertical party form, that they also need horizontal forms of expression. A new form of political organisation that articulates the two modes—that's how I conceive 'left-wing populism'. (Errejón & Mouffe 2016, p. 125)[22]

---

[21]See also Kitschelt (2006).
[22]See also Mouffe (2013, pp. 126–27).

ACTIVIST CITIZENSHIP IN SOUTHEAST EUROPE

Similarly, our analysis of the Slovenian case suggests that a simple division of labour between movements and parties, and between 'society' and 'politics', is unsound. Not only are horizontality and verticality closely entangled in any form of organisation—protest, movement or party—but there is a normative point here too about political parties that—like Syriza after the 2015 referendum—shift towards a more uniform and top-down structure, effectively cutting off vital ties with civil society groups and social movements. Horizontalist movements need to connect with vertical structures and use these for their own purposes, but vertical parties also need to stay plugged into horizontalist practices, not least because this is a more effective way of generating social and political change. With the institutions of representative politics facing a mounting challenge from new populist forces in Europe and across the Atlantic, reconceptualising the relationship between movements and parties may very well be the much needed answer for amending the social contract.

References

Bezjak, B. (2016) 'Štiri leta mariborskih radarjev', *Večer*, 14 December, available at: http://www.vecer.com/stiri-leta-mariborskih-radarjev-6243370, accessed 10 September 2017.

Bokovoy, M., Irivine, J. A. & Carol, L. S. (eds) (1997) *State-Society Relations in Yugoslavia, 1945–1992* (London, Palgrave Macmillan).

Caparini, M., Fluri, P. & Molnar, F. (eds) (2006) *Civil Society and the Security Sector: Concepts and Practices in New Democracies* (London, Lit Verlag).

Čuvar (2013) *Odbor VLV se bo udeležil tribune v Cankarjevem domu*, 27 January, available at: http://cuvar.si/manifest-vseslovenske-ljudske-vstaje, accessed 4 April 2016.

Day, R. (2005) *Gramsci is Dead: Anarchist Currents in the Newest Social Movements* (London, Pluto Press).

Della Porta, D. & Diani, M. (eds) (2015) *The Oxford Handbook of Social Movements* (Oxford, Oxford University Press).

Della Porta, D., Fernàndez, J. & Mosca, L. (2017) *Movement Parties Against Austerity* (Cambridge, Polity Press).

Errejón, Í. & Mouffe, C. (2016) *Podemos: In the Name of the People* (London, Lawrence & Wishart).

Figa, J. (1997) 'Socializing the State: Civil Society and Democratization from Below in Slovenia', in Bokovoy, M., Irivine, J. A. & Carol, L. S. (eds).

Fink-Hafner, D. (ed.) (2015) *The Development of Civil Society in the Countries on the Territory of the Former Yugoslavia since the 1980s* (Ljubljana, FDV).

Fisher, M. (2013) 'Indirect Action: Some Misgivings about Horizontalism', in Gielen, P. (ed.).

Gielen, P. (ed.) (2013) *Institutional Attitudes: Instituting Art in a Flat World* (Amsterdam, Valiz).

Gilbert, J. (2014) *Common Ground: Democracy and Collectivity in an Age of Individualism* (London, Pluto Press).

Golob, T. (2013) Uroš Lubej: Samo njim ni nič jasno, *Playboy.si*, 26 March, available at: http://www.playboy.si/branje/intervju/uros-lubej-samo-njim-ni-nic-jasno/, accessed 7 January 2016.

Gračner, B. (2013) '2013 Slovenia's "Zombie Uprising"', *Counterfire*, 1 March, available at: http://www.counterfire.org/international/16323-slovenias-zombie-uprising, accessed 27 July 2016.

Gregorčič, M. (2005) *¡Alerta roja! Teorije in prakse onkraj neoliberalizma* (Ljubljana, Študentska založba).

Horvat, S. & Štiks, I. (eds) (2015) *Welcome to the Desert of Post-Socialism: Radical Politics After Yugoslavia* (London, Verso).

IDS (2015) *O nas*, available at: http://www.demokraticni-socializem.si/o-nas/, accessed 24 February 2015.

IDS (2016) *Koraki k demokratičnemu socializmu*, available at: http://www.demokraticni-socializem.si/programski-dokumenti/program-ids-koraki-k-demokraticnemu-socializmu/, accessed 4 October 2016.

ACTIVIST CITIZENSHIP IN SOUTHEAST EUROPE

Isin, E. (2009) 'Citizenship in Flux: The Figure of the Activist Citizen', *Subjectivity*, 29.

Jelušič, L. (2006) 'Civil Society in Slovenia: A Watchdog against Militarisation of the Political State', in Caparini, M., Fluri, P. & Molnar, F. (eds).

Katz, R. S. & Crotty, W. (eds) (2006) *Handbook of Party Politics* (New York, NY, Sage).

Kioupkiolis, A. (2010) 'Radicalizing Democracy', *Constellations*, 17, 1.

Kirn, G. (2014) 'Slovenia's Social Uprising in the European Crisis: Maribor as Periphery from 1988 to 2012', *Stasis*, 2, 1.

Kirn, G., Kralj, G. & Piškur, B. (eds) (2009) *New Public Spaces: Dissensual Political and Artistic Practices in the Post-Yugoslav Context* (Maastricht, Jan van Eyck Academie).

Kitschelt, H. (2006) 'Movement Parties', in Katz, R. S. & Crotty, W. (eds).

Korsika, A. & Mesec, L. (2014) 'Slovenia: From Spontaneous Protest to the Renewal of the Socialist Left', *Kurswechsel*, 1.

Kraft, M. G. (2015) 'Insurrections in the Balkans: From Workers and Students to New Political Subjectivities', in Horvat, S. & Štiks, I. (eds).

Krašovec, P. (2013) 'The Slovenian Uprising in Retrospect', *Journal of Contemporary Central and Eastern Europe*, 21, 2–3.

Kurnik, A. & Beznec, B. (2009) 'Resident Alien: The Rog Experience on the Margin', in Kirn, G., Kralj, G. & Piškur, B. (eds).

Kriesi, H. (2015) 'Party Systems, Electoral Systems, and Social Movements', in Della Porta, D. & Diani, M. (eds).

Kurnik, A. (2013) 'Artikulacije rabijo neartikuliran bes', *Časopis za kritiko znanosti, domišljijo in novo antropologijo*, 254.

Kuzmanić, T. (2002) *Policija, mediji, UZI in WTC: antiglobalizem in terorizem* (Ljubljana, Mirovni inštitut).

Lorey, I. (2013) 'On Democracy and Occupation: Horizontality and the Need for New Forms of Verticality', in Gielen, P. (ed.).

Lukšič, I. (1990) 'K razpravi o civilni družbi: sprejem Gramscija v Jugoslaviji', *Časopis za kritiko znanosti, domišljijo in novo antropologijo*, 130, 1.

Maeckelbergh, M. (2009) *The Will of the Many: How the Alterglobalisation Movement is Changing the Face of Democracy* (London, Pluto Press).

Močnik, R. (2003) 'Social Change in the Balkans', *Eurozine*, 20 March, available at: http://www.eurozine.com/articles/2003-03-20-mocnik-en.html, accessed 4 October 2016.

Mouffe, C. (2013) *Agonistics: Thinking the World Politically* (London, Verso).

Mouffe, C. (2014) '"Democratise Democracy!"—Interview with Chantal Mouffe', *Transformations*, 16 April, available at: http://transformations-blog.com/we-propose-democracy-interview-with-chantal-mouffe/, accessed 3 October 2016.

Musić, G. (2013) 'Between Facebook and the Picket Line: Street Protests, Labour Strikes and the New Left in the Balkans', *Journal of Contemporary Central and Eastern Europe*, 21, 2–3.

Nemac, K. (2014) 'Vseslovenska vstaja—leto kasneje', *mojpogled.com*, 28 April, available at: http://mojpogled.com/vseslovenska-vstaja-leto-kasneje/, accessed 7 January 2016.

Prentoulis, M. & Thomassen, L. (2013) 'Political Theory in the Square: Protest, Representation and Subjectification', *Contemporary Political Theory*, 12, 3.

Prentoulis, M. & Thomassen, L. (2014) 'Autonomy and Hegemony in the Squares: The 2011 Protests in Greece and Spain', in Kioupkiolis, A. & Katsambekis, G. (eds) *Radical Democracy and Collective Movements Today: The Biopolitics of the Multitude versus the Hegemony of the People* (Farnham, Ashgate).

Razsa, M. & Kurnik, A. (2012) 'The Occupy Movement in Žižek's Hometown: Direct Democracy and a Politics of Becoming', *American Ethnologist*, 39, 2.

Sitrin, M. A. (ed.) (2006) *Horizontalism: Voices of Popular Power in Argentina* (Oakland, CA, A. K. Press).

Sitrin, M. A. (2012) *Everyday Revolutions: Horizontalism and Autonomy in Argentina* (London, Zed Books).

Sitrin, M. (2014) 'Goals without Demands: The New Movements for Real Democracy', *South Atlantic Quarterly*, 113, 2.

Sitrin, M. & Azzellini, D. (2012) *Occupying Language: The Secret Rendezvous with History and the Present* (New York, NY, Zuccotti Park Press).

Sitrin, M. & Azzellini, D. (2014) *They Can't Represent Us! Reinventing Democracy from Greece to Occupy* (London, Verso).

Slameršak, A. (2013) 'Slovenia on the Road to Periphery', The International Marxist–Humanist, 25 June, available at: http://www.internationalmarxisthumanist.org/articles/slovenia-road-periphery-aljoa-slamerak, accessed 14 October 2015.

Srnicek, N. & Williams, A. (2015) *Inventing the Future: Postcapitalism and a World Without Work* (London, Verso).

Štiks, I. (2015) '"New Left" in the Post-Yugoslav Space: Issues, Sites, and Forms', *Socialism and Democracy*, 29, 3.

ACTIVIST CITIZENSHIP IN SOUTHEAST EUROPE

Tormey, S. (2015) *The End of Representative Politics* (Cambridge, Polity).

Transparency International (2013) 'Holding Politicians to Account: Slovenia's Prime Minister Ousted', 4 March, available at: https://www.transparency.org/news/feature/holding_politicians_to_account_slovenias_prime_minister_ousted, accessed 9 September 2017.

Vidrih, P. (2014) 'Bili smo zelo naivni, politika nas je izigrala', *Primorske novice*, 18 April, available at: http://www.primorske.si/Priloge/7-Val/-Bili-smo-zelo-naivni,-politika-pa-nas-je-izigrala.aspx, accessed 7 January 2016.

Vodovnik, Ž. (2014) 'Demokratizacija in nova družbena gibanja', *Teorija in praksa*, 51, 2–3.

Zadnikar, D. (2002) 'Nato in globalizacija', in Gregorčič, M. & Kovačič, G. (eds) *Ne NATO—mir nam dajte!* (Ljubljana, Mirovni inštitut).

Zdravković, L. (2014) 'Misliti nemogoče: onkraj predstavništva, Editirana transkripcija pogovornega večera v anarhističnem socialnem centru', *Časopis za kritiko znanosti, domišljijo in novo antropologijo*, 257.

Contesting Neoliberal Urbanism on the European Semi-periphery: The Right to the City Movement in Croatia

DANIJELA DOLENEC, KARIN DOOLAN & TOMISLAV TOMAŠEVIĆ

Abstract

This essay is a case study of the Right to the City movement in Croatia, one of the largest citizens' struggles in the country's recent history. Firstly, we argue that the movement managed to avoid the supposedly unavoidable Michels's iron law of oligarchy. Outlining the movement's trajectory in five phases, we show how it always prioritised social impact over institutional self-preservation. Secondly, we analyse movement outcomes as viewed by activists. In interviews with activists we establish features of evolving activist citizenship as well as ways in which participation in the movement influenced the forging of alliances among organisations and initiatives.

THE CITY IS THE PRIMARY SITE OF SOCIAL CONFLICT WITHIN contemporary capitalism, at the same time exposing its relentless logic of commodification, as well as generating space for envisioning and mobilising towards its alternatives (Brenner *et al*. 2012). Analysing city dynamics is particularly insightful because it encapsulates larger processes of economic and political change, with urban struggles serving as 'detectors of the critical issues and conflicts of our time' (Jacobsson 2015, p. 12). We focus on one such struggle, the Right to the City (*Pravo na grad*) protest movement in Croatia, which started in the country's capital Zagreb in mid-2006, choosing its name to signal its relationship to critical urban theory and struggles against neoliberal urbanisation. Putting Harvey's (2008, p. 23) claim that the Right to the City 'is a right to change ourselves by changing the city' into action, the protest movement grew into the main source of opposition to neoliberal city transformations, subsequently moving the target of its contention to the national level, as well as supporting similar urban initiatives in Croatia and the region. In 2014, eight years after its inception, the Right to the City was instrumental in building a national alliance of organisations that successfully implemented a citizens' petition for a referendum aimed at preventing the long-term private concession of the national highway network.

We first situate the Right to the City movement in Zagreb within contemporary struggles against the neoliberalisation of cities. Given that the movement invoked a long tradition of

© 2017 University of Glasgow

urban struggles under the banner of the Right to the City, first captured by Henri Lefebvre in the 1960s (Lefebvre 1968; Brenner *et al*. 2012), we relate the movement's relationship to such urban struggles. We suggest that the Zagreb Right to the City movement is part of a global phenomenon of resisting neoliberal transformations, and that its local configuration relates to the context of the post-socialist semi-periphery, which shaped the movement's framing (Benford & Snow 2000) and repertoire of action (Tarrow 2011, 2012). Secondly, we analyse the trajectory of the movement with respect to its objectives, organisational forms, and repertoire of action. The Right to the City protest movement seems to have avoided the 'unavoidable' destiny that the literature on social movements predicts: 'routinising' into a conventional organisation under Michels's 'iron law of oligarchy', or dissipating as a result of 'burnout' (Tarrow 2011, 2012). Instead, this Right to the City movement has exhibited a remarkable capacity for metamorphosis, always managing to prioritise political confrontation over concerns for organisational self-preservation. Finally, we investigate dominant conceptions of successful protest outcomes alongside how the success of a given movement is understood from a participant perspective. In this part, we draw on interviews with Right to the City activists in order to problematise the 'productivist vision' of social action (Castells 2012), which reduces the success of protests to whether a concrete outcome has been achieved. Instead, we propose that an undervalued success of protest movements is their contribution to the development of activist citizens (Isin 2009).

We rely on five main sources in building this case study. The first is the archival material of the movement itself, which has kept records of its public activities, press releases, and other aspects of its work. We use this material in establishing key stages in the movement's trajectory and explaining the drivers of its capacity for metamorphosis in reaction to the changing political environment. Secondly, we draw on media sources that published reports on the demonstrations and other activities of the protest movement. Thirdly, we use interview material collected in September 2014. This material refers to responses obtained from ten Right to the City protesters who answered in writing 13 questions exploring their experience of protest participation.[1] The interviewees belonged to the inner circle of the Right to the City initiative who were intensely involved in the movement. This material is used to problematise understandings of protest movements' outcomes and conceptions of success. For confidentiality, we use pseudonyms in the interview extracts. Fourthly, we rely on written and oral accounts of the movement from the movement leaders themselves. Finally, one of the authors played a leadership role in the Right to the City movement and all three authors of this essay are part of a collective involved in knowledge production in support of the Right to the City and similar protest movements in Croatia.[2] In other words, this analysis is in part an activist self-reflection and at the same time part of a larger analytical endeavour, exemplifying Marcuse's (2009) understanding of critical theory as simultaneously aiming to illuminate existing emancipatory urban practices and informing their future course.

---

[1] The interview protocol was adapted from a study on the biographical consequences of participation in student protests in Croatia, reported in Ćulum and Doolan (2015).

[2] Group 22, available at: www.grupa22.hr, accessed 20 September 2017.

ACTIVIST CITIZENSHIP IN SOUTHEAST EUROPE

The political economy of protest on the European semi-periphery

Popular and scholarly attention regarding contemporary cycles of protest is focused on the arc from the Arab Spring (2011), to the Indignados (2011), Syntagma Square (2010) and Occupy Wall Street (2011) movements. However, the Balkans have also witnessed a growing cycle of contention since the mid-2000s, with the Right to the City movement in Zagreb turning out to be the harbinger of things to come. A cursory overview of the politics of contention in this region includes the Initiative for the Protection of Peti Park in Belgrade, followed by student protests and occupations in Zagreb and Belgrade in 2008 and 2009,[3] workers' strikes in 2011 in Bulgaria (Dolenec *et al.* 2014), violent protests against the Maribor mayor in Slovenia in 2012,[4] 'The Park is Ours' (*Park je naš*) protests in Banja Luka in 2012 (Bosnia & Hercegovina), protests against an open-cast gold mine in Romania in 2013 (Swyngedouw 2014), violent riots across Bosnia & Hercegovina in 2014,[5] as well as the 2015 anti-government protests in Macedonia, which were rekindled in the spring of 2016 amid a deep government crisis.[6] In 2015, a struggle very similar to that fought by the Right to the City movement in Zagreb emerged in Belgrade, against a large real-estate development project on the Sava waterfront, under the name 'Let's Not Drown Belgrade' (*Ne davimo Beograd*).[7]

Not all of these protests are focused on re-claiming public space, but they do exhibit certain commonalities. Across the Balkans, many social spheres are exposed to demands for privatisation and pressured into demonstrating their short-term economic value (Dolenec *et al.* 2014). The concept of the 'public' has been thoroughly vilified as synonymous with corruption and inefficiency, while private ownership is invariably presented as the superior solution that yields efficiency and productivity. As a result, the state is withdrawing from its role as provider of key social services and, following the neoliberal recipe, re-appearing as the enabler of 'a favourable economic climate' (Dolenec *et al.* 2014, p. 6).

Apart from being embedded in the context of these contemporary struggles in the Balkans, the Right to the City protest movement in Zagreb also draws on the legacy of other Right to the City movements. These date back to the 1968 protest cycle in Western Europe, when they were first captured in Henri Lefebvre's expression 'the right to the city', which he described as a right 'to urban life, to renewed centrality, to places of encounter and exchange, to life rhythms and time uses, enabling the full and complete usage of these moments and places' (Lefebvre 1996).[8] Mayer (2012) described the urban social movements of the 1960s as a struggle against bureaucratisation and in favour of increased participation, autonomy,

---

[3]In 2014, students occupied the University of Skopje in Macedonia.

[4]'Maribor Mayor Resigns after Violent Protests in Slovenia', *Bloomberg*, 6 December 2012, available at: http://www.bloomberg.com/news/articles/2012-12-06/maribor-mayor-resigns-after-violent-protests-in-slovenia, accessed 14 June 2016.

[5]'Bosnia–Herzegovina Hit by Wave of Violent Protests', *The Guardian*, 7 February 2014, available at: https://www.theguardian.com/world/2014/feb/07/bosnia-herzegovina-wave-violent-protests, accessed 14 June 2016.

[6]'Survey: Macedonians Lose Faith as Crisis Escalates', *Balkan Insight*, 10 June 2016, available at: http://www.balkaninsight.com/en/article/survey-macedonia-crisis-escalates-06-09-2016, accessed 14 June 2016.

[7]'Serbian Activists Plan Fresh Waterfront Protest', *Balkan Insight*, 25 May 2016, available at: http://www.balkaninsight.com/en/article/protest-in-belgrade-scheduled-for-wednesday-05-25-2016, accessed 14 June 2016.

[8]See also Schmid (2012).

and alternative lifestyles. In other words, these movements emerged in the specific political economic context of the Western European welfare state and its concomitant urbanism, which was marked by strong state intervention in organising urban life (Schmid 2012). Needless to say, the situation today is markedly different: contemporary urban social movements are reacting to ever-expanding commodification and a fundamentally changed role of the state in urban planning and development, which more often than not facilitates the reshaping of the city according to private rather than public interests.

In Kerbo's (1982) terms, the movements of the 1960s belonged to a period of affluence, which we associate with the development of post-materialist value orientations that emphasise individual autonomy and self-expression (Inglehart 1971; Inglehart & Welzel 2005). However, given the tectonic shifts in the political economy of European states since then, and the fact that European cities are experiencing a renewed rise in poverty and inequality, class contestation is back on the agenda of social struggles (Mayer 2012). One may say that with the rise of neoliberalism, even urban movements in the hyper-developed European core countries like Germany or France have started exhibiting features of Kerbo's (1982) 'movements of crisis', which appear in conditions that are life-disrupting, such as widespread unemployment, food shortages, or major social dislocations. Therefore, contemporary social movement analysis advocates 'bringing capitalism back into the analysis' in order to understand current cycles of contention (Della Porta 2015). By bridging political economy and social movement studies, we are able to analyse ways in which the neoliberal recipes for urban transformation, according to which the market is a 'solution looking for problems ... and usually finding them, in all sectors of society' (Olsen & Maassen 2007, p. 4), are resisted by protest movements and initiatives. In this analysis, we chart the trajectory of social resistance that emerges from the dynamic in which the state is re-shaped according to its neoliberal role as a service provider to capital and an enforcer of private property rights (Harvey 2005).

At the same time, if we follow Pickvance's (2003) reasoning, contemporary urban social movements can be understood as exhibiting features of both movements of affluence and movements of crisis. They oppose the exemplary, physically visible process of capitalist enclosure and dispossession, while at the same time articulating demands that social science would recognise as post-materialist—including demands for democratisation, participation, and alternative forms of governance. Urban struggles will therefore confound analysts who, applying the said dichotomy, look for pure forms of either anti-capitalist struggle or protests aimed at increased citizen participation and democratisation of city governance. Urban struggles are quite often both of these things simultaneously, and the Right to the City movement in Zagreb testifies to this hybridity. The movement framed its objective as fighting against 'the economic exploitation of space, governing public space against public interest, unsustainable urbanisation policy and excluding citizens from decision-making regarding urbanisation'.[9] The movement has therefore simultaneously engaged with economic and political domains, arguing that the citizens of Zagreb are experiencing economic exploitation as well as being excluded from decision-making. The fundamental catalyst that shifted the movement towards broader mobilisation was its opposition to a large private investment project that aimed to privatise public space and infrastructure, a process which is often identified in the literature as the crucial fault line sparking contemporary urban protest (Hackworth 2008; Mayer 2012). As

[9]The Right to the City website, available at: http://pravonagrad.org/, accessed 28 November 2015.

Hackworth argues, Right to the City movements oppose inequitable real-estate development in cities as 'the knife-edge of neoliberal urbanism' (Hackworth 2007, p. 192).

In 2008, the Right to the City initiative organised a conference in Zagreb, entitled 'The Neoliberal Frontline: Urban Struggles in Post-Socialist Societies', hosting leading theoreticians of neoliberal urban transformations, such as critical urban geographers Neil Smith and Jason Hackworth.[10] In a number of contributions, the conference thematised specific configurations of neoliberal city transformations in a post-socialist context. The Right to the City initiative published a conference newsletter[11] and the *Handbook for Life in Neoliberal Reality*.[12] The handbook made available Croatian translations of texts by Lefebvre, Foucault, Harvey, Smith and others, included a study of urban development of Zagreb, and displayed a series of art interventions in Zagreb public spaces that took place between November and December that year. The conference and accompanying events thematised numerous aspects of neoliberal urbanism in post-socialism, highlighting ways in which neoliberal urbanisation promoted private interests at the expense of the public. From this contextualisation it was clear that while many features of this transformation follow a similar logic both West and East, post-socialist neoliberal urbanisation suffers from a stronger democratic deficit, government corruption and the legacy of dubious privatisation projects from the 1990s,[13] which some analysts characterised as 'daylight robberies' (Eagleton 2011, p. 14). These conference conclusions echoed a growing body of research into the political economies of the European semi-periphery.[14] Cities in post-communist Europe have developed within a variety of capitalism characterised by the retrenchment of the welfare state and the vanishing power of organised labour on the one hand, and a structural dependency on investment strategies of multinational corporations on the other (King 2007; Nölke & Vliegenthart 2009; Bohle & Greskovits 2013). The fact that in the 1990s regime change in this region entailed simultaneous transformations of the economic and the political sphere created a particular morphology of power where political power was converted into economic gain, and *vice versa* (Dolenec 2013). In such a context, the application of the Washington Consensus recipe of liberalisation, deregulation, and privatisation led to 'privileged information, privileged access, privileged loan terms, and appropriations by dubious means' (Ramet & Wagner 2010, p. 22). With inside capture of the privatisation process (Gould 2003) being the rule rather than the exception, political corruption

---

[10]More information about the conference is available at: http://www.mi2.hr/programi-i-projekti/commons/#T2, accessed 28 November 2015.

[11]The newsletter is available at: https://monoskop.org/images/3/3d/Operation.City_2008_The_Neoliberal_Frontline_Urban_Struggles_in_Post-Socialist_Societies.pdf, accessed 27 June 2016.

[12]The handbook is available at: https://monoskop.org/images/f/f4/Operacija.Grad_Prirucnik_za_zivot_u_neoliberalnoj_stvarnosti.pdf, accessed 27 June 2016.

[13]Right to the City Newsletter, 2008, available at: https://monoskop.org/images/3/3d/Operation.City_2008_The_Neoliberal_Frontline_Urban_Struggles_in_Post-Socialist_Societies.pdf, accessed 27 June 2016.

[14]In employing the concept of the semi-periphery (Wallerstein 1979), we want to stress that we understand Southeast Europe not only with respect to its geographical location *vis-à-vis* Western Europe, but as possessing political economic features of both core and peripheral regions, and acting as a mediator and an 'in-between space' (Wallerstein 1979; Chase-Dunn & Hall 1997). More importantly, following Wallerstein's world systems theory, we consider the semi-periphery as carrying politically and socially transformative potential, making it not so much a geographical descriptor, but rather a position within the world hierarchy through which social and economic transformation can be interpreted (Domazet & Marinović Jerolimov 2014). In terms of what this means for our analysis, we do not approach social contention in Southeast Europe simply as an 'echo' of events taking place elsewhere, but as a phenomenon in its own right, which might carry important insights into informing future emancipatory practices.

became the primary manifestation of capitalism in the Balkans. As a result, compared to their Western counterparts, in post-socialist cities the demolition of the social in favour of the market has been met with fewer obstacles, resulting in far-reaching transformations of how the city is used and experienced.

As part of Yugoslavia, Zagreb grew within a socialist developmental logic which aimed to equalise life conditions across class boundaries. This urbanisation philosophy was rejected in the 1990s in favour of 'desolidarisation' (Brenner 2000). By putting their faith in the market, post-socialist cities have become more responsive to the interest of capital and more tolerant of illegal practices like collusion or bribery. The result was widespread corruption (Woolcock 1998), as well as a general lack of urban planning and development policies. Citizen participation is low, institutional mechanisms for participatory governance are lacking, and post-communist political elites have been unwilling to take into consideration the demands of civic groups (Petrović 2005). Furthermore, regulations pertaining to city planning in post-socialist cities have been particularly malleable. In Croatia, the relevant legislation underwent numerous amendments: between 1991 and 2006, the Building Act was changed eight times, while the Physical Planning Act was changed ten times (Šarić 2012). This has arguably contributed not only to the absence of coherent urban planning, but has encouraged the growth of grey markets in construction and real estate (Mišetić & Ursić 2010). The city being a place where global trends 'touch down' (Mayer 2012), the described post-socialist context affected the movement's configuration and framing of grievances towards a stronger emphasis on the protection of public interest and the fight against corruption.

The following sections engage with the movement's trajectory and outcomes. We reconstruct the movement's trajectory by addressing the supposedly unavoidable contradiction that social movements encounter, whereby due to the dynamic of competitive polarisation, they diverge over time either into institutionalisation or radicalisation (Tarrow 2011). The identified five phases of the movement shed light on the evolution of its targets and campaigns, its changing repertoire of contention, and the networks it was central in producing. Considering outcomes, we analyse the views and opinions of protesters who took part in the Right to the City movement, arguing that one of the most relevant long-term outcomes of the movement has been the strengthening of activist citizenship (Isin 2009). In this, we align with Castells's (2012) critique of the 'productivist vision' of social action according to which, if nothing concrete is accomplished by the action, particularly *vis-à-vis* state institutions, then the action has failed.

Contesting neoliberal urbanism on the European semi-periphery[15]

Tarrow (2011) has written about social movements' trajectories as diverging over time into either institutionalisation or radicalisation. The first trajectory was famously described by Michels (1968) and formulated as 'the iron law of oligarchy'. Michels studied the transformation of the German labour movement and the growth of the German Social Democratic Party, concluding that the growth of the movement inevitably necessitated organisation-building and hence bureaucratisation. This, in turn, set into motion an organisational logic of self-preservation

---

[15]A more detailed analytical narrative is provided in Appendix 1.

which killed off radicalism and the pursuit of substantial social change. Organisational bureaucratisation transposed to the substantive level meant de-radicalisation, with movements eventually becoming conventional players in the political arena, no longer posing a challenge to the *status quo* (Piven & Cloward 1977; Rucht 1999). The fact that Michels formulated his iron law by studying socialist organisations, which were supposed to embody participatory and democratic principles, made his conclusions particularly pertinent for progressive Left movements (Lipset 1969). According to Tarrow (2011), movements that wanted to stay true to their radical objectives and avoid this destiny decided, as a rule, to keep only loose organisational networks and eschew formal organisation. However, without the personal, financial, and logistical infrastructure that organisations secure for movements, they end up in the other trap—their voluntarism 'burns out' and the movement loses its capacity to mobilise. The most recent wave of Occupy movements around the world is a good illustration of this dynamic. Occupations of city squares were powerful demonstrations of direct-democratic, participatory culture, carrying the performative strength of lived alternatives, but the aversion of these movements to more permanent organisational forms and protest repertoires contributed to their quick dissipation (Gitlin 2013).

Though today most social scientists are uncomfortable with pronouncing social 'laws', Michels's thesis on oligarchisation has not only kept its theoretical relevance, but has also been confirmed empirically. Rucht (1999) analysed a large number of protest organisations and their tactics to find that Michels's thesis generally holds: movements become more bureaucratic with time and more moderate in their actions. Synthesising from various existing studies, Tarrow (2011) found that even though in principle movements strive to create organisational models that are sufficiently robust to structure contention but flexible enough to ensure vitality and a reliable grassroots base, in practice they either go down the 'bureaucratise and moderate' route, or they 'radicalise and dissipate'. Based on these propositions, we identify five stages that the Right to the City Zagreb movement has undergone, arguing that it escaped this trap by constantly reinventing its methods, objectives, and organisational base.

Escalating confrontation with the city of Zagreb

The roots of the Right to the City movement in Zagreb can be traced back to cooperation between independent cultural non-governmental organisations (NGOs) and youth NGOs in 2005. The period between May 2005 and June 2006 was the first phase of the movement, which we have named 'Claiming Rights'. It was marked by the issuing of a joint declaration on 'Independent Culture and Youth in the Development of the City of Zagreb', signed by national associations of cultural and youth NGOs as well as a number of other organisations. This declaration was presented at a round-table discussion and offered for signing to the main candidates for city mayor on the eve of the 2005 local elections in Zagreb. The declaration contained nine objectives, the most concrete of which was a call for the establishment of a multi-functional centre for independent culture and youth activity in abandoned factory sites owned by the City of Zagreb. The declaration was signed by most mayoral candidates, including Milan Bandić, who became mayor of Zagreb in May 2005 as a member of the Social Democratic Party (*Socijaldemokratska partija Hrvatske*).

With the city's permission, the coalition occupied the factory site of Badel-Gorica in September 2005, organising a two-week cultural event entitled 'Operation City' in order to demonstrate the potential of such a social centre for cultural and youth activity. This occupation was the spin-off of an earlier 2005 cultural project, 'Invisible Zagreb', which had mapped abandoned industrial sites in the city. The default plan for these former factories was a sell-off to private investors, and in order to contest this, the 'Invisible Zagreb' project advocated their restoration and public use. This project was probably the first instance of programmatic claims for citizens' right to the city in this case study. The project's stated objective was to 'show the public that they have the right to claim the city, that the city is the exclusive right of its citizens, and that they have the right and the opportunity to use it creatively'.[16]

During this event, the mayor promised that the city would establish a social centre for culture and youth on this industrial site, agreeing to the creation of a public–civic institution that would require the centre to be co-governed by the city and the coalition of independent culture and youth NGOs. In summary, during the first phase of the movement, the coalition employed a combination of negotiations and public pressure on the city administration in pursuit of its main objective—the establishment of a social centre for culture and youth in Zagreb. In terms of framing, in this first phase the coalition aimed to address the insufficient attention paid to youth policy and to negotiate for space and resources from the city for its activities. At the same time, some of the framing of grievances referenced the rights of citizens to the city, and the need for the city to include citizens in decision-making processes.

What happened next was that the mayor reneged on his promises. Six months later, the site was transformed into a commercial zone. In response, the coalition of NGOs moved to a more confrontational pressure tactic—in June 2006, they gathered under the name 'The Right to the City' and adbusted[17] billboards with the mayor's photo on them, provoking a lot of media attention (see Figures 1 and 2).

Apart from marking the decisive point that catalysed the conflict with the city government after which negotiations with the mayor were broken off, adbusting also served to broaden the scope of the movement from spatial demands for culture and youth NGOs to Zagreb's urban planning policy, whereby the movement entered its second phase.

The second phase of the movement began with the establishment of the Right to the City initiative, which formulated its objective explicitly as fighting against 'the economic exploitation of space, governing public space against public interest, unsustainable urbanisation policy and excluding citizens from decision-making regarding urbanisation'.[18] The initiative soon formed a partnership with the NGO *Zelena Akcija* (Green Action—Friends of the Earth Croatia). The entry of Green Action, a seasoned fighter in environmental and urban planning policy, decisively influenced the future trajectory of the movement. This partnership was not an easy decision, since it meant involving a large professional NGO with its complex decision-making procedures and parallel struggles that needed to be taken into consideration. However, cooperation with Green Action provided the movement with legitimacy and resources.

In its second phase, the movement was focused on opposing a developmental project in Zagreb in Petar Preradović Square, colloquially known as Flower Square. After realising that

---

[16]From an interview with the project coordinator, *Deutche Welle*, 21 March 2005, available at: http://www.dw.com/hr/nevidljivi-zagreb/a-2282374-1, accessed 28 November 2015.

[17]This expression originates from Adbusters, a Canadian-based organisation that publishes a magazine by the same title. They are known for their anti-consumerism, and in particular for 'busting' and subverting advertisements for well-known brands. See more at: https://www.adbusters.org/, accessed 28 November 2015.

[18]The Right to the City website, available at: http://pravonagrad.org/, accessed 28 November 2015.

FIGURE 1. RIGHT TO THE CITY MOVEMENT ADBUSTING THE MAYOR'S PHOTO, BILLBOARD ON TRG ŽRTAVA FAŠIZMA.
Source: Pravo na Grad/Right to the City Archive. Reproduced with permission.

the mayor had reneged on his agreement with them, activists had started investigating the city's development policies, discovering 'systematic mismanagement of public space and public resources for the benefit of private investors, and a complete disenfranchisement of the public in issues of urban development' (Medak *et al.* 2013).[19] This is how they learned about the proposed Flower Passage project, envisaged as the redevelopment of one of the blocks in Flower Square as upscale residences and a shopping mall. However, making the project profitable required numerous concessions by city authorities: amending planning regulations, rewriting the comprehensive urban plan (the so-called Master plan) to allow a garage to be built in the historic downtown, giving up part of a pedestrian public space for the garage entryway, and demolishing protected heritage buildings (Medak 2011). The initiative chose this particular redevelopment project as the focal point of its struggle in order to demonstrate the systematic trend towards the privatisation of public space happening in Zagreb and elsewhere. Flower Square occupies a central location in downtown Zagreb, only steps away from Zagreb's main square, Ban Jelačić Square. Once a leafy, quaint space for flower sellers, surrounded by cinemas, bookstores, and cafés, it is now a treeless space dominated by rows of café tables and chairs, and a shopping mall on its western side. However, despite its exaggerated commercialisation, the square

---

[19]Article written by the founders of the Right to the City movement.

FIGURE 2. RIGHT TO THE CITY MOVEMENT ADBUSTING THE MAYOR'S PHOTO, BILLBOARD ON VUKOVARSKA STREET.
Source: Pravo na Grad/ Right to the City Archive. Reproduced with permission.

remains a socialising hotspot. This second phase of the movement, which we named 'Flower Passage', lasted from December 2006 until January 2010.

In the second phase, the movement used both disruptive and symbolic public actions designed to attract media attention and mobilise support. In February 2007, it organised a petition, collecting 54,000 signatures against the construction of the 'Flower Passage'. In April, several hundred activists organised a sit-in at the crossroads between Gundulićeva and Varšavska streets, blocking traffic and provoking arrests.[20] Actions blocking city traffic around the Flower Square continued in 2008, together with the organisation of citizen demonstrations attended by several thousand people in January 2008.[21] In 2007, the movement renamed Flower Square as 'Victims of Milan Bandić Square' (*Trg žrtava Milana Bandića*)[22] (see Figure 3), and in 2008 they taped up the entrance to the Ministry of Environmental Protection, Spatial Planning, and Construction with police crime-scene tape. The latter action was designed to attract attention to the fact that the acting minister was also a significant shareholder in a

---

[20]'Activists Expand Pedestrian Zone in Varšavska', *Friends of the Earth Croatia*, 21 April 2007, available at: http://zelenaakcija.hr/hr/programi/info_centar_zelene_akcije/dan_planeta_zemlje/aktivisti_prosirili_pjesacku_zonu_na_gundulicevu, accessed 20 November 2015.

[21]*Kontrapunkt*, 28 January 2008, available at: http://old.kontra-punkt.info/print.php?sid=55845, accessed 20 November 2015.

[22]This pun plays on the fact that another central square in Zagreb is named 'Victims of Fascism'.

FIGURE 3. VICTIMS OF MILAN BANDIĆ SQUARE.
Source: Zelena Akcija/Friends of the Earth Croatia Archive. Reproduced with permission.

construction company which designed the entrance to the garage in Varšavska Street, while the same ministry was responsible for licensing this work.

As confrontation with the city authorities escalated, the Right to the City established an NGO in order to be able to fundraise, as well as pursue legal action against the mayor and the city administration. According to one of the leaders of the movement, this move was also made in order to insulate cultural and youth NGOs from the growing confrontation with the city, given that these organisations depended on the city for funding, working space, and programme permits. The previously mentioned conference, 'The Neoliberal Frontline: Urban Struggles in Post-Socialist Societies', took place during this time, in December 2008, which was important for the political articulation of the movement's objective: contesting neoliberal urbanism and the framing of the struggle in broader terms than the particular locality on Varšavska Street. In parallel, the movement was building a network of initiatives involved in urban struggles across the country, establishing *Nacionalni forum za prostor* (National Forum for Space) as a coordinating platform. The parallel reconfiguring of local organisations in Zagreb involved in the struggle against the Flower Passage project and this incipient national networking signalled a second morphing of the movement as it modified both its organisational form and objectives.

The catalyst for the third phase of the Right to the City protest movement came in January 2010 when construction works began on Varšavska Street, which was the crucial part of redevelopment on Flower Square. We named this phase 'We won't give up Varšavska'. The movement managed initially to stop and, thereafter, substantially delay the start of construction

FIGURE 4. THE 'TROJAN HORSE' IN THE FLOWER SQUARE.
Source: Marina Kelava. Reproduced with permission.

works, employing a combination of physical occupation of the square and surrounding streets, demonstrations and marches, as well as the initiation of legal actions against the project and the city administration. This is the phase of the protest movement which captured national media attention, drew in new supporters, and successfully mobilised the citizens of Zagreb for a number of demonstrations and marches.

Under the banner 'We won't give up Varšavska', the movement further radicalised its tactics and the confrontation with city authorities escalated. The movement organised the 'Live Wall for Varšavska', a mailing list of around 2,000 citizens who responded to calls to physically occupy Flower Square and Varšavska Street. Two converted shipping containers were illegally placed in Varšavska with the aim of keeping a vigil and physically occupying the street. This occupation of public space and sit-in was maintained for five days. As part of the occupation of Varšavska Street, during the protest that was attended by around 4,000 people, the movement wheeled a large wooden replica of the Trojan Horse into the square (see Figure 4),[23] to symbolise the fraudulent depiction of the development project as being 'in the public interest'.

The occupation of Varšavska Street led to the arrest of 23 non-violent activists in the middle of the night, ending the occupation but generating unprecedented media attention and citizen mobilisation. The movement continued to use the 'Live Wall' as a human shield against construction works.

---

[23]*Jutarnji List*, 10 February 2010, available at: http://www.jutarnji.hr/foto--cetiri-tisuce-ljudi-i--trojanski-konj-protiv-cvjetnog-prolaza/552360/, accessed 20 November 2015.

ACTIVIST CITIZENSHIP IN SOUTHEAST EUROPE

In parallel, in April 2010 the Right to the City and Green Action submitted a criminal lawsuit to the State Attorney's Office against the mayor of Zagreb for licensing the Flower Passage project. However, the project went ahead and in May 2010, in preparation for the start of construction works, Varšavska Street was fenced off and patrolled by private security guards. In response, the 'Live Wall for Varšavska' action destroyed the fence and began the second illegal occupation of Varšavska Street, which lasted for almost the whole month. It is worth noting here that while the Right to the City movement was by no means the first to introduce this tactic into the repertoire of protest movements, its occupation of Flower Square and Varšavska Street does predate the 15-M Spanish anti-austerity movement and the subsequent wave of occupations of public space epitomised by 'Occupy' movements.[24]

The following day, around 3,000 citizens gathered in Varšavska Street to support its physical occupation.[25] On average, around 100 citizens and activists guarded the street in shifts day and night, watched by police. After a few days, the movement again mobilised around 4,000 citizens in a march to the State Attorney General's office and to the City Council, requesting the mayor's resignation.[26] In June 2010, the State Attorney General announced that the amendments to the City Master Urban Plan that had allowed the Flower Passage project were illegal. As a result, the occupation of Varšavska was stopped. Despite this ruling, however, construction work on Varšavska Street began on 15 July 2010, guarded by around 200 police officers. Activists and citizens tried to stop it through a non-violent human shield but 142 of them were arrested.[27] This was the biggest mass arrest of non-violent protesters in Croatia's history, and it mobilised citizens in large numbers. Protesters were prevented from entering the street as the whole block was guarded by police. The beginning of construction and the mass arrest made this a top story in the Croatian media, and for five days, several thousand citizens marched through the city streets, creating spontaneous sit-ins at crossroads and illegally blocking vehicle traffic.[28] However, as Varšavska Street was heavily guarded by the police, the protests did not stop the construction work and the battle for Varšavska Street was lost.

Overall, the protest movement influenced the implementation of the development project significantly. Its efforts reduced the size of the garage in the pedestrian zone by almost half compared to the original plan, delayed the project for four years and reduced its scope by half (Medak 2011). Moreover, in February 2010 the City Assembly unanimously decided to reverse

---

[24]A student protest movement that originated at the University of Zagreb in 2009 and subsequently spread to other cities in Croatia also used the tactic of occupation, but with the important distinction that this was done within the university property, more akin to a sit-in. The Right to the City introduced the occupation of public squares, roads, and intersections into protest repertoires in Croatia.

[25]'Policija postavila novu ogradu u Varšavskoj, na prosvjedu tisuće ljudi', *Metro Portal*, 18 May 2010; available at: http://metro-portal.hr/policija-postavila-novu-ogradu-u-varsavskoj-na-prosvjedu-tisuce-ljudi/40333, accessed 20 November 2015.

[26]'Bandiću donijeli kofer s četkicom, sapunom i ručnikom za Remetinec', *Večernji list*, 20 May 2010, available at: http://www.vecernji.hr/zg-vijesti/bandicu-donijeli-kofer-s-cetkicom-sapunom-i-rucnikom-za-remetinec-143860, accessed 20 November 2015.

[27]'Konačni obračun: Aktivisti traže Karamarkovu smjenu', *Večernji List*, 17 July 2010, available at: http://www.vecernji.hr/zg-vijesti/konacni-obracun-aktivisti-traze-karamarkovu-smjenu-167987, accessed 20 November 2015.

[28]'Video: Bandić će biti prvi političar kojega su svrgnuli građani', *Index*, 19 July 2010, available at: http://www.index.hr/vijesti/clanak/video-bandic-ce-biti-prvi-politicar-kojega-su-svrgnuli-gradjani/502610.aspx, accessed 20 November 2015.

FIGURE 5. 'BURYING PUBLIC INTEREST' IN *VARŠAVSKA*.
Source: Zelena Akcija/Friends of the Earth Croatia Archive. Reproduced with permission.

the changes to Zagreb's Master plan that had enabled the Flower Passage project, preventing the realisation of other similar projects on downtown blocks. On a symbolic level, the Right to the City movement provoked a public apology from the Social Democratic Party that held the majority in the City Assembly at the time. The movement symbolically marked the end of this struggle by 'burying public interest' at the entrance to the garage built underneath Varšavska Street (see Figure 5).

Tactical shapeshifting

The first three phases of the protest movement were focused on the City of Zagreb's government and its mayor, who wields both formal power and wide discretionary informal power in the city. Between 2005 and 2010, the Right to the City movement grew from a coalition of cultural and youth NGOs pressuring the mayor to establish an independent cultural centre in the city, to one of the largest citizens' struggles in the country's recent history. The significance of the movement is reflected in the fact that it received two national activist awards and was voted by NGOs in Croatia as the most positive civil society initiative for three years in a row.[29]

---

[29]'Pravo na grad', *2010 GONG Award* to Right to the City, 27 May 2010, available at: http://www.gong.hr/hr/aktivni-gradani/nagrada-gong-a/pravo-na-grad/, accessed 20 November 2015; 'Krunoslav Sukić Nagrada za promicanje mirotvorstva', *2010 Centre for Peace Award* to the 'We Won't Give Up Varšavska' Campaign, available at: http://www.krunoslav-sukic.centar-za-mir.hr/priznanja/, accessed 20 November 2015; '5 + 5 Anketa civilno društvo 2010', *H-alter*, 24 December 2010, available at: http://www.h-alter.org/vijesti/5-5-anketa-civilno-drustvo-2010, accessed 20 November 2015.

Therefore, we agree with Stubbs that the fight for Varšavska had both immediate and long-term resonance, in part because it facilitated later protests in Croatia and the region, but crucially because this campaign managed 'to move discursively between the particular and the general, mobilising broad, popular concerns over corruption, the links between political and economic elites, the failure of ministerial regulation and control, the structural nature of "conflicts of interest", and the lack of public participation in urban planning' (Stubbs 2012, p. 23). As we have shown, although the movement initially operated in the context of a declaratively 'friendly' local government, the relationship quickly soured and led to open confrontation. In response to the enclosure of public space for the sake of private interests, the movement exposed city politics as collusive with the interests of capital, disregarding both citizens' demands and the broad legal framework that was supposed to guide city planning. The dynamic between the city government and the movement exhibited mutual radicalisation—as the movement employed ever more disruptive methods, the city authorities responded with growing repression.

Regarding the iron law of oligarchy, the first three phases of the movement exhibit a dynamic opposite to what Mayer (2012, p. 66) has termed 'from protest to program'. This is a feature she observes in the neoliberal era and describes as the increasing fragmentation and co-optation of urban movements into providing various services which used to be the city's responsibility. According to Mayer, as governments roll back from social service provision, NGOs and other civic initiatives jump in to fill that space, managing community centres, caring for the elderly and the children, or maintaining urban spaces. Thus, urban movements inadvertently move from 'protest to program' (Mayer 2012, p. 66). In a reversal of this dynamic, the Right to the City movement in Croatia started as a loose coalition of NGOs that focused its attention on the failures in the implementation of the city's youth policy. While in the beginning it used conventional forms of participation to address city authorities, it radicalised its objectives and tactics dramatically in response to the city's disregard of its demands.

Reflecting Tarrow's (2012) dynamic of competitive polarisation between institutionalisation and radicalisation, during the first three phases the Right to the City movement followed the radicalisation trajectory—but, instead of this leading to burnout, the movement grew substantially in strength during its first years. In 2010 it initiated new struggles, morphing first into a national network and, as we show in the following section, later into a coalition with trade union associations and new NGO partners. Though at one point it institutionalised itself as an NGO in order to be able to fundraise, the energy of the movement and its objectives were kept carefully separate from the organisational logic of self-preservation and growth. Bilić and Stubbs (2015, p. 127) attribute the contemporary shift away from conventional NGO formation to a broader set of movements that they understand as 'the new Left' in the Balkans, for which the 'NGO shape is either irrelevant, part of the problem, or a useful means of attracting project-based funding which can then be used for wider political aims' (Bilić & Stubbs 2015, p. 127). Acknowledging the fact that this new wave of activism in Croatia and elsewhere in the region has eschewed formal organisation, we contend that the Right to the City is unique in that, in principle, it sought any organisational form that best fitted its purpose at a given time. This pragmatism sets it apart from the principled 'anti-NGOism' of some of the new Left activism and, arguably, makes it politically more effective.

As we learned from the leaders of the movement, they understood the dangers of conventional institutionalisation and strove to achieve, in Tarrow's (2011) terms, the balance between the robustness necessary to structure contention and the flexibility that ensures vitality. According to an account provided by one of the leaders of the movement,[30] concrete decisions regarding targets, repertoires of contention, chosen framings, and partnerships that we described in this analytical narrative were based on two explicit principles. The first was 'tactical shapeshifting' whereby an organisation is understood as a framework rather than as being embodied in an institution. As a result, the movement deliberately relied on the hard and soft infrastructure, in terms of both organisational resources and expertise, of already existing organisations. When it established its own NGO, it was clear that its purpose was to serve as an interface for putting together campaigns in partnership with others. One measure taken to secure this objective was the decision that no one in the organisation was to be employed full-time. Instead, people were 'shared' through modular employment across several organisations.

The second principle was 'tactical networking' with actors and organisations across various domains; mostly in the sphere of civil society, but later also with trade unions and other institutional actors. The purpose was achieving greater social impact, which also meant that the repertoire of contention shifted in accordance with specific campaigns. As we have shown, the Right to the City movement in Croatia comprised a series of campaigns, each of which had a specific focus and objective. The principle was always the same—selecting targets which can be used to highlight systematic features of the political regime. Though networks are built around specific targets, partnerships across organisations are not maintained purely for pragmatic purposes, but represent conscious investment in longer-term partnerships. The principle of 'tactical networking' is captured in the second part of the analytical narrative in the following section.

Taking the fight elsewhere

The start of the fourth phase of the project was the activation of the National Forum for Space, a coordination network established back in 2006. This phase lasted from September 2010 until April 2013, during which the political struggle over public space was relocated to the city of Dubrovnik. The Right to the City movement supported the Srđ Is Ours (*Srđ je naš*) initiative in Dubrovnik, which then joined the National Forum for Space network. The support was in the form of funding, media visibility, and activist know-how, with the objective of jointly stopping a mega real-estate project, 'Golf Park Dubrovnik', on Srđ Hill above the Old City of Dubrovnik. Again, the campaign was shaped so as to signal the systemic character of neoliberal transformations of urban space.[31]

---

[30]Email interview with one of the leaders of the movement, 18 November 2015.

[31]Supported by the Right to the City, the 'Srđ Is Ours' initiative used protest actions and media communication to mobilise the citizens of Dubrovnik against the development project. The initiative decided to use the citizens' petition for a referendum as a mechanism to pressure the city government, and was successful in collecting the required number of signatures in February 2013. As a result, a local referendum took place in April 2013, with a significant majority of those who voted being against the building of Golf Park Dubrovnik. However, given that the turnout was 31%, which was lower than the legally required 50% turnout of all registered voters in Dubrovnik, the outcome of the referendum was not legally binding for the city government. After this battle was lost, the initiative Srđ Is Ours established an independent list to contest the local election that was held in 2013. They managed to secure three out of 25 seats in the city council, but were faced with the 'Dubrovnik Agreement', a broad coalition of left- and right-wing parties, pragmatically formed, among other objectives, to secure the passing of necessary legislation for the golf park. See 'Dubrovački dogovor okupio 16 vijećnika iz HDZ-a, HNS-a i SDP-a', *Slobodna Dalmacija*, 12 July 2013, available at: http://www.slobodnadalmacija. hr/dalmacija/dubrovnik/clanak/id/206415/dubrovacki-dogovor-okupio-16-vijecnika-iz-hdz-a-hns-a-i-sdp-a, accessed 20 September 2017.

As well as supporting the initiative Srđ Is Ours, the Right to the City networked with other similar initiatives against the enclosure of public space in Croatia and the region; for example, the project *Muzil* in Pula (Croatia), the 'Park Is Ours' initiative in Banja Luka (Bosnia & Hercegovina), 'Freedom Square' in Skopje (Macedonia), and 'Let's Not Drown Belgrade' (Serbia). This included the mutual exchange of information, skill-sharing, and activists travelling between locations. For instance, key activists involved in the Right to the City and Park Is Ours knew each other for years before both protests happened, given that partner organisations, Green Action and the Centre for Environment (Banja Luka), had a history of cooperation in joint environmental projects.

Parallel to supporting local struggles in Croatia and the region and building its network within the National Forum for Space, the Right to the City initiated another coalition in 2013 around a nationally relevant topic: the announced long-term private concession of the largest highway system in Croatia. The fifth and final phase of the Right to the City movement was therefore marked by the campaign 'We won't give up our highways'. We have named this phase after the campaign. It started in October 2013 and is still ongoing. Further developing its platform around the protection of public interest in urban planning and the use of natural and urban space in Croatia, as well as advocating for greater transparency and citizen participation in the governance of public infrastructure and utilities, the Right to the City movement initiated a campaign to oppose the government's plan to give around 1,000 km of highways in concession to a private company. According to the government's proposal, during the 40 years for which the concession would be awarded, the government would financially guarantee a profit return irrespective of actual traffic flows, funded with taxpayers' money. In October 2014, the campaign collected voters' signatures to initiate a national referendum that would ban private concessions on highways. The petition for the referendum collected around 500,000 signatures.[32] The campaign attracted national public attention and wide media coverage, as well as parliamentary debates and statements by the government.

The citizens' petition was successful despite the prohibitively high threshold for success (10% of registered voters needed to sign the petition within 15 days), which could at least in part be attributed to the organisational resources at the disposal of trade unions. It was *de jure* unsuccessful, given that the Constitutional Court ruled the referendum question inadmissible, but it was *de facto* a success since the government dropped the project. In the trajectory of the movement, the decision to use the citizens' petition for referendums as a tool for mobilisation can be interpreted as an attempt at reaching a wider constituency. Apart from that, however, turning to a referendum as a mobilisation tool was partly contingent on the fact that, prior to this one, there had been six national campaigns for citizens' referendums since 2010, two of which had been successfully organised by trade unions (Dolenec 2015). As we have argued elsewhere, since 2010 citizens' petitions have emerged as a powerful agenda-setting tool for influencing government actions, used by movements on both the left and the right of the political spectrum (Dolenec 2015).

Figure 6 visually summarises the five phases of the Right to the City movement. The trajectory of the movement reveals its persistent struggle against enclosures of public space and the commodification of public infrastructure.

---

[32]'Za referendum o autocestama prikupljen dovoljan broj potpisa', *Dnevnik*, 22 January 2015, available at: http://dnevnik.hr/vijesti/hrvatska/referendumska-inicijativa-ne-damo-nase-autoceste-prikupila-dovoljan-broj-potpisa---369552.html, accessed 20 November 2015.

FIGURE 6. THE FIVE PHASES OF THE RIGHT TO THE CITY MOVEMENT IN CROATIA.

The presented analytical narrative captures how, by carefully selecting the targets of their contention, the Right to the City movement managed over time to elaborate a coherent critique of privatisation and commodification of public space and expose the systemic trends of market-driven development behind ostensibly local political dynamics. By prioritising political confrontation and consciously applying its principles of tactical shapeshifting and networking, it exhibited a remarkable capacity for metamorphosis and hence managed to avoid both institutionalisation and dissipation. After the initial three phases, which evidenced a growing confrontation with the City of Zagreb, the movement shifted its attention to the national and regional arenas, providing resources and expertise to other urban struggles, as well as investing considerable efforts in engendering the 'We won't give up our highways' coalition with unions and national union associations.

Challenging the 'productivist vision' of social action

In their analysis of 843 protests that took place worldwide between 2006 and 2013, Ortiz *et al.* (2013) calculate that 63% of them did not achieve their specific demands in the short-term. At the same time, these same protests are often 'engaged with long-term structural issues that may yield results in time' (Ortiz *et al.* 2013, p. 6). An evaluation of the success of protests in terms of achieving specific demands in the short-term is what Castells (2012) has critiqued as a 'productivist vision' of social action, which is underpinned by the conviction that if nothing concrete is accomplished (particularly *vis-à-vis* state institutions), then the protest has failed. According to Castells (2012), some contemporary social movements reject this vision as a reproduction of the capitalist logic in the evaluation of the movement. We engage with this debate by analysing the views and opinions of protesters who took part in the Right to the City protests; in doing so, we argue that the most relevant long-term success of the protests has been the strengthening of activist citizenship (Isin 2009) on the European semi-periphery. Isin's (2009) conception of activist citizenship is characterised not by routine forms of participation in designated times and format, but instead by contentious acts of citizenship that question existing laws and regulations, challenge institutions, and demand a transformation of existing conceptions of citizens' rights. 'Activist citizenship' captures well the experience of Right to the City activists whom we interviewed, since it moves the discussion away from 'auditing' specific short-term outcomes and towards appreciating the long-term effects that arise from protest participation.

The interviews focused on protesters' experiences of the 'We won't give up Varšavska' protests elaborated earlier. Their responses suggest that the question of a protest's success is complex, multi-faceted, and process-sensitive, and that its evaluation requires longitudinal observation rather than being 'obvious', narrow, and outcome-oriented with success measured at one moment in time. Excerpts from three interviews reflect the tension between some aspects of these opposed understandings, implicitly criticising the 'productivist vision' of social action:[33]

---

[33]Interview extracts have been translated from Croatian into English by the authors.

ACTIVIST CITIZENSHIP IN SOUTHEAST EUROPE

I used to think protests were successful only if they resulted in the accomplishment of the desired goal. Having taken part in these protests I have become aware that things are not so black and white. (Ida)

If we look at it from a narrow perspective as opposition to the building of the shopping centre Flower Passage and the devastation of Varšavska Street, then the whole thing wasn't successful, which is a frequent cynical complaint made by different parts of the political and activist scene in Croatia. But one shouldn't look at it in such narrow terms. (Ana)

I think that the success of the Right to the City campaign is big, even though the controversial object was built at the very end. The end result of the campaign hasn't demotivated me because … I didn't have any large false hopes that we will be fully successful at the end. But I think that at the end the campaign was very successful because since then I can see a great improvement in civil society and society more generally. (Filip)

For the ten protesters who participated in our study, going beyond 'black and white' and 'narrow' understandings of success (in this case, the building of the shopping centre) entailed, among other things, influencing other actions, strengthening the civil society scene, influencing urban development policy more generally, raising consciousness on urban policy, highlighting the value of citizen engagement and alternative forms of political engagement, as well as the personal benefits of protest participation.

In terms of influencing other actions, several of the protesters who participated in our study mentioned initiatives that they felt drew inspiration and knowledge from the Zagreb Right to the City protests both in Croatia and regionally (although one interviewee mentioned that further research would be required to establish these links clearly). According to the protesters, these initiatives, some of which have already been mentioned as comprising the fourth phase of the movement, included the urban struggles mentioned above, as well as protests with a broader agenda, including the so-called Facebook protests in Croatia.[34] The following excerpts illustrate such protest interconnections:

Initiatives for [public] space started to multiply, not only in Croatia but also neighbouring countries, and many emphasised the struggle for Varšavska as an incentive for them to raise their voice in their local communities. Some of these struggles have managed to prevent the pillage and devastation of space. (Katarina)

I believe that the Facebook protests were partly inspired by Varšavska. (Ivana)

Strengthening the civil society scene in Croatia through intensified networking and trust-building was seen as integral to the protests' success. Protesters remarked:

What is particularly important is that the activist scene became stronger. (Ivan)

---

[34]The Facebook protests, named after the social media site through which they were predominantly organised, took place in 2011 as a reaction against the country's political elites. The Right to the City movement publicly supported the protests. See for instance 'Pravo na grad i Zelena akcija poduprli prosvjede', *Večernji list*, 8 March 2011, available at: http://www.vecernji.hr/hrvatska/pravo-na-grad-i-zelena-akcija-poduprli-prosvjede-262015, accessed 28 November 2015.

Different actors on the scene connected—'traditional' human rights civil society organisations had the opportunity to cooperate with the independent cultural scene, the latter with students who initiated the student sit-in, students with environmental organisations, etc. This wasn't the only such moment, but I think a basic trust was established between different actors on the civil society scene through this action. (Ana)

Our interviewees also noted protest success with regard to urban development. Protesters mentioned the tangible impact on decision-making processes in urban policies. According to one protester, new regulations on urban planning have been influenced by the action, which echoes a 'productivist vision' of success. A protester also stated that nepotism and the favouring of certain private investors will be less likely to happen in the future since politicians have been made aware of the damaging effect this can have on them. Although generally optimistic about the movement's impact, one of our interviewees—Filip—noted that there was a limit to how much urban policy could be influenced by urban struggles.

More abstractly, protesters framed success in terms of agenda-setting: drawing attention to injustice, introducing new ideas and concepts of the Left into the public sphere, and raising media and public consciousness regarding the governance of public space. The following three excerpts illustrate these points:

I think they raised people's awareness of the problem of governing public space, or at least I hope they have. (Ivana)

Problems of governing urban and other public goods became a normal topic in public. (Ana)

I have a feeling that the view that urban policy was of little relevance has changed significantly and has become one of the core themes of the activist scene in Croatia. (Ivan)

Echoing Isin's (2009) conception of activist citizenship, several interviewees mentioned how the protests highlighted the importance of alternative forms of political engagement. One protester noted that some people started to view citizen activism more positively, while another stressed that awareness was raised about the need for protests and their legitimacy. The importance of 'becoming aware of unconventional approaches to participating in the political life of one's community' (Ana), and the idea of non-violent resistance and protests as an occasion for a critical mass gathering are further examples of this understanding of success. One of our interviewees, Peter, noted that activism provides a rare chance for an individual to participate in the social life of his/her community. However, he also added that it can be exhausting and disappointing too.

Finally, for some of the protesters, success was also framed in terms of personal consequences. Research on the biographical impact of protest participation is empirically modest. Studies published in the 1970s and 1980s which explored the biographical consequences of participation in 1960s protests, such as Fendrich (1977), Whalen and Flacks (1980), and McAdam (1988, 1989), came to similar conclusions. Protesters tended to remain committed to a leftist agenda; they remained active politically, and many took up careers such as teaching and the 'helping professions', including social work. For several protesters in our study who reflected on their experience of protest participation four years later, the Right to the City protests were a personally transformative experience. For one protester, 'it (the protest) defined me and made me as a person' (Ivana); another described the protest as having 'an immeasurably great impact on me' (Filip). Personal consequences included 'learning a lot' (Sanda), meeting new people, professional effects, and a disposition to activism. One interviewee summed it up as follows: 'I think that participation in these protests ... was formative in an activist, professional, but also socialising sense' (Ana).

Protesting as a valuable learning experience involved acquiring knowledge of protest techniques and one's rights, communication and organisation skills, campaign management, and teamwork, as well as the importance of solidarity and democratic values. As already mentioned, many of our study participants emphasised deepening existing friendships and forging new ones. Tina noted that she 'met a lot of people, and those I knew from before I got to know better', while Sanda asserted that she 'met a lot of great, enthusiastic, smart people'. One person mentioned a negative consequence of protest engagement: some friendships ended because of disagreements about the protests.

Selected quotes illustrate the professional impact of protest participation for two of our study participants:

The experiences I acquired then are something I often use in everyday professional life. (Ana)

It changed my professional interests. I think it's indicative that, in various ways, I have tried to be involved in activism and to research it. (Ida)

Drawing on Bourdieu's concept of habitus, Crossley (2003) develops the concept of a 'radical habitus' to capture a transformed disposition to political activism resulting from protest engagement. In our study, this was reflected in participants' responses such as:

When I think back to certain moments—like the first big protest 'Give Up' or taking down the fence or 'sending' Bandić [Zagreb city mayor] to Remetinec [Zagreb city jail] with suitcases, my heart pounds and asks 'When shall we do it again'? (Sanda)

I have caught the activism virus ... the legacy is a generation ready to take to the streets again. (Tina)

An analysis of protests which reduces their success to measurable short-term outcomes overlooks both the multiple meanings protest success has for the protesters themselves, and the myriad ways in which this experience influences the forging of alliances among organisations and initiatives, strengthening the social fabric and making it more resilient. The cited experience of Right to the City protesters profoundly challenges the 'productivist vision' of social action. Going beyond narrow definitions of short-term success, participants' narratives illustrate the complex ways in which protest participation is productive of new subjectivities and meaningful beyond any specific objective. These findings echo those by Ćulum and Doolan (2015), who explored the biographical legacy of 2009 student protest participation in Croatia. In both cases, protesters share narratives of empowerment and personal change, suggesting that participation in protests had transformative effects on their biographies which the 'productivist vision' fails to capture.

Conclusion

The case study of the Right to the City movement in Croatia suggests that urban struggles often do not fit clear-cut typologies such as Kerbo's dichotomy between movements of affluence and movements of crisis. Instead, urban struggles tend to simultaneously engage both dimensions of 'old-style' class conflict and postmodern demands for broad participation in decision-making. Over its eight years of existence, the Right to the City movement has built a coherent critique of the processes of enclosure and commodification of public space, as well as articulated demands for democratising public sector governance. The fact that, in comparison with Western Europe, post-socialist neoliberal urbanisation suffers from a stronger democratic deficit and more pervasive government corruption has created an even greater urgency to go beyond critique and into articulating alternative models of public sector governance.

In this essay we provided an analytical narrative of the trajectory of the Right to the City movement. Between 2005 and 2010, the Right to the City movement grew into one of the largest citizens' struggles in the country's recent history. It initially encountered declaratively 'friendly' local authorities, but with time this turned to increasing confrontation with the City of Zagreb, which peaked with the occupation of Varšavska Street in opposition to the Flower Passage development project. Though the contested project was in the end implemented, it was significantly influenced by the movement, which both delayed it for several years and substantially reduced its scope. Overall, however, the most important legacy of this protest action was probably that it 'changed the game' when it came to large development projects in Zagreb and elsewhere. As our interviewees suggested, both the movement's framing of grievances as a fight against the enclosure of public space and its repertoire of action inspired other protest movements and affected civil society more generally. Investors and city authorities, meanwhile, have observably started to anticipate grassroots opposition to large-scale development projects, which will, we hope, with time result in more participatory processes of city planning. After 2010, the Right to the City supported several local struggles in Croatia and the region, continued building its network within the National Forum for Space, and in 2013 initiated another coalition to oppose the concession of the largest highway system in Croatia. In October 2014, the movement collected sufficient signatures in a citizens' petition for a referendum to oppose this government project. Though in the end the referendum did not take place due to a ruling of the Constitutional Court, the campaign was successful because the government decided not to move forward with the project.

This analytical narrative is intended to illuminate features of the Right to the City movement that helped it avoid the outcome of Michels's iron law of oligarchy. As we showed, during its first three phases, the Right to the City movement followed the radicalisation trajectory, but at the same time, it managed to secure the organisational robustness necessary for maintaining long-term political confrontation. As conveyed by one of the leaders of the movement, this was no accidental outcome, but the result of implementing organisational principles with the explicit objective of prioritising social impact over institutional self-preservation. Tactical shapeshifting was achieved, for instance, through reliance on the infrastructure of existing organisations and the decision to create long-term links between partner organisations through modular employment. Tactical networking meant investing considerable efforts into building relationships of trust with different actors across civil society and beyond, such as between large NGOs (such as Green Action), radical Left groups, professional associations (for example, architects and urban developers), and trade unions. Building such platforms in order to broaden its reach meant that the movement redefined its primary target several times in the observed period. Though the target changed, the principle of selection was always the same: highlighting the systematic character of enclosure and commodification of public space and infrastructure. The fact that the movement began in 2005 as a challenge to the City of Zagreb's youth policy, while its last campaign was a national petition for a referendum which mobilised half a million people, suggests it has indeed managed to avoid the iron law of oligarchy.

The fact that the Right to the City was not a one-off confrontation, but has become a decade-long civic-political phenomenon probably in part accounts for the way the protesters we interviewed understand its impact. Apart from reflecting on the struggle for Varšavska Street, they highlighted several other outcomes they consider to have emerged from the Right to the City movement. The outcomes they mentioned, such as strengthening civil society, influencing urban development policy, and encouraging citizen engagement and political participation, can be read as important indicators of bottom-up democratisation. If the Right to the City is a movement advocating the management of public space and infrastructure through principles of participatory governance and democratic accountability, the features of evolving activist citizenship that we recorded in interviews with protesters suggest that it has engendered forms of political subjectivity necessary for such democratisation to happen in the future.

References

Benford, R. D. & Snow, D. A. (2000) 'Framing Processes and Social Movements: An Overview and Assessment', *Annual Review of Sociology*, 26.

Bilić, B. & Stubbs, P. (2015) 'Unsettling "The Urban" in Post-Yugoslav Activisms: Right to the City and Pride Parades in Serbia and Croatia', in Jacobsson, K. (ed.) *Urban Grassroots Movements in Central and Eastern Europe* (Farnham & Burlington, VT, Ashgate).

Bohle, D. & Greskovits, B. (2013) *Capitalist Diversity on Europe's Periphery* (Ithaca, NY & London, Cornell University Press).

Brenner, N. (2000) 'Building Euro-Regions: Locational Politics and the Political Geography of Neoliberalism in Post-Unification Germany', *European Urban and Regional Research*, 7, 4.

Brenner, N., Marcuse, P. & Mayer, M. (2012) *Cities for the People, Not For Profit* (London, Routledge).

Castells, M. (2012) *Networks of Outrage and Hope. Social Movements in the Internet Age* (Cambridge, Polity Press).

Chase-Dunn, C. & Hall, T. D. (1997) *Rise and Demise: Comparing World- Systems* (Boulder, CO, Westview Press).

Crossley, N. (2003) 'From Reproduction to Transformation: Social Movement Fields and the Radical Habitus', *Theory, Culture & Society*, 20, 6.

Ćulum, B. & Doolan, K. (2015) '"A Truly Transformative Experience" the Biographical Legacy of Student Protest Participation', in Klemenčič, M., Bergan, S. & Primožič, R. (eds) *Student Engagement in Europe: Society, Higher Education and Student Governance* (Strasbourg, Council of Europe).

Della Porta, D. (2015) *Social Movements in Times of Austerity* (London, Polity).

ACTIVIST CITIZENSHIP IN SOUTHEAST EUROPE

Dolenec, D. (2013) *Democratic Institutions and Authoritarian Rule in Southeast Europe* (Colchester, ECPR Press).

Dolenec, D. (2015) 'The Rise of Organized Intolerance in Croatia', paper presented at the EUSA Fourteenth Biennial Conference, 5–7 March, Boston, MA.

Dolenec, D., Majstorović, D., Medarov, G., Sekulić, D., Simović, V. & Tomašević, T. (2014) 'The Struggle for the Commons in the Balkans', in Bibić, V., Milat, A., Horvat, S. & Štiks, I. (eds) *The Balkan Forum: Situations, Struggles, Strategies* (Zagreb, Bijeli Val).

Domazet, M. & Marinović Jerolimov, D. (2014) 'Sustainability on the Semi-Periphery: An Impossible Topic in a Non-Existent Place?', in Domazet, M. & Marinović Jerolimov, D. (eds) *Sustainability Perspectives from the European Semi-Periphery* (Zagreb, IDIZ).

Eagleton, T. (2011) *Why Marx Was Right* (New Haven, CT, Yale University Press).

Fendrich, J. M. (1977) 'Keeping the Faith or Pursuing the Good Life: A Study in the Consequences of Participation in the Civil Rights Movement', *American Sociological Review*, 42, 1.

Gitlin, T. (2013) 'Occupy's Predicament: The Moment and the Prospects for the Movement', *The British Journal of Sociology*, 64, 1.

Gould, J. A. (2003) 'Out of the Blue? Democracy and Privatization in Post-Communist Europe', *Comparative European Politics*, 1, 3.

Hackworth, J. (2007) *The Neoliberal City* (Ithaca, NY, & London, Cornell University Press).

Hackworth, J. (2008) 'The Neoliberal City: Governance, Ideology, and Development in American Urbanism', *Economic Geography*, 84, 1.

Harvey, D. (2008) 'The Right to the City', *New Left Review*, 53.

Harvey, D. (2005) *A Brief History of Neoliberalism* (Oxford, Oxford University Press).

Inglehart, R. (1971) 'The Silent Revolution: Intergenerational Change in Post-Industrial Societies', *The American Political Science Review*, 65, 4.

Inglehart, R. & Welzel, C. (2005) *Modernization, Cultural Change, and Democracy: The Human Development Sequence* (Cambridge, Cambridge University Press).

Isin, E. (2009) 'Citizenship in Flux: The Figure of the Activist Citizen', *Subjectivity*, 29.

Jacobsson, K. (ed.) (2015) *Urban Grassroots Movements in Central and Eastern Europe* (Farnham & Burlington, VT, Ashgate).

Kerbo, H. R. (1982) 'Movements of "Crisis" and Movements of "Affluence": A Critique of Deprivation and Resource Mobilization Theories', *The Journal of Conflict Resolution*, 26, 4.

King, L. P. (2007) 'Central European Capitalism in Comparative Perspective', in Hancké, B., Rhodes, M. & Thatcher, M. (eds) *Beyond Varieties of Capitalism* (Oxford, Oxford University Press).

Lefebvre, H. (1968) *Le droit à la ville* (Paris, Anthropos).

Lefebvre, H. (1996) *Writings on Cities* (London, Blackwell).

Lipset, M. S. (1969) *Revolution and Counterrevolution* (London, Heinemann).

Marcuse, P. (2009) 'From Critical Urban Theory to Right to the City', *City*, 13, 2–3.

Mayer, M. (2012) 'The "Right to the City" in Urban Social Movements', in Brenner, N., Marcuse, P. & Mayer, M. (eds) *Cities for the People, Not For Profit* (London, Routledge).

McAdam, D. (1989) 'The Biographical Consequences of Activism', *American Sociological Review*, 54, 5.

McAdam, D. (1988) *Freedom Summer* (New York, NY, Oxford University Press).

Medak, T. (2011) *Right to the City Zagreb*, unpublished.

Medak, T., Domes, T. & Celakoski, T. (2013) 'Right to the City Zagreb', *Cultural Policy and Management Yearbook 2012–2013* (Istanbul, Istanbul Bilgi University).

Michels, R. (1968) *Political Parties: A Sociological Study of the Oligarchical Tendencies of Modern Democracy* (New York, NY, Free Press).

Mišetić, A. & Ursić, S. (2010) '"The Right to the City": An Example of a Struggle to Preserve Urban Identity in Zagreb', *Sociologija i prostor*, 48/186, 1.

Nölke, A. & Vliegenthart, A. (2009) 'Enlarging the Varieties of Capitalism: The Emergence of Dependent Market Economies in East Central Europe', *World Politics*, 61, 4.

Olsen, J. P. & Maassen, P. (2007) 'European Debates on the Knowledge Institution', in Maasen, P. & Olsen, J. P. (eds) *University Dynamics and European Integration* (Dordrecht, Springer).

Ortiz, I., Burke, S., Berrada, M. & Cortes, H. (2013) *World Protests 2006–2013*, Initiative for Policy Dialogue (New York, NY, Columbia University and Friedrich Ebert Stiftung).

Petrović, M. (2005) 'Cities After Socialism as a Research Issue', Discussion Papers (South East Europe Series), DP34, Centre for the Study of Global Governance (London, London School of Economics and Political Science).

Pickvance, C. (2003) 'From Urban Social Movements to Urban Movements: A Review and Introduction to the Symposium on Urban Movements', *International Journal of Urban and Regional Research*, 27, 1.

ACTIVIST CITIZENSHIP IN SOUTHEAST EUROPE

Piven, F. F. & Cloward, R. A. (1977) *Poor People's Movements: Why They Succeed, How They Fail* (New York, NY, Pantheon).

Ramet, S. P. & Wagner, F. P. (2010) 'Post-socialist Models of Rule in Central and Southeast Europe', in Ramet, S. P. (ed.) *Central and Southeast European Politics Since 1989* (Cambridge, Cambridge University Press).

Rucht, D. (1999) 'Linking Organization and Mobilization: Michels's Iron Law of Oligarchy Reconsidered', *Mobilization: An International Journal*, 4, 2.

Šarić, D. (2012) *Urban Renewal, Entrepreneurialism and the Right to the City: a Research of the Social Actors and their Contestation of the Gentrification of Post-socialist Zagreb*, MA thesis, Central European University, Budapest.

Schmid, C. (2012) 'Henri Lefebvre, the Right to the City, and the New Metropolitan Mainstream', in Brenner, N., Marcuse, P. & Mayer, M. (eds) *Cities for the People, Not For Profit* (London, Routledge).

Stanilov, K. (2007) *The Post-Socialist City* (New York, NY, Springer).

Stubbs, P. (2012) 'Networks, Organisations, Movements: Narratives and Shapes of Three Waves of Activism in Croatia', *Polemos*, 2.

Swyngedouw, E. (2014) 'Insurgent Architects, Radical Cities and the Promise of the Political', in Wilson, J. & Swyngedouw, E. (eds) *The Post-Political and its Discontents: Spaces of Depoliticisation, Spectres of Radical Politics* (Edinburgh, Edinburgh University Press).

Tarrow, S. (2011) *Power in Movement. Social Movements and Contentious Politics* (Cambridge, Cambridge University Press).

Tarrow, S. (2012) *Strangers at the Gates. Movements and States in Contentious Politics* (Cambridge, Cambridge University Press).

Wallerstein, I. (1979) *The Capitalist World-Economy* (Cambridge, Cambridge University Press).

Whalen, J. & Flacks, R. (1980) 'The Isla Vista "Bank Burners" Ten Years Later. Notes on the Fate of Student Activists', *Sociological Focus*, 13.

Woolcock, M. (1998) 'Social Capital and Economic Development: Towards a Theoretical Synthesis and Policy Framework', *Theory and Society*, 27, 2.

Appendix 1. Right to the City 5 key phases

Timeline	Actions	Actor	Stage	Phase
May 2005	Round-table discussion with civil society and political leaders on needs of independent culture and youth NGOs in Zagreb.	Informal coalition of independent culture and youth NGOs in Zagreb.	Objective—committing candidates for mayor of Zagreb to nine demands in the declaration 'Independent Culture and Youth in Development of City of Zagreb'.	**Claiming Rights**
September 2005	'Operation City' cultural manifestation in former industrial complex Badel-Gorica, demanding establishment of centre for independent culture and youth.	Informal coalition of independent culture and youth NGOs in Zagreb.	Method—legal physical occupation of former industrial complex by independent culture and youth NGOs for cultural event.	
June 2006	Founding assembly of 'Alliance for Centre for Independent Culture and Youth' in Zagreb.	Formal association of NGOs 'Alliance for Centre for Independent Culture and Youth'.	Outcome—foundation of formal association of youth and independent culture NGOs to establish centre for independent culture and youth in Zagreb.	
June 2006	Illegal adbusting action of posters with mayor's photo by Right to the City after mayor's unfulfilled promise to establish Centre for Independent Culture and Youth in Zagreb.	Informal coalition 'Right to the City' comprising independent culture and youth NGOs in Zagreb.	Catalyst—mobilisation of around 60 activists for illegal action resulting in media coverage and public support which motivates 'Right to the City' to work on spatial issues beyond the needs of culture and youth NGOs.	
December 2006	Illegal action 'Total Sale': banner over the whole building announcing sell-off of publicly owned spaces and buildings, such as the 'Flower Passage' project.	Informal coalition of independent culture and youth NGOs, Right to the City, and Green Action.	Objective—coalition between Right to the City and Green Action with the objective of stopping the 'Flower Passage' project.	**Flower Passage**
February 2007	Beginning of petition 'Stop the devastation of Flower Square and Downtown'.	Informal coalition 'Right to the City' in partnership with Green Action.	Method—the first activity in which citizens could participate; in three months, 54,000 citizen signatures were collected in opposition to the 'Flower Passage' project.	
April 2007	Illegal 'Reclaim the Streets' protest action in which Gundulićeva Street was temporarily transformed into a pedestrian zone to obstruct the 'Flower Passage' project.	Green Action in partnership with Right to the City.	Method—mobilisation of 150 activists who for the first time used physical occupation of space as a protest method. First arrest of an activist.	
July 2007	Legal action 'Defending the block with signatures'. The block was surrounded by 150 activists holding banners made of petition signatures.	Initiative Right to the City as partnership of informal coalition Right to the City and Green Action.	Method—first larger action with legal permit. First use of 'Right to the City' as the name of the initiative on T-shirts.	

(Continued)

Timeline	Actions	Actor	Stage	Phase
November 2007	Round-table discussion and establishment of coalition of initiatives against commodification of space—National Forum for Space.	Informal coalition of NGOs and individuals—National Forum for Space.	*Outcome*—spatial issues get national coverage and become inspiration for citizen initiatives on the Adriatic coast.	
January 2008	Mass citizen protest 'Give up' in Varšavska Street to protest against adoption of Detailed Urban Plan for 'Flower Passage' by the City Assembly.	Initiative Right to the City as partnership between informal coalition Right to the City and Green Action.	*Method*—first protest to which citizens were invited; more than 4,000 gathered to protest against the 'Flower Passage' plan.	
November 2008	Illegal march shutting down car traffic in front of city government building to protest permits for 'Flower Passage' in Varšavska Street.	Initiative Right to the City as partnership of informal coalition Right to the City and Green Action.	*Method*—illegal secret action involving 500 activists which blocked car traffic in front of the city government building.	
December 2008	Conference 'The Neoliberal Frontline: Urban Struggles in Post-Socialist Societies'; thematised configurations of neoliberal city transformations in post-socialist context.	Initiative Right to the City.	*Catalyst*—The conference and accompanying events thematised numerous aspects of neoliberal urbanism in post-socialism.	
June 2009	Founding assembly of NGO Right to the City as association of key activists of initiative Right to the City from independent culture, youth NGOs, and Green Action.	NGO Right to the City.	*Outcome*—establishment of Right to the City as NGO to enable fundraising and legal actions, and to separate the initiative formally from independent culture and youth NGOs in Zagreb.	
January 2010	Temporary occupation of Varšavska Street to prevent illegal construction in pedestrian zone.	Initiative Right to the City as partnership of NGO Right to the City and Green Action.	*Catalyst*—first temporary occupation of public space to stop construction works led to establishment of citizens' watch and human shield called 'Living Wall for Varšavska'.	
February 2010	Illegal placement of two converted shipping containers in Varšavska Street to enable permanent physical occupation to stop construction works and beginning of 'Living Wall for Varšavska'.	Initiative Right to the City as partnership of NGO Right to the City and Green Action.	*Objective*—first permanent physical occupation of space by activists and citizens with objective of stopping the expected beginning of construction works in Varšavska Street.	**'We won't give up Varšavska'**
February 2010	Mass citizens' protest with Trojan Horse sculpture in Varšavska Street, followed by night arrests of activists who occupied the containers and destruction of the sculpture by riot police.	Initiative 'We won't give up Varšavska' led by Right to the City and Green Action.	*Method*—protest of 4,000 citizens followed by first mass arrest of 23 non-violent activists, which generated unprecedented media coverage and massive mobilisation of citizens into 'Living Wall for Varšavska'.	

(Continued)

Timeline	Actions	Actor	Stage	Phase
April 2010	Protest action 'Zagreb calls you' in front of the State Attorney General's Office, where a criminal lawsuit is lodged against the mayor of Zagreb.	Initiative 'We won't give up Varšavska' led by Right to the City and Green Action.	*Outcome*—Right to the City and Green Action submit criminal lawsuit against the Zagreb mayor in company of 300 activists and citizens symbolising beginning of direct conflict with the Zagreb mayor.	
May 2010	Citizens' protest against the fencing-off of Varšavska Street: citizens and activists spontaneously decide to destroy the fence and permanently occupy Varšavska Street.	'Living Wall for Varšavska' and Right to the City and Green Action.	*Catalyst*—for the first time 300 citizens took the lead from NGOs and destroyed the fence after which permanent physical illegal occupation of Varšavska Street began.	
May 2010	Mass citizens' protest to support occupation of Varšavska Street against the beginning of construction works.	Movement 'We won't give up Varšavska' facilitated by Right to the City and Green Action.	*Objective*—around 3,000 citizens supported illegal occupation and camping by 100 citizens in Varšavska Street to stop construction works.	
May 2010	Mass protest in front of city government building demanding that Zagreb mayor resign.	Movement 'We won't give up Varšavska' facilitated by Right to the City and Green Action.	*Method*—around 4,000 citizens marched from Varšavska Street to mayor's office asking the mayor to resign and prepare for prison as the criminal investigation was in process.	
June 2010	After one month, the end of the continuous physical occupation of Varšavska Street after State Attorney General announced that Zagreb Master plan changes that allowed 'Flower Passage' project were illegal.	Movement 'We won't give up Varšavska' facilitated by Right to the City and Green Action.	*Outcome*—End of physical occupation when State Attorney General confirms that 'Flower Passage' is illegal and that construction work should not begin on Varšavska Street.	
July 2015	Beginning of construction works in Varšavska Street met with human shield of activists and citizens followed by mass arrests and police occupation of Varšavska and surrounding streets.	Movement 'We won't give up Varšavska' facilitated by Right to the City and Green Action.	*Catalyst*—Arrest of 142 non-violent activists and citizens sparks mass non-violent protests for five days with 3,000–4,000 people attending but because of police guarding Varšavska Street construction works continue.	
September 2010	Establishment of citizens' initiative 'Srđ Is Ours' at public debate in Dubrovnik with support of initiative 'Right to the City' within National Forum for Space.	Initiative 'Srđ Is Ours' in partnership with Right to the City and Green Action.	*Objective*—Citizens' initiative 'Srđ Is Ours' is established at the public debate with support of initiative 'Right to the City' to fight against real-estate project 'Golf Park Dubrovnik' at Srđ Hill above Dubrovnik.	**National Forum for Space**

(Continued)

Timeline	Actions	Actor	Stage	Phase
February 2011	Publication and distribution of newspaper 'Srđ Is Ours' with articles and analysis by activists of the National Forum for Space.	Initiative 'Srđ Is Ours' in partnership with Right to the City and Green Action.	*Method*—with support of the initiative 'Right to the City', newspapers used for the first time as a method to inform and mobilise citizens with 4,000 copies distributed in Dubrovnik.	
April 2011	Mass citizens' protest for the opening of 'Flower Passage' shopping centre ending with private security guards using physical force against some protesters, followed by arrest of protesters by police.	Initiative 'We won't give up Varšavska' led by Right to the City and Green Action.	*Outcome*—End of initiative 'We won't give up Varšavska' by symbolic protest of 1,000 citizens at the opening of the shopping centre in which private security guards used force against some protesters with the support of police.	
February 2011	Initiative 'Srđ Is Ours' collects signatures to initiate local referendum on 'Golf Park Dubrovnik' project.	Initiative 'Srđ Is Ours' in partnership with Green Action and Right to the City.	*Catalyst*—Initiative 'Srđ Is Ours' supported by initiative 'Right to the City' starts collection of voter signatures in the legal timeframe of 15 days to initiate referendum and manages to collect more than required.	
April 2013	Referendum on golf park project at Srđ. Citizens vote against the project but do not reach legally required turnout.	Initiative 'Srđ Is Ours' in partnership with Green Action and Right to the City.	*Outcome*—31% mobilisation of citizens to vote. The majority vote against Golf Park Dubrovnik but legal threshold of 50% turnout is not reached, which allows the project to progress legally.	
October 2013	Coalition of NGOs and trade unions submits request to the Croatian government for access to the study which recommends concession of Croatian highways.	Right to the City in partnership with two trade unions and three NGOs including 'Green Action'.	*Objective*—established coalition of trade unions and NGOs, including Right to the City, to fight the government's plan to give Croatian highways away as a concession.	**'We won't give up our highways'**
December 2013	Protest action 'Give up on concession' against Croatian government by the coalition of trade unions and NGOs.	Right to the City in partnership with two trade unions and two NGOs including Green Action.	*Method*—first protest action of the coalition, involving around 100 activists.	
October 2014	Establishment of initiative 'We won't give away our highways' and collection of voter signatures to initiate national referendum that would ban new concessions on highways in Croatia.	Initiative 'We won't give away our highways' led by Right to the City on behalf of NGOs and Independent Roads Trade Union on behalf of trade unions.	*Catalyst*—Initiative 'We won't give away our highways' co-led by Right to the City starts collection of voter signatures in legal timeframe of 15 days to initiate referendum and manages to collect more than 500,000 voters' signatures.	
April 2015	Decision of Croatian Constitutional Court to block national referendum that would ban new concessions on highways after the decision of Croatian government to give up the concession plan.	Initiative 'We won't give away our highways' led by Right to the City on behalf of NGOs, and the Independent Roads Trade Union on behalf of trade unions.	*Outcome*—Initiative 'We won't give away our highways' co-led by Right to the City forced the Croatian government to rescind the concession, but the national referendum to legislate ban on future concessions will not be held.	

'We Are All Beranselo': Political Subjectivation as an Unintended Consequence of Activist Citizenship

BOJAN BAĆA

Abstract

Drawing on Jacques Rancière and Engin F. Isin, this essay discusses the success of a citizen-led mobilisation in rural Montenegro that eschewed the country's predominant ethnopolitical identity cleavages by using innovative repertoires of contention. As a result, this grassroots movement unintentionally brought into being a transcendent political subjectivity that was based on civic principles rather than ethnic values. The essay explores how the Beranselo movement embodied a democratic practice radically different from already available institutional practice of politics, in the process transforming the local *ethnos* into a *demos* and creating a dynamic of cross-ethnic, civic-minded mobilisation, organisation, and solidarity.

TO DATE, MONTENEGRO IS THE ONLY EUROPEAN COUNTRY THAT HAS not seen a change of regime through the ballot box. The most recent transfer of power happened within the League of Communists of Montenegro when, through mass street protests in January 1989, the party's youth wing—later rebranded as the Democratic Party of Socialists (*Demokratska partija socijalista*—DPS)—forced the old *nomenklatura* out of office (Bieber 2003, p. 14; Morrison 2009, pp. 81–8). This event was, at the same time, the last politically consequential large-scale popular movement in the country. During the DPS's uninterrupted reign, Montenegro has developed a socio-political configuration that severely constrains bottom-up mobilisations challenging the governing party or its policies. As a result, it has been effective at containing unconventional forms of participation and interest articulation 'from below' to rare instances (Jovanović & Marjanović 2002, pp. 161–72; Komar 2015, p. 146).[1] Understandably, by keeping a strong grip over state organs and resources for such a long period of time, the DPS has perfected not only a clientelistic model for maintaining popular support (Hockenos

---

This essay was written during my research stay at the University of Gothenburg, thanks to a Swedish Institute scholarship. I would like to thank Marina Antić, Katherine Bischoping, Engin F. Isin, Kerstin Jacobsson, Konstantin Kilibarda, James C. Scott, Lesley J. Wood, the editors of the special issue, and the two anonymous reviewers for their constructive comments on previous drafts of this essay. All errors and opinions are mine alone.
    [1]When compared to other post-Yugoslav countries, Montenegro shows significantly lower levels of extra-institutional political activism (Bešić 2014, pp. 240–41).

© 2017 University of Glasgow

& Winterhagen 2007, p. 43; Komar 2013, pp. 44–8; Kovačević 2014, pp. 3–4), but also a repertoire of intimidation and harassment tools designed to influence election outcomes (Mochťak 2015; Milovac 2016). When the state is established as a mechanism for reproducing patron–client relations, citizens can use personal and party connections to bend the formal rules in their own favour (Komar 2015, pp. 157–58; Sedlenieks 2015, pp. 210–12). Political, economic, and social grievances that might otherwise inspire engagement in collective (direct) action may instead be addressed through these informal (clientelistic) channels that play a central role in defining state–society relationships.

As statehood status emerged at the end of the 1990s as the central political question in Montenegro, political competition and public discourse were gradually realigned from left to right ideological disputes to reflect a new ethnonational identity fault line within the Slavic-Orthodox population (Sekelj 2000, p. 60; Bieber 2003; Milivojević & Bešić 2006; Morrison 2009, pp. 89–204). By 2001, this cleavage had become entrenched as the principal political division in Montenegro, in which 'Montenegrin identity' came to be associated with support for state independence, whereas 'Serb identity' signalled support for continued union with Serbia (Caspersen 2003, pp. 115–18; Jenne & Bieber 2014, pp. 447–52; Troch 2014, pp. 25–9).[2] Not only did independence fail to alter the nature of Montenegrin politics, but it was now reframed as the DPS's brainchild, further entrenching the link between ethnonational and political cleavages (Morrison 2011; Brković 2013; Džankić 2014). Aware of the fact that ethnic-cum-political identification is the key determinant of voter behaviour (Komar 2013), the DPS has framed its reign as the *conditio sine qua non* of Montenegrin independence by continuously representing Montenegro's current statehood (and the peaceful cohabitation of diverse ethnic groups within it) as precarious and reversible if the opposition comes to power. In that way, any activity seeking to contest DPS rule or its policies is framed—or, better yet, depoliticised and thus delegitimised—as 'anti-state', 'anti-Montenegrin', or 'anti-European', which in effect undermines the potential for cross-ethnic solidarity, mobilisation, organisation, and coalition-building.[3]

The 'non-anonymous' nature of Montenegro's society exacerbates these political constraints on non-institutional political participation. Montenegro is a country of roughly 620,000 people, condensed into a small territory and characterised by high degrees of interpersonal relationships and close kinship ties, and thus extremely dense and personalised social relations (Jovanović & Marjanović 2002; Komar 2013; Sedlenieks 2015). As a result of being a 'community of communities' in which 'everyone knows everyone', it has been observed that the social forces that would mobilise the masses, and subsequently produce particular dynamics of contention in large 'anonymous' societies, are extremely weak in Montenegro (Jovanović 2009, p. 39). In other words, public space—understood as the physical site of social interactions—in this 'micro-society' is not a space of difference, but a space in which encounters are with familiar faces rather than strangers; public opinion is thus

---

[2]Prior to the 2000s, the identity categories of 'Montenegrin' and 'Serb' were not mutually exclusive or antagonistic; rather, they were often interchangeable, as there was substantial overlap between them (Caspersen 2003; Džankić 2014; Jenne & Bieber 2014; Troch 2014).

[3]Both the anti-austerity/anti-corruption protests in 2012 (organised by civil society organisations, trade unions and student groups) and the anti-government protests in 2015 (after a violent police raid on protesting political parties) organised by both political parties and activist civic groups were delegitimised in the eyes of the public through state propaganda (as nationalistic, anti-systemic, anti-state and anti-EU), thus preventing the spread of these mobilisations outside their core constituencies and supporters.

never sufficiently anonymous. Within this configuration, a citizen of Montenegro is always 'embedded in a set of assumptions that link him or her ... in the political web' through his/her personal connections and kinship ties (Sedlenieks 2015, p. 204). Consequently, the citizen is never an anonymous person, but rather a concrete individual whose political affiliation and loyalties—whether perceived through political affinities or personal/family ties with political actors—are always 'known' in society. In such a non-anonymous society, based on a patron–client system and divided along ethnopolitical lines of conflict, everyone is always already 'labelled', which in effect severely lowers the social trust necessary for bottom-up mobilisation and movement-building outside existing social and political networks.

Furthermore, as a country whose strategic goal is European integration, an aim that is based on the consensus of all parliamentary parties since the early 2000s (Vujović & Komar 2008, pp. 230–34), Montenegro's citizens are often reminded by European Union (EU) officials of the need to practise politics through the institutions of liberal democracy (regardless of the ability of these institutions to actually uphold the rule of law or provide credible venues for dissenting opinion). The EU's position thus reinforces the general delegitimation of collective action and protests found in post-socialist societies (Císař 2013; Jacobsson & Saxonberg 2013; Gagyi 2015; Jacobsson 2015a; Piotrowski 2015). The result is democratic polities that are solely based on regular elections and narrowly institutionalised conceptions of 'the political'. This vision of 'politics' has become largely the norm among Montenegro's political, societal, and intellectual elites. With contentious and non-institutional forms of political participation rendered a non-option, the political agency of citizens in Montenegro is reduced to voting as their only legitimate activity and obligation towards the political community.

Against this backdrop, this essay discusses the emergence of a social movement in Montenegro which, by using innovative repertoires of contention, managed to overcome the aforementioned constraints and create a venue for hitherto unseen bottom-up cross-ethnic mobilisation to fight government policy. My case study is a four-year struggle, waged from August 2010 to March 2014, by residents of Beranselo in the municipality of Berane who protested against local and national plans to use the Vasove Vode site in their village as a dumping ground.[4] I explore the question of why and how acts of resistance in Beranselo succeeded in circumventing existing socio-political constraints on grassroots mobilisation to create a nationwide inclusionary space for cross-ethnic, civic-minded solidarity and contentious political action. The essay contributes to debates on 'how, why, and when certain patterns of relations produce full-scale mobilisation rather than accommodation or unobtrusive resistance' (Polletta 1999, p. 8), by showing how localised acts of resistance can, unintentionally, bring into being a transcendent political subjectivity that functions as a symbolic unifier for hitherto estranged, even antagonistic individuals, groups, and organisations.

The first part of the essay proposes a series of theoretical arguments that allow political 'subjectivation' to be framed as an unintended consequence of activist citizenship. The second part explores the genealogy of activist citizenship in Beranselo through three stages of political subjectivation. At the end of the essay, I then discuss the empirical and theoretical contributions of this case study to the analysis of activist citizenship, contentious politics, and political subjectivity in broader terms.

---

[4]Vasove Vode is a location in Beranselo, a meadow in a forest, known for eight springs of clean, drinkable water. It literally translates as Vaso's Waters.

ACTIVIST CITIZENSHIP IN SOUTHEAST EUROPE

Activist citizenship, everyday resistance, and political subjectivation

If we take voting as the 'only game in town', then Montenegro possesses 'active' citizens only in a narrow sense. Scholarly work shows that Montenegrin citizens follow already existing trajectories of 'obedient' political participation (Komar 2013).[5] Yet, the available forms of exercising the 'political self' in Montenegro through circumscribed electoral processes tend to tie citizens even more 'into governmental practices through which conduct is produced' (Isin 2009, p. 383). The current polity thus appears to lack manifestations of what Engin F. Isin calls 'activist citizenship'. According to this definition, citizenship is not to be understood in a legal manner as a 'status', but in political terms as an 'act', during which 'subjects constitute themselves as citizens'—that is, 'claimants of rights'—by demanding justice through unconventional, and often contentious, participation (Isin 2008, p. 18; 2009, p. 383). Montenegro's current social, political, and cultural dispensation severely limits the possibility for 'acts of citizenship' outside institutional channels that produce new sites of political enunciation, new forms of political participation, and new modes of political being (Isin 2008, 2009). However, rather than focusing entirely on the 'activist citizens' of Beranselo, I am more interested in exploring why and how their localised 'acts of citizenship' in a rural setting gradually grew into a nationwide social movement.

By the time the struggle in Beranselo started, in August 2010, there had already been several citizen-led mobilisations around issues of environmental protection in both rural and urban Montenegro, but Beranselo's residents were the only ones to gain state-wide mass support without the initial brokerage of political parties, non-governmental organisations (NGOs), and/or mainstream media.[6] The potential of environmental degradation—often perceived as an apolitical issue in post-socialist societies—to motivate contentious grassroots initiatives (that eventually grow into nationwide movements) has been well documented in the cases of Ruse (Bulgaria) and Roşia Montană (Romania) (Baumgartl 1993; Mercea 2014).[7] Fagan and Sircar (2010, p. 815), on the other hand, showed how 'the dominance of nationalist cleavages and the ethnicisation of party competition, political space and discourse … constrain the political opportunities for environmental issues and activism' in the ethnopolitically divided society of Bosnia & Hercegovina.

While Montenegro is also ethnopolitically divided, the situation regarding environmental movements in the country is more akin to the cases found in Bulgaria and Romania. As Komar (2015, p. 156–57) observed, environmental issues have the power to override dominant ethnopolitical frames and mobilise Montenegrin citizens to protect their common interests. Some of the most prominent examples of environmental activism transcending ethnopolitical frames include: the citizens' initiative to protect Tara Canyon from being exploited for its

---

[5]Montenegro experiences high voter turnout in elections in spite of high levels of mistrust in the electoral process, a result of the DPS's misuse of public resources for ensuring better election results (Kovačević 2014, p. 3).

[6]Since 2010, when the political contestation in Beranselo began, several comparable popular mobilisations against environmental degradation have taken place in rural Montenegro (for example, in Golija, Gradac, Lješevići, Mahala, Maljevac, Mislov Do, Omerbožovići, Potoci, Prijelozi, Rujište, Tisova Greda, Trešanjski Mlin, and Zbljev), but none of these gained support outside their local communities or municipalities.

[7]See also Komar (2015). In the first instance, the environmental movement unintentionally served as a catalyst for the fall of the Bulgarian communist regime (Baumgartl 1993), while in the second example the environmental campaign on social media to save Roşia Montană unintentionally expanded the movement by creating a new category of non-activist 'casual participants' (Mercea 2014).

hydro-electric potential (2004); organisation at grassroots level to protect Valdanos Bay from privatisation and commercial exploitation (2008–2014); and a citizen-led mobilisation to stop the building of a tunnel in the Gorica urban park in the capital (2012). The protection of Tara was articulated and backed by a wide network of NGOs, political parties, media, and international organisations, while the protection of Valdanos and Gorica are examples of successful grassroots campaigns that, nevertheless, remained local issues, even though local residents were professionally supported by the most influential Podgorica-based NGOs, media outlets, and public intellectuals. When compared to these citizen-led mobilisations, the Beranselo movement is unique, because it not only became a nationwide movement, but also built its social and symbolic capital by motivating non-activist 'ordinary citizens' to join its cause. These were citizens who were not necessarily affected by the environmental degradation in Beranselo and who were often cynical towards the donor-funded 'civil sector'.[8] Put more simply, before they drew the attention of civil society organisations, Beranselo's residents first worked to build support among citizens, gaining the support of voters before that of their political representatives and communicating grievances on social media already before these grievances became a 'hot topic' for the mainstream media.

In terms of repertoires of contention, what differentiated the Beranselo movement from other popular mobilisations was its use of 'symbolic resistance'—understood as a form of everyday resistance that primarily operates through signs and visuals (Hall & Jefferson 1976; Hebdige 1979)—to communicate grievances. Without symbolic resistance as part of their daily repertoire, Beranselo's residents would probably have started yet another publicly invisible (unsuccessful) local grassroots initiative. For that reason, I investigate how activists' usage of images to communicate grievances on social media brought into being a new political subjectivity that gradually developed into a nationwide social movement. For the purposes of this essay, I understand social movements as a constellation of diverse individuals, groups, and organisations—held together by shared beliefs and solidarity—that engage in contentious, non-institutional, and collective action in order to promote or resist social change (Della Porta & Diani 1999, pp. 20–2; Tilly & Wood 2012, pp. 35–7). While the collective that defended Beranselo never had an official name, I refer to it as the 'Beranselo movement' throughout the essay. Its direct actions were coordinated predominantly by the Council of the Local Community of Beranselo and its Coordinating Committee for Environmental Protection, but the movement built around the protection of Beranselo cannot be reduced solely to 'acts of citizenship' in Beranselo, since numerous individuals, groups, and organisations (from diverse class, ideological, political, ethnic, geographical, gender, and generational backgrounds) joined the cause over the course of four years.[9]

---

[8]It is not uncommon for people in Montenegro to view the activism of prominent NGO figures negatively, as 'personal promotion' (Brković 2013, p. 147).

[9]It was noted that, in 2010 and 2011, despite '[lacking] support and interest from the most influential Podgorica-based civil society organizations' (USAID 2012, p. 149), Beranselo's residents, unlike the instigators of other grassroots initiatives, gained widespread public attention (USAID 2013, p. 149). The most influential civil society actors, as well as certain political parties, started supporting and providing assistance to Beranselo in 2012. However, besides concerned citizens and smaller activist groups, during the early stages of contention in Beranselo, only the Nikšić-based environmental organisation Ozon provided the Beranselo movement with legal and logistical assistance, while the Berane-based journalist Tufik Softić was the sole mainstream media voice showing genuine interest in the movement's struggle.

For that reason, my methodological focus is on the everyday acts of symbolic resistance used by the movement's wider constituency, rather than solely on the villagers' repertoires of collective action. I argue that day-to-day acts of resistance—such as posting and sharing photographs of the injustices that Beranselo's residents had to endure—unintentionally created a political subjectivity that could not be reduced to any existing ethnic-cum-political identity, and subsequently opened a hitherto unprecedented space of inclusion. In this section, I will provide a theoretical rationale and conceptual framework for understanding how localised acts of resistance can unintentionally develop into a nationwide social movement. To do so, I employ Jacques Rancière's concept of 'political subjectivation'.[10] While I recognise the importance of collective identities that are protected, defended, and/or (re)affirmed through collective action (Cohen 1985; Buechler 1995; Melucci 1996), I move beyond the New Social Movement paradigm, in not only focusing on identity, but also asking how activist citizens came to be constituted as political subjects in the first place. Therefore, one must distinguish subjectivation from identification, since the former is a process through which social actors refuse to identify with the existing (politicised) identity categories, but create themselves anew, in spite of their differences (May 2010; Prentoulis & Thomassen 2013).

According to Rancière (1999, 2010), every society is highly hierarchised: who can speak/act politically and how, when, and where are clearly defined through institutionalisation by the state (for example, based on legitimacy, competence, qualifications). As a result, only certain political actors are made visible and audible to the general public at any given moment, while numerous social actors (both individual and collective) are not identified, legitimised, or recognised as political. In this case, Beranselo's residents were deemed by the state to be 'unqualified' and 'incompetent' to speak on environmental policies and infrastructure projects. When they decided to contest this logic by speaking out publicly against the injustice, disagreement manifested itself. As Rancière (2007, p. 60) argues, disagreement between the state and its people possesses the 'capacity to shift the sites and forms of participation', that is, to create public spaces in which those ordinarily thought to be unequal can demonstrate their equality by speaking with the authorities on an equal footing (Rancière 1992, 1999, 2010, pp. 27–111; May 2010; Prentoulis & Thomassen 2013). Political subjectivation, therefore, is enacted when activist citizens performatively stage their equality by interacting with the state directly, as those who are unrepresented in the polity. This democratic process should not be understood as 'a rational debate between multiple interests, but the struggle for one's voice to be heard and recognised as the voice of a legitimate' and equal partner (Žižek 1999, p. 188).[11] From a Rancièrian perspective, in order for an activist citizenship to bring into being a new political subjectivity, it must: first, disagree that already existing trajectories of civic and political participation are the only available venues for addressing 'what is at stake'; second, create new scripts and sites for political enunciation/participation in order to interact with authorities on an equal footing; and third, be identified/recognised by other invisible, exploited, and/or disrespected groups as their 'symbolic representation', even though they are not (directly) involved in 'acts of citizenship' that are taking place.

---

[10]I have opted for 'subjectivation' as the most straightforward translation of Rancière's 'subjectivation', though it has also been translated as 'subjectification' and 'subjectivisation'.

[11]This is also how emancipation comes into being, understood by Rancière as the 'verification of the equality of any speaking being with any other speaking being' (Rancière 1992, p. 59).

While I acknowledge the impact and importance of repertoires of organised collective action (such as road blockades, street protests, and public performances) in acquiring public attention and influencing government policies (Tilly & Tarrow 2007), this essay nevertheless demonstrates how, in the Beranselo case, political subjectivity unintentionally arose as the cumulative outcome of uncoordinated similar actions (for example, posting and sharing photographs on social media) performed consecutively by a number of non-activist 'ordinary people'. Therefore, instead of focusing entirely on 'acts of citizenship' that entail purposive or affective disruption of the routinised flow of everyday life, I explore the decentralised, uncoordinated and, essentially, individual acts of everyday defiance and resilience that cannot be viewed as part of organised collective action (De Certeau 1984; Scott 1985, 1990). As my interviewees explained, there was no coordination in the use of visuals in their everyday life routines, especially not in terms of a purposive framing of Beranselo's problems in a particular way on social media (for example, as a non-ethnic, civic framework). Their goal was to raise awareness of the issue, but they were also surprised when, in 2012, it became evident that their struggle was widely recognised and supported by Montenegrin civil society as a political event of historical significance. The choice of images and social media was also not a matter of strategising, but of necessity: these were used, in the first place, because of their affordability and accessibility in making problems and injustices visible and, in the second place, because everyday experience revealed these methods to be the least susceptible to political manipulation and state control.

Therefore, in order to theoretically bridge Isin's 'activist citizenship' and Rancière's 'political subjectivation', I introduce two sociological concepts: 'the everyday' and 'the unintended'. As stated before, the Beranselo movement became publicly visible, identifiable, and recognisable through the posting and sharing of images on social media—that is, through routinised activity that was practised daily, from homes, workplaces, bars, and schools. I am thus focusing on these uncoordinated, spontaneous 'microsubversions' (Smith 1996) and their day-to-day 'modes of operation or schemata of action' (De Certeau 1984, p. xi) that were a part of the everyday life routine of the Beranselo movement's widest constituency, and thus were not necessarily (self-)perceived as activism. Following Scott (1990), the aim of this essay is to illustrate how these low-key, uncoordinated individual acts of everyday resistance complement the public resistance of collective actors by strengthening shared values and creating new venues for collective experiences or, in this case, political subjectivation. Moreover, the literature on everyday acts of resistance shows that the resulting patterns of cultural, political, or social change are, in many cases, purely unintentional (De Certeau 1984; Scott 1985, 1990, 2012). Analysis of 'unintended social phenomena' is predominantly found in sociology (Portes 2000). According to Merton (1936), purposive social (inter)actions and collective decisions can have unintended consequences. The general idea is that since social activity is mediated by social structures and culture toolkits, social actors are prevented from realising the outcomes of their activity: they often have incorrect expectations regarding their own actions because their actions do not have only consequences for the actors themselves, but also for other individuals and collectives. Unintended consequences, hence, 'figure as an explanatory bridge between the "human" character of action and the "alien" character of history' (Vernon 1979, p. 57). In other words, the intended goal of activist citizenship is not the issue here, rather, its unintended transformative impact.

I will frame the following empirical section through three stages of political subjectivation. In the first segment, I discuss disagreement between the locals and the authorities on who can speak on the issue of environmental degradation. In the second part, I illustrate how Beranselo's residents engaged in organised 'acts of citizenship' to speak on an equal footing with the authorities. Finally, I analyse how uncoordinated acts of everyday resistance unintentionally brought into being a hitherto unidentifiable political subjectivity. In doing so, I rely on three available data sources: archival news articles, to establish key stages in the Beranselo movement's development and to interpret the movement's reception in the Montenegrin public sphere; interviews with the movement activists who were most prominent on social media—Jovan Lončar, Gojko Cimbaljević, and Nebojša Babović—to understand the purposive use of images in their daily routines;[12] and photographs shared on social media, to analyse the public voice of the movement from the perspective of the knowledge-production method of 'photovoice' (Wang & Burris 1997).

Political subjectivation of the Beranselo movement

As stated in the introduction, the movement emerged when the villagers protested against local and national plans to use a location in Beranselo as an illegal dumping ground. The selection of a site for a sanitary landfill facility serving northern Montenegro began in 2004, when the development organisation CHF Montenegro financed a report titled *Study for Regional Landfill Site Selection*.[13] It recommended seven locations in Berane for this purpose: four sites were nominated by the Institute of Hydrometeorology and Seismology of Montenegro, two by CHF itself, while the municipal government of Berane later added a seventh location, Vasove Vode in Beranselo.[14] CHF assessed an abandoned quarry on Berane's outskirts as the optimal location.[15] Nevertheless, the local authorities informed CHF that this location—close to the mayor's home and the DPS's municipal stronghold—was subject to an ongoing restitution dispute and that, even before the process of evaluating different sites had been completed, the acquisition of the land at Vasove Vode was already in motion (Softić 2012b). The environmental organisation Ozon estimated that, as a consequence of this decision, by 2011, 500,000 tonnes of unprocessed hazardous waste had been stored at the site in a way that did not fulfil the legal and technical requirements prescribed by the Law on Waste Management, the Veterinary Law, the Environmental Law, the Constitution, and a number of by-laws and international conventions (Softić 2011b).[16] Waste disposal practices at this location were eventually universally criticised as a severe violation of Montenegro's constitutional identity as an 'ecological state',[17] and were categorised by prominent environmental organisations in

---

[12]While Lončar was the *spiritus movens* of the Beranselo movement, Cimbaljević and Babović joined the movement out of solidarity, as discontented citizens.

[13]This study is not available online, but details of its contents can be found in 'Borba protiv planine od smeća', *Vijesti*, 24 January 2011, p. 11; 'Vasova Voda za deponiju', *Dan*, 7 April 2007, p. 16.

[14]'Borba protiv planine od smeća', *Vijesti*, 24 January 2011, p. 11.

[15]'Vasova Voda za deponiju', *Dan*, 7 April 2007, p. 16.

[16]'Lukšiću pomagaj', Environmental movement Ozon, 21 February 2011, available at: http://www.pcnen.com/portal/2011/02/21/luksicu-pomagaj/, accessed 16 November 2015. Since 2005, waste has been accumulating at the Vasove Vode site without treatment or selection, including not only municipal solid waste but more dangerous types of waste, such as biomedical and electronic.

[17]In its Constitution, in Article 1, Montenegro is defined as 'a civil, democratic and ecological state based on social justice and the rule of law'. Montenegro thus prides itself as being the first constitutionally defined 'ecological state'.

Montenegro as 'the most severe example of environmental harm' in the country,[18] verging on 'ecocide' and representing an 'unprecedented systematic use of terror' against public health.[19] Even the expert who conducted the aforementioned study would later confirm that the local authorities had manipulated him with fabricated documents and falsified evidence, and concluded that Vasove Vode was not an acceptable site for the regional landfill.[20] Ultimately, the unregulated waste storage site in Beranselo has taken a considerable toll on residents and their health.[21]

Disagreement between the people and the state

The contention between Beranselo's residents and the authorities had been building gradually since 2007.[22] According to Lončar, documents sanctioning the temporary waste storage area at the Vasove Vode location were hidden from the public until 2010.[23] The locals eventually conducted their own survey in order to show the Montenegrin public that the dump violated several criteria set by the government's *Study for Regional Landfill Site Selection.*[24] This act of 'citizen science'—in which ordinary citizens used scientific facts to bypass political representation and directly inform and communicate with the public (Kullenberg 2015, p. 67)—signalled the beginning of disagreements between villagers and the municipal and national authorities. In August that same year, the local community of Beranselo held an assembly and organised a petition signed by 191 households with the aim of establishing a dialogue with the local authorities over the proposed site.[25] However, their petition was ignored as 'illegitimate' and their measurements mocked as 'incompetent' by the local authorities.[26] The DPS decided to proceed with a regional sanitary landfill and recycling centre at Vasove Vode in October 2010.[27] The official rationale for building a regional landfill at Vasove Vode was that it was the most economical and efficient way of bringing European waste-management standards to Montenegro, dismissing the voices of Beranselo's residents as reflecting uninformed opposition to the country's economic development and overall progress (Baća 2013). Without any legal basis, the municipal authorities continued to pile up hazardous

---

[18]'Saopštenje povodom 20. septembra, Dana Ekološke države Crne Gore', 2012, available at: http://www.greenhome.co.me/index.php?IDSPIDSp=539&jezik=lat, accessed 18 November 2015.

[19]'Nezapamćen sistemski teror i ekocid', *Vijesti*, 17 September 2013, p. 10.

[20]'Ministar ima freške slike', *Vijesti*, 6 May 2011, p. 23.

[21]The waste dump poisoned the soil, nearby streams, and the River Lim. It also affected the air: in the warmer months, the accumulated waste would periodically catch fire and release dioxins, thereby resulting in a measurable increase in lung disease in Beranselo ('Naslage smeća uništavaju imanja', *Dan*, 1 August 2015, p. v). From the dump's establishment up to 2015, ten Beranselo residents were diagnosed with cancer that was attributed to the extra pollution ('Kancer "jede" Beranselo', *Večernje novosti*, 13 May 2015, p. 26).

[22]'Vasova voda za eko-katun, ne za smetlište', *Dan*, 9 July 2007, p. 17.

[23]Vasove Vode was originally intended to be only a temporary dumping ground, until a more suitable permanent site could be found. However, contrary to the law it became a permanent facility. Interview with Jovan Lončar, a Beranselo Movement activist, Berane, 14 September 2013.

[24]It is important to point out this was not a local example of a NIMBY ('Not In My Back Yard') movement. The villagers' main demand was to halt waste disposal until independent experts could determine whether Vasove Vode fulfilled the criteria for a landfill, and if it was indeed the best location out of the seven proposed. If these experts confirmed the findings of the authorities, Beranselo's residents agreed not to protest the decision ('Borba protiv planine od smeća', *Vijesti*, 24 January 2011, p. 11).

[25]'Nemoćni ste u Beranselu', *Vijesti*, 24 August 2010, p. 20.

[26]Interview with Jovan Lončar, a Beranselo Movement activist, Berane, 14 September 2013.

[27]'Deponija na Vasovom dolu', *Vijesti*, 8 October 2010, p. 23.

ACTIVIST CITIZENSHIP IN SOUTHEAST EUROPE

waste at this location, giving no indication that they were building any technical infrastructure to process the accumulated garbage.[28]

From the very beginning, the contention was not only about stopping waste disposal on Vasove Vode, but also about 'having a say'—the engagement of people in decision-making and having control over their own destinies. Lončar explains that since 2007, Beranselo's residents had been trying to establish a dialogue with their political representatives, but their grievances were met with indifference.[29] When attempts to communicate with the local authorities failed, Lončar wrote to the Ministry of Health, but was dismissed harshly for 'abusing Montenegrin democracy'.[30] The villagers nonetheless demanded public disclosure of the persons who were responsible for authorising the hazardous project without previously consulting the citizens whose lives were directly endangered by the decision (Softić 2010).

The disagreement between Beranselo's residents and the local authorities reached its peak in August 2010, when Lončar rented a billboard in the town square, on which he displayed four disturbing images of the dump accompanied by one word: 'Dokle?!' (Enough?!).[31] As much as his 'photovoice' was driven by anger and desperation, it was also an act of awareness-raising (see Figure 1).[32] This act immediately turned the subjective gaze of a marginalised group into an objective concern of the local community. When townspeople began to ask questions about Vasove Vode, local authorities illegally removed Lončar's billboard in the early hours of the morning.[33] He took photographs of this violation and posted them on discussion forums and social media, which provoked further outrage in Berane.[34] Coming to terms with the fact that complaining through institutional legal and political channels would not resolve the problem of illegal waste-dumping, the villagers reacted by giving the authorities 90 days' notice to find another location for the dump or more radical measures of resistance would be employed.[35] One resident summed up their position succinctly: '[The authorities] are stubbornly refusing to talk to us about anything. They continue to plan the landfill project as if we don't exist and show disrespect to us as their fellow citizens. They sue us, so what else can we do but respond with new protests and blockades!'[36]

Throughout the four-year period of contention, Beranselo's residents made resolutions collectively, organising their decision-making through horizontal consensus-based models

[28]In January 2011, the Environmental Protection Agency of Montenegro determined that dangerous medical waste was being stored illegally at the Vasove Vode site ('Hronologija aktivnosti Ekološke inspekcije u vezi sa neuređenom privremenom deponijom komunalnog otpada u Beranama', 2011, available at: http://www.gov.me/naslovna/vijesti-iz-ministarstava/102381/Hronologija.html, accessed 17 November 2015). In June 2013, the Administrative Court of Montenegro invalidated the decision of the municipality of Berane to make Vasove Vode a temporary waste storage site, thus effectively declaring any future waste dumping illegal ('Opština na sudu', *Vijesti*, 15 June 2013, p. 37).

[29]For instance, Radosavović (2013, p. 2) provides an account on how the movement activists retained animosity and expressed cynicism towards the parliamentary opposition who visited Beranselo in 2013. They wrote off the politicians' 'support' as an opportunistic 'scoring of political points' now that the Beranselo movement had become a national news story.

[30]'Sačuvati zdravlje ljudi i životnu sredinu', *Pobjeda*, 5 December 2010, p. 10.

[31]'Dokle?!' can also be translated as 'When (will it end)?!' or 'For how long (is this going to go on)?!'.

[32]Interview with Jovan Lončar, a Beranselo Movement activist, Berane, 14 September 2013.

[33]'Zaboljelo ih ruglo', *Večernje novosti*, 11 August 2010, p. 22.

[34]The residents of Beranselo won a court case against the local authorities and the billboard was returned to its original position in September 2012 ('Pobijedila demokratija', *Vijesti*, 5 September 2012, p. 36).

[35]'Ističu vam 90 dana', *Vijesti*, 26 August 2010, p. 23.

[36]'Sami ste tražili', *Vijesti*, 13 May 2011, p. 23.

FIGURE 1. A SMALL PART OF THE ILLEGAL 'MOUNTAIN OF RUBBISH' ON THE VASOVE VODE SITE IN BERANSELO.
Source: Photo courtesy of Beranselo movement activists. Reproduced with permission.

based on principles of direct democracy. In June 2012, they organised a referendum as the legal instrument of last resort, since it was the statutory right of the local community to organise such a poll when the environment was being endangered.[37] The referendum was supposed to be organised by the municipal government, but the petition signed by Beranselo's residents was ignored, even though the authorities were obliged to act once the minimum number of signatures was reached (Softić 2012a). Out of 1,171 adult residents of Beranselo, 53.45% used their voting rights, and 623 eventually voted against the building of the regional landfill in their municipality, with just two voting in favour.[38] The authorities did not recognise the referendum as legitimate, with the mayor of Berane dismissing it as 'violence' against the legal system and referring to it as 'a circus'.[39] Since the disagreement could not be resolved through institutional channels, Beranselo's residents worked proactively on complementing these attempts at 'obedient' citizenship with collective acts of civil disobedience.

[37]'Referendum o deponiji', *Vijesti*, 9 June 2012, p. 37.
[38]'NE deponiji na Vasovim vodama', *Vijesti*, 11 June 2012, p. 11.
[39]'Jasno "ne" deponiji', *Dan*, 11 June 2012, p. 17.

ACTIVIST CITIZENSHIP IN SOUTHEAST EUROPE

Performative staging of equality

The first collective act of resistance began in November 2010 when—together with other concerned citizens from Montenegro, Serbia and Bosnia & Hercegovina who lived in the endangered Lim river basin—the villagers organised the first blockade of access roads to the dump.[40] The local authorities reacted by accusing the locals of trespass and the Basic Court identified 42 residents whom it forbade to engage in blockades. The next morning, approximately 50 villagers who had not been issued a court order continued to block the dump (Softić 2011a). From that moment on, the villagers organised daily pickets (*straže*) on access roads to the dumping ground. This 'power play' between the locals and the authorities continued until March 2014, when the government finally stopped using the site for dumping. During this period, access roads to the dump were collectively blocked 17 times,[41] with the police violently raiding the site 14 times,[42] arresting pregnant women, children and the elderly, among others, in the process (see Figure 2). Overall, more than 80 activists were fined, and many of these fines were translated into prison sentences.[43] Discussions with local activists suggest this was because people refused to pay.

Beranselo's residents expanded their repertoire of contention in January 2011, when they began to publicly mock the authorities and the system by holding, together with activists from coastal Montenegro, a 'garbage polo match' at the landfill.[44] They continued their performative acts of dissent, such as putting road signs saying 'Welcome to Beranselo, your garbage is already here!', and organising public events at the dump, including a musical performance in March 2013, where numerous activists, prominent individuals, artists, and concerned citizens came to Vasove Vode to spend 'some quality family time in polluted nature' and 'adopt' the *Civic Declaration*.[45] The document was written as a reminder that human dignity and the constitutional idea of Montenegro as an 'ecological state' must be defended.[46] However, since 'environmental issues were never part of the official political discourse and were never a topic for the political elites' in Montenegro (Komar 2015, p. 157), local and especially national political elites based in the capital showed little interest in the grievances and demands of Beranselo's residents.[47] Contempt for the alienated system of political representation culminated in November 2013, when movement activists arrived in chains in front of the Parliament of Montenegro to stage a performance in which they symbolically declared what Gramsci (1971, p. 210) calls 'detachment'—people taking things into their own hands because they no longer recognised political elites as representing them. MPs were told that they should be ashamed of themselves for keeping silent while the innocent people of Beranselo were arrested and harassed. In the name of the sentenced villagers, the protesters ripped up the subpoenas they had received and stated that they did not recognise the judiciary that was

---

[40]'Stop ekološkom genocidu', *Dan*, 18 November 2010, p. 17.

[41]'Nije bilo dobre struje', *Vijesti*, 22 January 2014, p. 35.

[42]'Policija ponovo privela meštane', *Večernje novosti*, 22 January 2014, p. 28.

[43]'Za novi početak', *Vijesti*, 18 November 2013, p. 37.

[44]'Obračun s prljavom politikom', *Vijesti*, 30 January 2011, p. 7.

[45]Interview with Gojko Cimbaljević, a Beranselo Movement activist, Berane, 14 September 2013. For details on the *Civic Declaration* see 'Zeleno gumno protiv smeća', *Vijesti*, 24 March 2013, p. 8.

[46]'Zeleno gumno protiv smeća', *Vijesti*, 24 March 2013, p. 8.

[47]Interview with Jovan Lončar, a Beranselo Movement activist, Berane, 14 September 2013. See also, 'Branićemo tijelima ako treba', *Vijesti*, 26 August 2010, p. 22.

FIGURE 2. BERANSELO'S RESIDENTS BLOCKING ACCESS ROADS TO THE RUBBISH DUMP.
Source: Photo courtesy of Beranselo movement activists. Reproduced with permission.

prosecuting innocent people for defending their dignity and Montenegro's constitutional identity as an 'ecological state'.[48] While professional NGO activists tend to be very critical of such radical acts of disobedience, the Beranselo movement showed exceptional success in bridging these middle-class notions of 'civil(ised)' activism with the allegedly 'uncivil(ised)' acts of defiance.[49]

The 'ethics of *tenacity*' and the 'esthetics of *"tricks"*' (De Certeau 1984, p. 26) demonstrated in these collective acts of resistance gradually motivated Montenegro's citizens to show hitherto unseen solidarity with the villagers and declare 'fidelity' (Badiou 2005, p. 233) to the event(s) in Beranselo. These would, however, have remained invisible if Beranselo's residents had not drawn attention to the wrongs they had to suffer.[50] More than anything else, the ease of using social media in communicating grievances and rendering injustices visible made the collective in Beranselo identifiable, '[a]nd once identifiable, they could become identified with' (May 2010, p. 40).

---

[48]'Stidite se što ćutite', *Dnevne novine*, 8 November 2013, p. 15.

[49]Bilić and Stubbs (2015) show that the middle-class habitus of NGO activists in the post-Yugoslav space often equates 'civic' with 'urban'—a term often used to denote an educated, middle-class, and liberal urbanite. At the same time, the term is used to draw demarcation from 'rural', which in turn becomes a container of 'primitive traditionalism', 'uncivilised ethnonationalism' and, ultimately, 'unenlightened people'. While Montenegro is no exception to this trend, the Beranselo movement was successful in deconstructing 'civic activism' by showing that it cannot be reduced to the middle-class habitus and its 'civility', but rather is a manifestation of progressive—and often disruptive—political activity by all citizens, the majority of whom were peasants, senior citizens, and (laid-off) workers at the time.

[50]According to Perović (2014), more than 350 illegal waste-dumping grounds were identified in Montenegro in 2014, the majority of which were not publicly visible.

FIGURE 3. DISCONTENTED CITIZENS AND ACTIVISTS FROM OTHER MONTENEGRIN TOWNS IN BERANSELO HOLDING 'WE ARE ALL BERANSELO' BANNER.
Source: Photo courtesy of Beranselo movement activists. Reproduced with permission.

Enacting impossible identification

According to Rancière (2007, p. 48), emancipation essentially 'means escaping from a minority', implying that political subjectivation requires a certain degree of intersubjectivity: a problem experienced by a certain group of people needs to be acknowledged and reaffirmed by those who are not directly affected by it. References to Beranselo at protests elsewhere in Montenegro (Softić 2012a, 2013c) were acts of solidarity and recognition in which the grievances of Beranselo's residents were accepted by others as their own (see Figure 3). This is what Rancière (1992, pp. 61–2) calls 'impossible identification', whose ultimate effect is to render a particular injustice universal (Žižek 1999, p. 188). The outcome of the disagreement between Beranselo and the state was that the hitherto unrepresented 'we' effectively cha(lle)nged the meaning of the noun denoting a resident of Beranselo: as opposed to being merely a geographically determined identity, *Beranselac*[51] became a designation for a new political subjectivity, encapsulating all those disappointed in or wronged by the system, disenchanted with the electoral democracy (partitocracy), and deprived of the right to control their own destinies.

What differentiated the Beranselo movement from other citizen-led mobilisations against the abuse of state power happening at that time was that, instead of waiting for their political representatives, mainstream media, NGOs, and experts to react and come to their aid, the Beranselci used social media to disseminate upsetting visuals of injustices they had to suffer. Images capturing their tenacity and resilience in fighting decisions that denied their human dignity pushed the broader Montenegrin public to recognise these as genuine acts of

---

[51]'Beranselac' designates resident of Beranselo, while the plural is 'Beranselci'.

citizenship. Therefore, unlike in other protest events, the public spoke on both mainstream and social media of contention in Beranselo as 'a problem for the whole of Montenegro', a place in which 'Montenegro's constitutional order and civil society are being defended'.[52] As anti-establishment sentiment grew throughout the country in 2012 (Kilibarda 2013), activists of diverse profiles, prominent public figures, and ordinary people from various towns in Montenegro joined the barricades at Vasove Vode.[53] When 32 residents of Beranselo were given fines by the courts, a group of 31 NGOs signed a (ultimately rejected) 'Petition for Pardon', which claimed that the '[p]unishment of Beranselo's residents represents an obvious injustice because they were ... defending the legal order of the ecological state Montenegro', pointing out that 'Beranselo's residents did not have any other option but to try to prevent, through nonviolent protest, further threats to the environment and people's health'.[54] The political subjectivity of the Beranselci also became visible and identifiable throughout Montenegro: their catch phrase 'Dokle?!' appeared on t-shirts as an act of support for civil disobedience (Softić 2012b); cries of 'We are all Beranselo!' were heard at various protests (Softić 2013c); the anti-government protest walks of 2012 (see above) were frequently headed by the 'Beranselo is Democracy!' banner (Softić 2012a); and the word 'Beranselo' became a threat in the discourse of other wronged and discontented groups; for example, 'If you don't fulfil our demands, you will have another Beranselo!' (Nikolić 2013, p. 33), and 'Beranselo will be nothing compared to us!'.[55]

The Beranselo movement was declared a nationwide symbol of resistance to political oppression (Perović 2013; Perović-Korać 2013; Softić 2013a, 2013b) and a paradigmatic example of civic responsibility and civil courage (Baća 2012a; Perović 2012; Kalezić 2013; Milačić 2014). In the emerging media discourse, Beranselo's residents were not only defending their right to a healthy environment, but also to constitutional order, civil society, and human dignity: their disobedience was understood as 'proof of being the only genuine citizens of Montenegro' (Radosavović 2013, p. 2). They were praised for uniting Montenegro and returning political power to the local community (Davidović 2013). Participants of the 'March Against Corruption' in Podgorica emphasised that their protests show that 'Montenegro has become one big Beranselo'.[56] Moreover, in October 2015, Ozon initiated a national award for civic activism named after the oldest member of the Beranselo movement—Đorđije Tomović, who had died earlier that year at the age of 96. The stated rationale for the award was that Tomović had served as an example of civic responsibility and political courage, becoming a symbol of the fight against political practices that reduced citizens to obedient subjects (see Figure 4).[57] Aleksandar Perović, a prominent Montenegrin

---

[52]See the documentary film *Između rijeke i ljudi* (directed by Mladen Ivanović, 2014). Since the Anti-bureaucratic Revolution of 1988–1989, the Beranselo movement has been the only social movement in Montenegro to serve as a topic of a feature-length documentary, as well as of two short films.

[53]'Vještaci da obezbijede dokaze', *Vijesti*, 17 April 2013, p. 36.

[54]'Inicijativa za pomilovanje', *ozon*, 14 October 2013, available at: http://www.ozon.org.me/wp-content/uploads/2013/10/Inicijativa-za-pomilovanje.pdf, accessed 17 November 2015.

[55]'Zaboraviće Beranselo pri Potocima', *Dan*, 17 April 2014, p. xi.

[56]'Podgorica: Oko 60 građana učestvovalo u maršu protiv korupcije', *Cafe del Montenegro*, 2 November 2013, available at: www.arhimed.me, accessed 2 December 2015.

[57]'Čovjek koji se nije uplašio režima', *Vijesti*, 4 October 2015, p. 13.

FIGURE 4. THE OLDEST RESIDENT OF BERANSELO, ĐORĐIJE TOMOVIĆ (94 AT THAT TIME), BLOCKING THE POLICE VEHICLE TO BREAK UP THE BLOCKADE.
Source: Photo courtesy of Beranselo movement activists. Reproduced with permission.

environmental activist and expert, explains why his organisation Ozon became a part of the Beranselo movement:

> While their fight wasn't the fight of my local community, it was the way in which institutions underestimated the initiative of Beranselo's residents that gave us necessary civil courage, solidarity, defiance, and creativity to recognise their fight as our own and to fight the power on different fronts …. Local and state authorities tried to downgrade this issue to an unimportant local nuisance, but we were persistent in showing that it was a systemic problem …. This never became a grant-supported project, there was no financial gain for anyone involved, which largely contributed to creating mutual trust and gaining the sympathy of the common people and organisations that still believe in change.[58]

Just as residents of Berane saw what was happening in Beranselo on the billboard, the rest of the Montenegrin public became aware of it through images on social media, predominantly Facebook. The everyday symbolic resistance employed by the Beranselo movement can be classified into two categories: first, the dissemination of upsetting visual representations of the dump, of performances/protests, and of confrontations with the police (as discussed above); and second, the creation of a virtual 'alternative Berane', known as *Luka Berane* (Port Berane), on Facebook.[59] Port Berane was an autonomous community art project aimed at mocking the establishment, initiated by Babović and Cimbaljević, among others. However, it was (mis)perceived by the public as a constitutive element of the Beranselo movement, so on a national level it unintentionally framed the struggle of the Beranselci in more political terms:

[58] Email correspondence with Aleksandar Perović, 26 June 2015.
[59] It was only later that 'Port Berane' became the name of an activist rock band.

ACTIVIST CITIZENSHIP IN SOUTHEAST EUROPE

it situated their resistance within a wider context and deconstructed its apparent localised particularism, subsequently rendering Vasove Vode a symptom of the structural violence common throughout post-socialist Montenegro.[60]

Cimbaljević speaks of activists' photographs as proof that 'the authorities were lying' and that Beranselci 'were not standing in the way of progress, [but] preventing the [environmental] apocalypse'.[61] Moreover, he points out the viscerality of photographs: unlike textual descriptions of the problem, which are often uninteresting to the general public or ideologically mystified by the regime along ethnopolitical cleavages, visual representations had a guaranteed emotional impact. The dump thus served the function of the 'punctum'—a part of the photograph that cannot be disinterestedly observed, because of its ability to establish the spectator's direct relationship with the object (or person) within it (Barthes 1981). The 'photovoice' of the Beranselci had the same effect on everyone who witnessed it: the evident environmental harm and the negated human dignity of those residents who were depicted rendered the spectator's own identity and ideology irrelevant, as there was no (political) narrative that could defend the injustices shown.[62] Babović posited that visual tools were used to 'provide evidence of injustice directly', unmediated by 'words that can be twisted and turn everything into another [ethnopolitical] identity issue'.[63]

Mitchell (2011) emphasises how photographs are often used to better communicate abstract concepts such as injustice or marginalisation. Visuals are, for that reason, frequently used by those whose voices cannot be heard in the public sphere to challenge power structures, dominant narratives, and hegemonic discourses (Freedberg 1989; Azoulay 2008). As such, photographs become 'social actants': 'by viewing them, persons are constituted into audiences that become responsible to alleviate the suffering of those depicted as victims' (Kurasawa 2015, p. 2). The Beranselci's 'photovoice' had thus interpellated their fellow citizens to become political and 'do something'. By showing the (post-)transition traumas that were supposed to remain hidden, the Beranselci articulated problems that were never or rarely spoken of in the Montenegrin polity as a whole, thus effectively reconfiguring the field of political experience. In other words, their photographs functioned as the public's encounter with the traumatic 'repressed' of the neoliberal state-building process (Baća 2012b).

The field of everyday symbolic struggle was additionally expanded through the creation of an online virtual town of Berane named 'Port Berane'.[64] It is a speculative, 'photoshopped' history of the town—an 'alternative history Berane' that imagines all unfulfilled election promises of the transitional period to have been fulfilled, a Berane in which privatisation, cronyism, and corruption have not destroyed the town's infrastructure, industry, and middle and working classes. It also expresses the marginalised position of the northern region of Montenegro. Lončar explains that 'in the south, towns [were or are being transformed into] trade, tourist, business or even financial centres', while 'the north had become the "Third

---

[60]In this essay, 'structural violence' is understood in the broadest terms as the physical, psychological, and emotional harm that results from the country's exploitive and unjust social, political, and economic system.

[61]Interview with Gojko Cimbaljević, a Beranselo Movement activist, Berane, 14 September 2013.

[62]See the documentary film *Između rijeke i ljudi*.

[63]Interview with Nebojša Babović, a Beranselo Movement activist, Berane, 14 September 2013.

[64]The name 'Port Berane' is an allusion to the mainstream development narrative that Montenegro is a potential 'tourism giant' due to its coast. Berane is, on the other hand, a former industrial town, located in the harsh continental and mountainous area. It is a paradigmatic example of a post-socialist, (post-)transition 'loser-town'.

FIGURE 5. 'INFRASTRUCTURE PROJECTS' PROMISED DURING ELECTION CAMPAIGNING OF DPS 'REALISED' IN PORT BERANE.
Source: Photo courtesy of Beranselo movement activists. Reproduced with permission.

World" within Montenegro with Berane as its "garbage centre"'.[65] What was absent in reality, therefore, became present in Port Berane (see Figure 5). Babović explains the relevance of their project as 'how Berane would now look like if [DPS's] election promises about infrastructure projects had come to be, if the government was doing its job. Instead, the only "infrastructure project" we got was the hazardous dump'.[66]

Among other problems of the Berane community, the contention around the Vasove Vode dumpsite was recast within popular culture to appeal to the widest audience through the Port Berane project as a representation of problems associated with the transitional experience. Unlike pictures of the dump, Cimbaljević looks at these photoshopped images of Port Berane as products of an inclusive creative work that gave (political) voice to Montenegrin citizens: 'in an oppressive society such as this, only a small number of people are ready to criticise something under their own name, [but through an image] anyone can say something and remain anonymous. ... It wasn't important who made the photos, but what they were showing—critique, difference and change'.[67] This project carried a radical emancipatory potential for

---

[65]Interview with Jovan Lončar, a Beranselo Movement activist, Berane, 14 September 2013.
[66]Interview with Nebojša Babović, a Beranselo Movement activist, Berane, 14 September 2013.
[67]Interview with Gojko Cimbaljević, a Beranselo Movement activist, Berane, 14 September 2013.

ACTIVIST CITIZENSHIP IN SOUTHEAST EUROPE

democratic participation in the non-anonymous society of Montenegro, as it became an affordable, but effective weapon in the hands of the marginalised and the discontented.[68]

Essentially, Port Berane was a sarcastic but emancipatory project—a midpoint between what Berane was and what it could have been, if only the transition period from state socialism to the market economy had not destroyed its present. When the Beranselo dump became a part of Port Berane's satirical imaginarium, it was eventually re-signified as a symptom of injustices committed in the name of the government's strategic goals that effectively benefit only ruling elites. Juxtaposed with Port Berane's iconography, images of the dump served as a traumatic reminder of the DPS's manipulation strategies and political incompetence. The dissemination of these images exposed the structural injustices and structural violence inscribed in top-down state-building, politicised ethnonational divisions, neoliberal privatisation, and European integration, among which the concentration of capital in central and southern parts of Montenegro was the most neglected instance. With the Beranselo movement, the critique of the negative effects of these 'strategic goals' of the Montenegrin government was clearly and cleverly articulated, consequently making it a voice for numerous politically unrepresented social groups that were wronged in the name of 'progress' and denied a voice in the polity.[69]

The Beranselo movement was a fight by discontented 'ordinary people' waged in the name of equality: they were not defending their rights as a particular identity, but as universal human subjects, demanding to have their fundamental human rights respected and to be treated equally to other citizens of Montenegro. Their pleas were thus made in the name of shared human dignity rather than an identity associated with Beranselo. That is to say, even though the movement assumed a name that implies a certain identity, that identity did not have 'any particular borders', due to the fact that political subjectivation 'binds together the individuals in a democratic group' through equality (May 2010, p. 49). 'Beranselo' thus became a signifier of democratic practice radically different from the already available institutional practice of politics, and denoted the politics of citizens who had no part in Montenegro's political order.

The relevance of the Beranselo Movement

In February 2014, the conservative People's Party (*Narodna stranka*—at that time not represented in parliament) that claims to represent the interests of the Serb ethnic group made a 'guarantee' to the residents of Beranselo that the dump would be closed. The guarantee was presented as a 'joint effort' with the municipal government and national authorities to 'put an end to the problem' (Softić 2014, p. 42). A few days later, the DPS announced that 'not a single gram of waste will be unloaded at the illegal dump' and that 'no one will be mistreated and harassed' from that point on.[70] The dump was officially closed on 3 March,[71] and remediation

---

[68]In addition to creating memes and photomontages, people from around the world expressed solidarity by holding up 'We Want Port Berane!' signs, or placing it next to famous monuments, landmarks or celebrities, as well as posting their 'Port Berane' photomontages to social media.

[69]For instance, the political subjectivity of the Beranselo movement was not created solely through 'disidentification' (declassification) in relation to ethnopolitical categories. Beranselo's residents also expressed solidarity with the country's LGBT population by tying a rainbow flag to several national flags, an expression of unity among the wronged and the marginalised in Montenegro. Later, prominent LGBT activists would express their support for the struggle of the Beranselci by holding a 'We Want Port Berane!' banner.

[70]'Mi tu odluku nismo vidjeli', *Vijesti*, 6 March 2014, p. 35.

[71]'Pokušavaju da zataškaju ekološku katastrofu', *Dan*, 4 March 2014, p. 12.

(*sanacija*) began two years later.[72] For the first time in four years, the public service broadcaster Radio–Television of Montenegro 'showed the mountain of garbage [in Beranselo]' (Softić 2014, p. 42). The Beranselo movement publicly condemned political parties for attempting to exploit the grievances of the Beranselci for election campaigning, saying, 'Vasove Vode is not a political story, but a life story', in which 'no one has the right to negotiate on this issue in [Beranselo's] name'.[73] Essentially, three months before the local elections, the DPS tried to capitalise on what had already been achieved by the Beranselo movement—solidarity among and mobilisation of people across ethnopolitical lines of conflict.

However, what political elites did not recognise was that claims made by the Beranselo movement were not the grievances of Serbs or Montenegrins; neither was the movement a deliberate attempt to reconcile these politicised ethnic/national groups. Whereas the political parties aimed at political profit by simulating cross-ethnic collaboration that, nevertheless, was articulated in the names of abstract Montenegrins and Serbs, the Beranselo movement could not be reduced to any of these identities, as it was acting in the name of a social group that could not be sociologically identified at the point of its emergence. Unlike political parties, the Beranselci refused to be reduced to any existing ethnic-cum-political identity, or to be confined to any place where they could 'legitimately' express their grievances or exercise their political being. They created spaces, both real and virtual, in which they could performatively demonstrate their political subjectivity by exposing the state's inegalitarian practices.

As an emergent phenomenon, this political subjectivity could not be represented in the polity, so it was performed through activist citizenship (by resisting, in the name of justice against injustice, decisions that affected the Beranselci) and direct democracy (by demanding control over their lives through participatory decision-making forums and a referendum). The Beranselo movement created a different, radical form of politics: its tactics of resistance erased the demarcation between participatory and representative democracy, creating an egalitarian, inclusive space for anyone to express solidarity and practise civil disobedience. In other words, it was not just an articulation of a new political message, but of a new, inclusive place of political enunciation. The movement showed that politics is an emergent phenomenon that can arise anywhere and everywhere, but through political subjectivation becomes the symbol of the whole of society. Their act was, therefore, an assertion of shared humanity, civic responsibility, and civil rights under the rubric of 'Beranselo'. While demanding recognition of its members' human dignity, the movement was fundamentally political as it questioned the corrupt, oligarchic, clientelistic/nepotistic, and bureaucratic order of the Montenegrin state, its malignant (neoliberal) policies, and the arbitrary decisions of party *apparatchiks*.

The case of Beranselo becomes more interesting in light of recent literature on contentious politics in post-socialist societies that criticises the Western theoretical bias that focuses on Western models of social movements or 'eventful protests' (such as mass demonstrations) and calls for more nuanced understandings of context-specific forms of activism, resistance, and contention (Gagyi 2015; Jacobsson 2015a; Piotrowski 2015; Pleyers & Sava 2015). However, while the scholarly work on contentious politics in Central and Eastern Europe focuses predominantly on urban movements, this essay discusses the political consequentiality of localised rural grassroots activism. It also moves away from analysing political subject-formation solely in terms of 'political becoming'—that is, activists' 'gaining of a sense of

---

[72]'Saniraju Vasove vode', *Dan*, 2 June 2016, p. 12.

[73]'Sraman pokuštaj predizborne prevare', *Dan*, 25 February 2014, p. 13.

agency and political efficacy' through resistance and resilience (Jacobsson 2015b, p. 19). Conversely, this essay shows how democratic subject-formation also works as disidentification through performativity: when people disconnect from their already existing identities and 'perform' equality and solidarity that are not already present in a given field of experience, thus creating new social bonds between hitherto estranged, often antagonistic individuals and groups under a new symbolic unifier.

When the Beranselci installed the billboard, blocked access roads to the dump, held performances, or shared photographs, they simultaneously staged equality and exposed the inegalitarian practices of the regime, in spite of its claims to uphold a constitutional order committed to democracy and an 'ecological state'. However, it was their 'photovoice'— through which they demanded the 'part of those who have no part' (Rancière 2010, p. 33)— that ruptured the discursive field and helped turn the political voice of the Beranselci not simply into that of a local movement, but a voice for all Montenegrin citizens wanting a greater say in decision-making.

The theoretical contribution of this essay, applied to the case of Beranselo, is threefold. First, the Beranselci extracted themselves from the dominant (ethnonational and political) categories of identification and classification. To paraphrase Foucault (1997, pp. 114–15), the 'we' of the Beranselci did not precede the problem it attempted to solve, but was constituted in relation to, or as a consequence of, the problem itself. The injustice in Beranselo was not an identity question to be approached from the political positions related to it; rather, it was an injustice that did not discriminate along identity lines. Therefore, what the movement asserted was essentially a misnomer: rather than simply representing the residents of Beranselo, it came to represent a new social bond between multitudes of individuals and collectives demanding respect for human dignity and protection of the environment, questioning official policies and narratives, and renouncing the elite's definition of politics in which the primary function of the political system is to serve the (economic) interests of the few.

Second, the Beranselci created a new space for fighting injustice that was 'not a place for a dialogue or a search for a consensus in Habermasian fashion', but 'a polemical commonplace for the handling of a wrong and the demonstration of equality' that manifests as an interruption or rupture in the phenomenological experience (Rancière 1992, p. 62). In the case of Beranselo, that 'commonplace' occupied a gap between ethnic/national identities, ideological orientations, party affiliations, places of residence, and citizenship statuses, among other positionalities, in which this emerging political subject could interact with the authorities on an equal footing. In other words, the equality claimed by the Beranselo movement was 'not an expression of an already existing equality' in the institutional makeup of Montenegrin society, but a 'performative act' that created 'the equality of the speaker' (Prentoulis & Thomassen 2013, p. 180). Beranselo, both real and virtual, became a place in which diverse groups, failed by electoral democracy, could address the public and fight the authorities without being seen as 'anti-state', 'anti-Montenegrin', or even 'anti-European' elements. It became an inclusive space of civic autonomy, a place in which citizens dared to contest the inegalitarian logic of the order, question political authorities and national dogmas, and provide (policy) solutions.

Third, the Beranselci established a trajectory for an impossible identification. As I have shown, others unaffected by the environmental harm declared unprecedented fidelity to the struggle of the Beranselci, and thus publicised and universalised a geographically specific inegalitarian practice. Their resistance created a 'we' that appealed to all those in Montenegro who were wronged in the name of the country's so-called 'strategic goals'. The claim that 'We are all Beranselo' could not be embodied by those who uttered it, since they could not actually identify with Beranselci and their concrete problem. However, what they could do is question their identification with existing categories—for instance, with the dominant political rhetoric supporting a 'independent' and/or 'European' Montenegro that served as symbols of unquestionable progress—in whose name the Beranselci were wronged. In other words, through everyday symbolic resistance, the movement unintentionally rendered visible and audible a new inclusive political subjectivity in Montenegro, with which anyone (exploited and/or disrespected) could identify, regardless of his/her ethnonational background or political affiliation.

Contrary to the general tendency of activists in the post-socialist region to emulate Western models of activism without taking into account the local context (Gagyi 2015, pp. 19–20), the contentious acts of Beranselci were recognised by the Montenegrin public as an authentic and autonomous civic struggle against injustice precisely because of their emphasis on the local reality of a negated universal human dignity. By communicating their grievances through images, the Beranselo movement unintentionally motivated Montenegro's citizens to question their identification with abstractions (for example, state, nation, transition, economic development, European integration) in whose name Beranselo's residents had been wronged. This tactic effectively circumvented the dominant ethnopolitical framework and brought the question of universal human dignity, civic responsibility, and social equality to the core of political debate. This 'new' politics, based on civic values, created a new 'we' in Montenegro's socio-political landscape: instead of expressing solidarity with a particularly politicised version of identity and the values specific to it, Montenegro's citizens could identify instead with a poignant human struggle. If the grievances of the Beranselci were understood as 'noise' by the authorities, their collective actions and, more importantly, uncoordinated tactics of everyday symbolic resistance turned into a powerful voice of the people. The localised struggle against injustice thus became the representation of the people as a whole, expressed through the democratic claim 'We are all Beranselo'. While the Beranselo movement's purposive actions were aimed at stopping illegal waste-dumping, its unintended consequence—transforming the *ethnos* into a *demos* by setting a trajectory for cross-ethnic, civic-based solidarity, mobilisation, organisation, and alliance-building—had an emancipatory effect on Montenegrin society.

References

Azoulay, A. (2008) *The Civil Contract of Photography* (New York, NY, Zone Books).
Baća, B. (2012a) 'U Mordoru, kraj Berana', *Art Vijesti*, 18 February.
Baća, B. (2012b) 'Beranski masakr toksičnim otpadom', *Art Vijesti*, 4 August.
Baća, B. (2013) 'Poslednji tango i keš u Beranama', *Art Vijesti*, 9 March.
Badiou, A. (2005) *Being and Event* (London, Continuum).
Barthes, R. (1981) *Camera Lucida: Reflections on Photography* (New York, NY, Hill and Wang).
Baumgartl, B. (1993) 'Environmental Protests as a Vehicle for Transition: The Case of Ekoglasnost in Bulgaria', in Vari, A. & Tamas, P. (eds) *Environment and Democratic Transition: Policy and Politics in Central and Eastern Europe* (Dordrecht, Kluwer Academic Publishers).

ACTIVIST CITIZENSHIP IN SOUTHEAST EUROPE

Bešić, M. (2014) *Tranzicione traume i promene vrednosnih orijentacija—generacijski pristup: Komparativna empirijska studija vrednosti u zemljama bivše Jugoslavije* (Belgrade, Čigoja štampa).

Bieber, F. (2003) 'Montenegrin Politics since the Disintegration of Yugoslavia', in Bieber, F. (ed.) *Montenegro in Transition: Problems of Identity and Statehood* (Baden-Baden, Nomos).

Bilić, B. & Stubbs, P. (2015) 'Unsettling "the Urban" in Post-Yugoslav Activisms: "Right to the City" and Pride Parades in Serbia and Croatia', in Jacobsson, K. (ed.) (2015a).

Brković, Č. (2013) 'Ambiguous Notions of "National Self" in Montenegro', in Brunnbauer, U. & Grandits, H. (eds) *The Ambiguous Nation: Case Studies from Southeastern Europe in the 20th Century* (Munich, Oldenbourg Verlag).

Buechler, S. M. (1995) 'New Social Movement Theories', *The Sociological Quarterly*, 36, 3.

Caspersen, N. (2003) 'Elite Interests and the Serbian-Montenegrin Conflict', *Southeast European Politics*, 4, 2–3.

Císař, O. (2013) 'Postcommunism and Social Movements', in David, A. S., Della Porta, D., Klandermans, B. & McAdam, D. (eds) *The Wiley-Blackwell Encyclopedia of Social and Political Movements* (New York, NY, Blackwell).

Cohen, J. (1985) 'Strategy or Identity: New Theoretical Paradigms and Contemporary Social Movements', *Social Research*, 52, 4.

Davidović, B. (2013) 'Nagrada "21. Jul" mjesnoj zajednici Beranselo za fanatičnu borbu protiv ilegalnog smetlišta', *Javniservis.me*, 6 June 2013, available at: http://javniservis.me/2013/06/06/blazo-davidovic-nagrada-21-jul-mjesnoj-zajednici-beranselo-za-fanaticnu-borbu-protiv-ilegalnog-smetlista, accessed 2 December 2015.

De Certeau, M. (1984) *The Practice of Everyday Life* (Berkeley, CA, University of California Press).

Della Porta, D. & Diani, M. (1999) *Social Movements: An Introduction* (Oxford, Blackwell).

Džankić, J. (2014) 'Reconstructing the Meaning of Being "Montenegrin"', *Slavic Review*, 73, 2.

Fagan, A. & Sircar, I. (2010) 'Environmental Politics in the Western Balkans: River Basin Management and Non-Governmental Organisation (NGO) Activity in Herzegovina', *Environmental Politics*, 19, 5.

Foucault, M. (1997) 'Polemics, Politics and Problematizations', in Rabinow, P. (ed.) *Ethics: Subjectivity and Truth* (New York, NY, The New Press).

Freedberg, D. (1989) *The Power of Images: Studies in the History and Theory of Response* (Chicago, IL, University Of Chicago Press).

Gagyi, Á. (2015) 'Why Don't East European Movements Address Inequalities the Way Western European Movements Do? A Review Essay on the Availability of Movement-Relevant Research', *Interface: A Journal For and About Social Movements*, 7, 2.

Gramsci, A. (1971) *Selections from the Prison Notebooks* (New York, NY, International Publishers).

Hall, S. & Jefferson, T. (eds) (1976) *Resistance Through Rituals: Youth Subcultures in Post-War Britain* (New York, NY, Holmes and Meier).

Hebdige, D. (1979) *Subculture: The Meaning of Style* (London, Methuen).

Hockenos, P. & Winterhagen, J. (2007) 'A Balkan Divorce that Works? Montenegro's Hopeful First Year', *World Policy Journal*, 24, 2.

Isin, E. F. (2008) 'Theorizing Acts of Citizenship', in Isin, E. F. & Nielsen, G. M. (eds) *Acts of Citizenship* (London, Zed Books).

Isin, E. F. (2009) 'Citizenship in Flux: The Figure of the Activist Citizen', *Subjectivity*, 29.

Jacobsson, K. (ed.) (2015a) *Urban Grassroots Movements in Central and Eastern Europe* (Farnham, Ashgate).

Jacobsson, K. (2015b) 'The Development of Urban Movements in Central and Eastern Europe', in Jacobsson, K. (ed.) (2015a).

Jacobsson, K. & Saxonberg, S. (eds) (2013) *Beyond NGO-ization: The Development of Social Movements in Central and Eastern Europe* (Farnham, Ashgate).

Jenne, E. K. & Bieber, F. (2014) 'Situational Nationalism: Nation-building in the Balkans, Subversive Institutions and the Montenegrin Paradox', *Ethnopolitics*, 13, 5.

Jovanović, P. (2009) 'Neke odlike političke kulture u Crnoj Gori', *Ljetopis crnogorski*, 4.

Jovanović, P. & Marjanović, M. (2002) *Politička kultura u Crnoj Gori* (Podgorica, SoCEN).

Kalezić, J. (2013) 'Odgovornost za bolesni prostor i ljude', *Vijesti*, 27 September.

Kilibarda, K. (2013) 'An Anatomy of the Montenegrin Spring: Mobilizing Workers and Civic Networks against Austerity', Paper Presented at the 45th Annual Convention of Association for Slavic, East European and Eurasian Studies, Boston, USA, 21–24 November.

Komar, O. (2013) *Birači u Crnoj Gori: Faktori izborne i partijske preferencije* (Belgrade, Čigoja štampa).

Komar, O. (2015) 'The Development of Civil Society in Montenegro', in Fink-Hafner, D. (ed.) *The Development of Civil Society in the Countries on the Territory of the Former Yugoslavia since the 1980s* (Ljubljana, Faculty of Social Sciences).

Kovačević, M. (2014) *Legal and Transparent Use of Public Resources—A Precondition for Building Trust in Elections* (Podgorica, Center for Democratic Transition).

Kullenberg, C. (2015) 'Citizen Science as Resistance: Crossing the Boundary between Reference and Representation', *Journal of Resistance Studies*, 1, 1.

Kurasawa, F. (2015) 'How Does Humanitarian Visuality Work? A Conceptual Toolkit for a Sociology of Iconic Suffering', *Sociologica*, 1/2015.

May, T. (2010) *Contemporary Political Movements and the Thought of Jacques Rancière: Equality in Action* (Edinburgh, Edinburgh University Press).

Melucci, A. (1996) *Challenging Codes: Collective Action in the Information Age* (Cambridge, Cambridge University Press).

Mercea, D. (2014) 'Towards a Conceptualization of Casual Protest Participation: Parsing a Case from the Save Roşia Montană Campaign', *East European Politics and Societies*, 28, 2.

Merton, R. K. (1936) 'The Unanticipated Consequences of Purposive Social Action', *American Sociological Review*, 1, 6.

Milačić, M. (2014) 'Beranski šamar', *Vijesti*, 13 March.

Milivojević, A. & Bešić, M. (2006) 'Wither the Union? Interim Findings on the "Changing" Ethnic Makeup of Montenegro and the Independence Referendum', *Newsletter of the Institute of Slavic, East European, and Eurasian Studies*, 23, 1.

Milovac, D. (2016) 'Montenegro: Democratic Deficits Persist Instead of Progressing Euro–Atlantic Integration', *Südosteuropa Mitteilungen*, 56, 1.

Mitchell, C. (2011) *Doing Visual Research* (Thousand Oaks, CA, Sage Publications).

Mochťak, M. (2015) 'Democratization and Electoral Violence in Post-Communism: A Study of Montenegro', *Southeast European and Black Sea Studies*, 15, 1.

Morrison, K. (2009) *Montenegro: A Modern History* (London, I.B. Tauris).

Morrison, K. (2011) 'Change, Continuity and Consolidation: Assessing Five Years of Montenegro's Independence', *LSEE Papers on South Eastern Europe*, 2, 1.

Nikolić, P. (2013) 'Novo Beranselo', *Monitor*, 8 November.

Perović, A. (2013) 'Vijesti iz zone (su)mraka', *Vijesti*, 29 May.

Perović, A. (2014) 'Insistirajmo na istini', *Vijesti*, 18 November.

Perović, V. (2012) 'Deponija obećanja', *Dnevne novine*, 23 July.

Perović-Korać, M. (2013) 'Kad Ćoćo bije zakonom', *Monitor*, 20 December.

Piotrowski, G. (2015) 'What are Eastern European Social Movements and How to Study Them?', *Intersections: East European Journal of Society and Politics*, 1, 3.

Pleyers, J. & Sava, I. N. (eds) (2015) *Social Movements in Central and Eastern Europe: A Renewal of Protests and Democracy* (Bucharest, Editura Universităţii din Bucureşti).

Polletta, F. (1999) '"Free Spaces" in Collective Action', *Theory and Society*, 28, 1.

Portes, A. (2000) 'The Hidden Abode: Sociology as Analysis of the Unexpected. 1999 Presidential Address', *American Sociological Review*, 65, 1.

Prentoulis, M. & Thomassen, L. (2013) 'Political Theory in the Square: Protest, Representation and Subjectivation', *Contemporary Political Theory*, 12, 3.

Radosavović, Đ. (2013) 'Smeće je govorilo za sebe', *Art Vijesti*, 28 September.

Rancière, J. (1992) 'Politics, Identification, and Subjectivization', *October*, 61.

Rancière, J. (1999) *Disagreement: Politics and Philosophy* (Minneapolis, MN, University of Minnesota Press).

Rancière, J. (2007) *On the Shores of Politics* (London, Verso).

Rancière, J. (2010) *Dissensus: On Politics and Aesthetics* (New York, NY, Continuum).

Scott, J. C. (1985) *Weapons of the Weak: Everyday Forms of Peasant Resistance* (New Haven, CT, Yale University Press).

Scott, J. C. (1990) *Domination and the Arts of Resistance: Hidden Transcripts* (New Haven, CT, Yale University Press).

Scott, J. C. (2012) *Two Cheers for Anarchism: Six Easy Pieces on Autonomy, Dignity, and Meaningful Work and Play* (Princeton, NJ, Princeton University Press).

Sedlenieks, K. (2015) 'Buffer Culture in Montenegro: Bratstvo, Kumstvo and Other Kin-Related Structures', in Cvetičanin, P., Mangova, I. & Markovikj, N. (eds) *A Life For Tomorrow: Social Transformations in South-East Europe* (Skopje, Institute for Democracy 'Societas Civilis').

Sekelj, L. (2000) 'Parties and Elections: The Federal Republic of Yugoslavia—Change Without Transformation', *Europe-Asia Studies*, 52, 1.

Smith, M. B. (1996) 'Michel de Certeau's Microsubversions', *Social Semiotics*, 6, 1.

Softić, T. (2010) 'Vlast ignorište mještane', *Monitor*, 26 November.

Softić, T. (2011a) 'Beranselo simbol otpora', *Monitor*, 14 January.

Softić, T. (2011b) 'Policija protiv građana', *Monitor*, 27 May.

Softić, T. (2012a) 'Osvajanje slobode', *Monitor*, 6 July.

Softić, T. (2012b) 'Dokle', *Monitor*, 3 August.

Softić, T. (2013a) 'Otporom protiv zakona sile', *Monitor*, 22 March.

Softić, T. (2013b) 'Opasni virus pobune', *Monitor*, 6 September.

Softić, T. (2013c) 'Za sjeme', *Monitor*, 22 November.

Softić, T. (2014) 'Vasove, Pecove il' Svetove vode', *Monitor*, 28 February.

Tilly, C. & Tarrow, S. (2007) *Contentious Politics* (Boulder, CO, Paradigm Publishers).

Tilly, C. & Wood, L. J. (2012) *Social Movements, 1768–2012* (3rd edn) (Boulder, CO, Paradigm Publishers).

Troch, P. (2014) 'From "And" to "Either/Or": Nationhood in Montenegro during the Yugoslav Twentieth Century', *East European Politics and Societies*, 28, 1.

USAID (2012) 'Montenegro Country Report', in *The 2011 CSO Sustainability Index for Central and Eastern Europe and Eurasia* (15th edn) (Washington, DC, USAID).

USAID (2013) 'Montenegro Country Report', in *The 2012 CSO Sustainability Index for Central and Eastern Europe and Eurasia* (16th edn) (Washington, DC, USAID).

Vernon, R. (1979) 'Unintended Consequences', *Political Theory*, 7, 1.

Vujović, Z. & Komar, O. (2008) 'Impact of the Europeanization Process on the Transformation of the Party System of Montenegro', *Journal of Southern Europe and the Balkans*, 10, 2.

Wang, C. & Burris, M. A. (1997) 'Photovoice: Concept, Methodology, and Use for Participatory Needs Assessment', *Health Education and Behavior*, 24, 3.

Žižek, S. (1999) *The Ticklish Subject: The Absent Centre of Political Ontology* (London, Verso).

Post-Yugoslav Everyday Activism(s):
A Different Form of Activist Citizenship?

PIOTR GOLDSTEIN

Abstract

Activism is typically associated with work within charities/NGOs or participation in social movements. This essay highlights activism different from these forms in that it happens without funding or mass mobilisation. Instead, it is powered by the longer-term perspective and day-to-day efforts of 'activist citizens'. Based on interviews and participant observation in bookshop-cafés and other donor-independent initiatives in Novi Sad, Serbia, the essay argues that such 'everyday activism' is significant not only because it supports the development of other, more visible, forms of activism, but also in its own right, as a counter-space contributing to social change.

ACTIVISM IN THE POST-YUGOSLAV CONTEXT TENDS TO BE EXAMINED from two perspectives. On the one hand, some studies focus on 'civil society' understood in myriad ways, but usually explored through research on non-governmental organisations (NGOs) (Helms 2003; Jeffrey 2007). On the other hand, other studies are concerned with social movements and popular protest (Fagan & Sircar 2013; Jacobsson & Saxonberg 2013; Sardelić 2013; Štiks & Horvat 2014). This essay aims to supplement these two understandings of activism by looking at forms of activism which are less obvious because they seek neither financial support (which distinguishes them from NGOs), nor recognition (which distinguishes them from social movements and popular protest). These forms of activism aim to create counter-spaces and counter-practices gradually and discreetly.

The essay scrutinises everyday, discreet activisms, that is, alternative forms of activism in contexts where other forms of activism appear unsatisfactory or ineffective, and where

The fieldwork which informed this essay was conducted thanks to an Erasmus Mundus (Action 2–Strand 1–Lot 6 JoinEU-SEE IV) six-month postdoctoral fellowship at the Institute of Sociology, University of Novi Sad. The author would like to thank the funder for the grant and Zsolt Lazar for his mentorship throughout the fellowship. This work was also supported by the British Academy [grant number PF150021]. The author is very grateful to Indraneel Sircar and Adam Fagan for their feedback which greatly helped to shape this essay. A very early version was presented at the 'Voluntary Associations in the Yugoslav Space' workshop at Collège de France in December 2015. The author is grateful to the organisers for this opportunity, and to Paul Stubbs, Chiara Bonfiglioli, and Bojan Bilić for their useful suggestions. Last but not least, the author is very grateful to the two anonymous reviewers for their valuable recommendations. All errors are the sole responsibility of the author.

This is an Open Access article distributed under the terms of the Creative Commons Attribution-NonCommercial-NoDerivatives License (http://creativecommons.org/licenses/by-nc-nd/4.0/), which permits non-commercial re-use, distribution, and reproduction in any medium, provided the original work is properly cited, and is not altered, transformed, or built upon in any way.

activists choose a less radical and more long-term approach. My interest is threefold: to what extent these activisms form, for engaged individuals, a stage between (or perhaps beyond) engagement in NGOs and social movements in 'genealogies of activism' (Stubbs 2012); whether they are performed independently of such engagements; and whether they form a link between different activisms or catalyse them. Examples of such activisms include efforts aimed at goals similar to those of NGOs and social movements (for example, opposing growing social inequalities, nationalism, and capitalist usurpations of public space) but take on different organisational forms or remain altogether informal.

Theorising everyday activism

The activist citizen and her 'sites'

The starting point of this essay is the 'figure of the activist citizen' developed by Engin F. Isin (2009). While active citizenship has been traditionally connected to interest and engagement in the political affairs of one's country (Kearns 1995; Marinetto 2003) or, more broadly, to economic activity or any other 'productive contribution to society' (Fuller *et al.* 2008, p. 157), Isin's activist citizens go further.[1] They not only fulfil their civic duties and responsibilities (Carens 1986; Deigh 1988) but also 'make claims to justice … break habitus and act in a way that disrupts already defined orders, practices and statuses' (Isin 2009, p. 384). The actions of an activist citizen are stimulated not only by responsibility but also by 'militant commitment' (Balibar 2004, pp. 49–50).[2] Robert Putnam used two Yiddish terms to distinguish between *schmoozers*—people who are engaged by talking (*schmoozing*) about things—and *machers*— 'those who do', that is, engage in community projects, vote, and protest, for example (Putnam 2000, pp. 93–4). An activist citizen is a *macher*, one who makes things happen, and it is her or his acts (Isin 2008, 2009, p. 372), whether grand (starting a revolution) or (seemingly) small (blogging), that allow us to recognise him/her as an activist citizen.

Isin's activist citizen operates within 'sites' and 'scales' of citizenship. Sites are 'fields of contestation around which certain issues, interests, stakes as well as themes, concepts and objects assemble' (Isin 2009, p. 370). 'Scales' in turn denote the focus of such contestation: 'cities, empires, nations, states, federations, leagues' (Isin 2009, p. 372). It is through sites, scales, and their own acts that '"actors" claim to transform themselves (and others) from subjects into citizens as claimants of rights' (Isin 2009, p. 368). It is important to stress that sites and scales, more often than not, are conceptual rather than physical, and that they often overlap and depend on each other (Isin 2009, p. 372). In the context of protest and/or contestation of the dominant order, sites in particular become conceptually close to Henri Lefebvre's 'counter-spaces'.

Counter-spaces

For Lefebvre, 'counter-spaces' are 'spaces occupied by the symbolic and the imaginary'; 'forces that run counter to a given strategy'; an 'initially utopian alternative to actually existing "real" space' (Lefebvre 1991, pp. 366, 367, 349). In the context of the ever-present

---

[1] For a less traditional treatment of active citizenship, see Goldstein (2016).
[2] See also Isin (2009, p. 383).

commodification of public space, counter-spaces become an important element of activist de-commodification of the city. These are more and less temporary, physical and non-physical 'spaces' which, as Fran Tonkiss put it, 'refuse a predatory logic of capital' (Tonkiss 2005, p. 64). Lefebvre explains:

> What runs counter to a society founded on exchange is a primacy of *use*. What counters quantity is quality …. When a community fights the construction of urban motorways or housing developments, when it demands 'amenities' or empty spaces for play and encounter, we can see how a counter-space can insert itself into spatial reality: against the Eye and the Gaze, against quantity and homogeneity, against power and the arrogance of power, against the endless expansion of the 'private' and of industrial profitability; and against specialized spaces and a narrow localization of function. (Lefebvre 1991, pp. 381–82)

Similarly to acts of citizenship, counter-spaces must not be grand. On the contrary, Lefebvre himself asserts that one should not see them as an extreme, as a total opposite of desires of political power, a grand counter-force. He argues that 'everything (the "whole") weighs down on the lower or "micro" level, on the local and the localizable—in short, on the sphere of everyday life' (Lefebvre 1991, p. 366). The power of counter-spaces lies not in their ability to turn things upside down in an instant, but in that they 'open up cracks in the totalizing logic of the capitalist city' (Tonkiss 2005, p. 64).

Everyday utopias

Focus on daily practice is also characteristic of what Davina Cooper (2014) calls 'everyday utopias'. She uses this term for

> networks and spaces that perform regular daily life … in a radically different fashion. Everyday utopias don't focus on campaigning or advocacy. They don't place their energy on pressuring mainstream institutions to change, on winning votes, or on taking over dominant social structures. Rather they work by creating the change they wish to encounter, building and forging new ways of experiencing social and political life. (Cooper 2014, p. 2)

Examples of such 'everyday utopias' include spaces as diverse as a feminist bathhouse in which volunteers teach fellow women to appreciate and enjoy their bodies, a time-trading scheme in which participants exchange services rather than currency, or the Speakers' Corner in London. According to Cooper, the function of these spaces is twofold. On the one hand, 'against the assumption that anything outside the "normal" is impossible', they reveal their own possibility (Cooper 2014, p. 4), and on the other hand, they constitute spaces 'from which to critique the world as it currently is' (Cooper 2014, p. 5). As such, one could argue, even if they seem not to be particularly successful in creating a sustainable alternative to the current order, they can still be perceived as successful in creating a starting point for further action but also, like Lefebvre's counter-spaces, in 'opening up cracks' and undermining the universality of the current state of affairs.

Micro-politics/infrapolitics

Finally, this essay engages with two theories which foreground non-evident, less visible, and not particularly dynamic, yet significant, avenues forming an integral part of citizens' engagement in broader political change. These are Jeffrey C. Goldfarb's theory of politics of small things, or micro-politics (Goldfarb 2006, 2008) and James C. Scott's theory of infrapolitics (Scott 1990). Goldfarb's theory arose from his study of student theatres in Poland in the late 1970s and his observations of various everyday practices which escaped full control of the state, such as clandestine poetry evenings in private apartments at that time (Goldfarb 1980, 2006). In the late 1970s, both the work of student theatres, formally controlled by the state, and practices such as poetry readings seemed completely insignificant. However, argues Goldfarb, a couple of years later, during the upsurge of the *Solidarność* (Solidarity) movement, it became clear that this movement would not have been possible without the 'electricity' created by the multiplicity of seemingly small and insignificant actors and practices, such as those he studied. Similarly, Scott points to historical examples of subordinate groups engaging in activities such as 'poaching, squatting, desertion, evasion, foot-dragging', as well as more symbolic ones, such as creating folktales of revenge. He calls such activities 'infrapolitics', because infrapolitics create the 'cultural and structural underpinning of the more visible political action' (Scott 1990, pp. 183–84) in the same way that appropriate infrastructure is indispensable for any serious business. Both authors argue that the less visible, not particularly dynamic, and seemingly insignificant practices on which they focus are in fact extremely important. They argue that such practices are not a 'safety valve' or a substitute for real anger and real action, nor are they necessarily direct stimulators of change. Instead, in their multiplicity and diversity, they form an environment without which change would not happen.

Place and method

The research on which this essay is based was conducted in Novi Sad—Serbia's second biggest city (with a population of about 340,000) and the regional capital of Vojvodina, an autonomous province of Serbia that has for centuries been part of various Hungarian kingdoms and Austria–Hungary. Novi Sad is a relatively young city (hence *Novi*—new—in the name) established in the time of Austria–Hungary, as a result of cooperation between local Danube Swabians, Hungarians, and a large Serbian minority. Despite large population shifts after World War II and throughout recent conflicts, the city remains multi-ethnic: it is now home to a Serbian majority and a multitude of minorities, most notably Hungarians, but also Croats, Ruthenians, Romanians, Slovaks, Roma, Jews, and others. Unlike many other cities across the western Balkans it was not directly affected by fighting during the recent Yugoslav wars. Novi Sad's bridges were bombed, not by civil fighting, but by NATO, an external enemy. It would be wrong, however, to think of Novi Sad as untouched by war—many of the city's men were incorporated in the Serbian army and a huge influx of refugees became the root of many of today's conflicts. Minorities have experienced 'low-level violence' (Bieber & Winterhagen 2006), enough to incur long-lasting resentment and mistrust. The psychological trauma is only a part of what makes Novi Sad a post-war city. Here, as elsewhere in the former Yugoslavia, the wars have shaped post-communist 'triple transitions'—political, economic, and the nation-building that has seen the emergence of powerful national elites (Offe 1991 p. 871). In the new successor states of the former Yugoslavia, even more than elsewhere in Eastern Europe, the situation was 'replete with opportunities ... to improve one's "original endowment," or to take revenge' (Offe 1991, p. 872). The rise of nationalism went hand-in-hand with non-transparent privatisation and the development of *nouveau riche* elites. Today, the wars of the 1990s remain for the inhabitants of Novi Sad the key point of rupture between a better past and an insecure present. For many, an invisible map of unwanted monuments, changed street names, and businesses which they know flourished as a result of the arms trade, other war-profiteering, or corrupt processes of privatisation, is a constant remainder of the conflicts.

Method

The core of the data for the research presented here was collected between January and June 2014 through interviews and ethnographic observation.[3] The research first focused on bookshop-cafés—places which, during an earlier four-year project (2009–2013), appeared to be particularly important for activists in Novi Sad—and later included other similar initiatives. Regular participant observation was conducted in two bookshop-cafés, while four other similar venues were visited less regularly. The managers or owners of most of these venues were interviewed, as well as some of their customers. These data were complemented by a follow-up visit and participant observation in November 2015, interview and ethnographic data collected during earlier research visits to Novi Sad between 2010 and 2013, and by information obtained online.

Not for profit

This study started from the author's astonishment at the operations of some of Novi Sad's bookshop-cafés. These venues operate as businesses but, because of their ambitious choice of books, they have little chance of being successful in economic terms and therefore could also be seen as charities. The observed bookshop-cafés sold books by respected foreign and local authors, books on philosophy, books tackling current social and political questions, dictionaries of the local minority languages, and books for children which aimed not only to entertain but also to educate and instil values in the youngest generation.[4] Some of these books sold slowly and some (such as books in Hungarian—the language of the city's largest ethnic minority) seemed not to sell at all. In relation to local pay, books in Serbia are expensive and even more so if they are published by independent publishers. In the UK, a new copy of Plato's *Republic* sells for approximately the equivalent of one hour's work on the minimum hourly wage; in crisis-hit Spain or in Poland, for approximately two hours of such work. In Serbia, however, a copy costs the equivalent of over seven hours of minimally paid work.[5] At the same time, as in many other post-communist countries, the cultural capital typical of Western middle-, upper-middle-, or even 'upper' classes—a taste for poetry, an inclination towards books on difficult subjects, a distaste for television (Bourdieu 1984; Bourdieu & Passeron 1990)—often does not correlate to the financial resources typical of such classes in the West (Eyal *et al.* 1998; Goldstein 2011; Cvetičanin *et al.* 2012; Salmenniemi 2012). Thus, what could seem a well-thought-out marketing plan—the use of books as symbolic capital (Bourdieu 1984) able to attract the well-read who are at the same time well-off—is not an effective strategy in Serbia. That is because the well-read and the well-off are to a

---

[3]The interviews were originally conducted, transcribed, and encoded in Serbian. Citations for this essay were translated by the author.

[4]That is, books such as *Winnie the Pooh* or *The Little Prince* or even more ambitious titles such as *Why Do People Make War?* rather than, for example, books with protagonists from current television series.

[5]Using prices from some of the most popular online bookshops in these countries. Author's own calculations.

large extent two different groups.[6] In this context, stocking shelves almost exclusively with quality, hard-to-sell books seemed to be a naïve business model. Indeed, during the course of my research, several of the places I observed went bankrupt, changed owners, or were forced to leave their premises, subsequently selling their stock online. However, for the owners of these bookshop-cafés, their choice of books, the location of the venue, and even the size of their shop, were all part of a struggle. They considered their activity as a struggle against the primacy of quantity over quality, the reduction of value to profitability, the occupation of central spaces in the city by banks, chain-stores, and shops for the super-rich, and the commodification of public space. Thus, while the method they chose was very different as they did not expect instant change, the claims that they made were in many respects similar to those of protesters on Varšavska Street in Zagreb (see Dolenec, Doolan and Tomašević's contribution to this collection) or other Right to the City movements. These claims were also very political: in a post-Yugoslav region which for more than two decades has been undergoing a 'seemingly endless transition to liberal democracy and neoliberal economy' (Štiks & Horvat 2015 p. 1) and where the word 'transition' has 'brought into both public and political discourse quasi-biblical connotations of acceding to the "land of plenty"' (Horvat & Štiks 2012), to question the rules of the free market or the ethos of making ever-growing profits is fundamentally political.

Books as tools and symbol

In some cases, the very choice of venue for the bookshop-café was meaningful. *Serendipiti* was, for instance, a large, three-storey modern bookshop-café located in the most central part of the city, surrounded by banks and expensive restaurants. Roman, the owner, believed that the books he wanted to offer deserved to be in the most central part of the city, even if this was not the best idea business-wise. At the same time, he saw being in the centre as a way of reaching a wide audience and playing a role in changing local society. He declared that he was happy even when people only read the books in the bookshop without actually buying them.[7] When he started the business, he also tried to encourage reading (also among those who only came for the coffee) by leaving books on all coffee tables, and using them as menu-holders. This had to be stopped, as many people hesitated to come in, believing that the tables were reserved. For Roman, the ambitious choice of books that he offered and his various efforts to get the books read were about 'building taste' in the local community. He did this in opposition to bookshop chains:

> Bookshop chains participate in creating taste. In the same way as we experience 'tabloidisation' of media, we have in the same way the 'tabloidisation' of publishing, because books that people look for, these are books of low profile, these are hits, these are books which are completely meaningless … and all these tastes are dictated by licensing agencies, through their branches here, that's it![8]

---

[6]At the time of my research, there was at least one café-restaurant in Novi Sad that did use books as symbolic capital—part of a larger marketing and interior-design plan. In that restaurant, books, alongside expensive Italian or Spanish ham, cigars, and quality wines, contributed to the overall elegant ambience of the venue. In fact, these books were placed too high to be accessible and their choice, which clearly showed that they were chosen for their covers and not for their content, indicated that this was a very different place from the ones that I investigated.

[7]Interview #8, Roman, owner of *Serendipiti* bookshop-café, Novi Sad, 18 June 2014.

[8]Interview #8, Roman, owner of *Serendipiti* bookshop-café, Novi Sad, 18 June 2014.

Engin F. Isin points out that citizenship 'involves practices of making citizens—*social, political, cultural* and *symbolic*' (Isin 2008, p. 17, emphasis added). Roman's activity involved a variety of such practices: providing books on social and political topics, providing space—the top floor of his venue—for cultural events, and bringing all these into the city centre to symbolically break the dominance of banks, exclusive shops, and other sites of consumerism.

Lemi, owner of *Lemijeva Knjižara* (Lemi's Bookshop), used ideologically similar but in reality very different practices for 'making citizens'. His was a small family business, a bookshop with new and second-hand books, where he and his closest family would treat some of the guests to a cup of coffee and/or a glass of *rakija*, sit with them, and discuss books, art, politics or, as I observed during one of my visits, his and his guests' experiences of activism. The place was very modest, located in a residential neighbourhood away from the city centre. There seemed to be two main types of visitors to the bookshop: people from the neighbourhood, mostly schoolchildren passing by with their parents; and seasoned readers (including Novi Sad's activists), some of whom would come to the bookshop from other parts of the city or even other cities. Similar to Roman, Lemi presented his idea of a bookshop in contrast to the chains and saw it as something necessary for the city, for both authors and society:

> I wanted to keep one ordinary bookshop in Novi Sad. Ordinary, in the sense that it would not be led by this commercial moment. To say … there are some publishers which … are completely not known but which do some very interesting things. And if these things, if they are not found by someone from this commercial sphere and if they are not offered to potential buyers, to literary magazines, to readers, then they remain unknown …. You know, if someone works with poetry today … this may sound, who knows how, but … this is very important, it is important for the whole society. There should always be these … these dear lunatics who … who write poetry and those who read it, who appreciate it in any case.[9]

It is instructive to ask whether these activities should really be taken as micro-politics or infrapolitics. Without a doubt, being an ineffective businessperson is not itself a form of activism. Asef Bayat calls for distinguishing between everyday resistance and simple everyday coping (Bayat 1997, p. 70). Similarly, Roger Mac Ginty who examines everyday peace, which comprises uncoordinated everyday practices allowing for the creation of 'islands of civility' in conflicted societies, stresses that 'in order for everyday peace to be taken seriously as a meaningful practice, it needs to be conceived of as more than an aggregation of coping mechanisms' (Mac Ginty 2014, pp. 11, 12). But the activities of Roman and Lemi went beyond coping: they had the potential to make more money and were aware of it. For instance, Lemi could sell coffee instead of offering it for free and Roman could easily have installed television screens during the 2014 football World Cup to attract more customers. However, both of them argued that such compromises would hurt the ethos of their respective places.[10] When balancing between the 'commercial moment' and creating spaces which, in their eyes were socially, culturally and, in the longer term, politically enriching their city, they chose the latter. It is this choice which allows us to see them as activist citizens, ones who are actively resisting, not just coping.

[9]Interview #6, Lemi (Miljenko), owner of *Lemijeva Knjižara*, Novi Sad, 17 June 2014.
[10]Interview #8, Roman, owner of *Serendipiti* bookshop-café, Novi Sad, 18 June 2014; interview #6, Lemi (Miljenko), owner of *Lemijeva Knjižara*, Novi Sad, 17 June 2014.

As with other independent booksellers examined during the research, Roman and Lemi intended to sell books in local minority languages, particularly Hungarian. Despite the fact that the city has a relatively large Hungarian minority (officially around 4%, but probably more), these books are hardly ever bought.[11] This might be due to the fact that many of Novi Sad's Hungarians do not actually know Hungarian; also, that those who do read it are used to buying books online, during trips to Hungary, or directly from the local publisher. Nevertheless, both Lemi from *Lemijeva* and Roman from *Serendipiti* felt that it was important for them to have books in minority languages. Having books written in Hungarian was only insubstantially related to potential sales. However, as Roman explained, they were there out of respect towards the city's largest minority: 'we keep these books because we consider it a question of respect to have books in Hungarian in Novi Sad. This is normal. I wish we also had books in Romanian'.[12] For Lemi too, keeping books in Hungarian was simply the 'right thing to do',[13] as was almost certainly the case for managers of *Knjižara Gradska* (City Bookshop), another large bookshop-café in the very centre of the city, which went bankrupt before *Serendipiti* opened. *Knjižara Gradska* had an entire section devoted to books in Hungarian, and kept a very large (and very expensive) Romani–Serbian dictionary in the most prominent place in the bookshop. Just like the people participating in the 'everyday utopias' studied by Cooper, for owners and managers of these places, these practices were simply 'normal and right' (Cooper 2014, p. 5).

The efforts of these bookshop-café owners to keep the languages of the local minorities visible in the bookshop space can be seen as symbolic statements. Such symbols may have little immediate significance, but they do create a counter-voice to that of ever-growing nationalist sentiment on the one hand, and the primacy of what Lemi called 'the commercial moment' on the other.[14] In fact, the two seem to be interconnected, particularly in Novi Sad where commercialisation of the public space often goes hand-in-hand with erasing the city's multi-ethnic and multicultural heritage. The German cemetery, the Jewish cemetery, and the centrally located Armenian Church had already been destroyed during communist times to make space for wider streets and buildings of 'public utility'. The post office constructed in 1961 was built diagonally between the octagonal grid of buildings and made so high that it obscures the view of the otherwise very large synagogue from both the main pedestrian area and the road from Belgrade running through the city centre (Stevanović 2013). More recently, sites testifying to the city's multicultural heritage have been destroyed in the name of making space for commercial development. In March 2016, the marble gravestone of an Armenian family erected in 1790 was destroyed to make space for the construction of a 13-storey building.[15] The grave was not only the last material testimony to the former Armenian community of Novi Sad, but was also a centrally located and highly visible reminder

---

[11]According to the 2011 census (Statistical Office of the Republic of Serbia 2012, pp. 36–7) there are 3.9% of Hungarians in Novi Sad. However, according to the same census 9.25% of citizens of Novi Sad declared their ethnicity as 'Yugoslav', 'Other', 'Regional affiliation', 'not known', or did not declare it. It is likely that also some of the city's Hungarians adopted these categories.

[12]Interview #8, Roman, owner of *Serendipiti* bookshop-café, Novi Sad, 18 June 2014.

[13]Interview #6, Lemi (Miljenko), owner of *Lemijeva Knjižara*, Novi Sad, 17 June 2014.

[14]For discussion on this and other 'narratives of diversity' see Goldstein (2015).

[15]'Počela gradnja solitera: Srušena zaštićena zgrada, uklonjen stari jermenski spomenik', *mojnovisad.com*, 26 March 2016, available at: http://www.mojnovisad.com/vesti/pocela-gradnja-solitera-srusena-zasticena-zgrada-uklonjen-stari-jermenski-spomenik-id8655.html, accessed 28 April 2016.

ACTIVIST CITIZENSHIP IN SOUTHEAST EUROPE

that at one time Novi Sad was so multicultural that German and Latin words, alongside Serbian names written with Hungarian spelling, could all coexist on a single tombstone. In this context, maintaining public spaces where the multilingual heritage of the city is exposed and promoted is distinctive and potentially empowering from the perspective of minorities and those who care about their city's multi-ethnic character.

(Counter) space

The abovementioned *Serendipiti*, *Lemijeva*, and *Knjižara Gradska* were not the only places in Novi Sad that combined books and coffee with a social mission. *MaTerra Mesto* was a joint initiative of a second-hand bookshop—*Prostorija* (Room)—and Novi Sad Lesbian Organisation (NLO)—an organisation known not only for promotion of LGBT rights but also for its broader activist engagement in the city, for example, with questions of freedom of artistic expression or the rights of ethnic minorities. The house, formerly a film studio, was rented to the NLO for a symbolic amount of money by Želimir Žilnik, a well-known film director and public intellectual. Apart from the bookshop, a gallery managed by *Prostorija* and a café and Lesbian Reading Room Lepa Mlađenović (*Lesbejska Čitaonica Lepa Mlađenović*) both operated by the NLO, it also hosted a music studio used by a collective of local musicians and rooms for artistic residencies. At the time of the fieldwork, these rooms were occupied by a group of German artists who transformed books into sculptures and artistic installations, and worked on other artistic projects in the city. For the NLO, running the place together with a bookshop and turning it into an independent cultural centre was part of their activism, no less important than the protests or events that they would regularly organise. Their cooperation with a bookshop was by no means incidental. According to Jelena, an NLO leader, 'the books themselves and the idea of reading, I think one does not need to comment on how important they are'.[16] Like Roman and Lemi, and also the theorists of the role of education for democracy such as Martha Nussbaum (2010), Jelena had no doubts about the importance of promoting readership in general and in the arts and humanities in particular, for a healthy and peaceful democracy. Nussbaum argues that the arts and humanities play a crucial role in developing a society which is critical of populism, open to difference, and prepared for constructive political dialogue, because they develop both the skill and the inclination to ask questions, to take account of different perspectives, and to argue rationally (Nussbaum 2010, pp. 27–77). Focusing on such potential, long-term results rather than immediate and quantifiable outcomes motivated the NLO activists to cooperate with *Prostorija*. This cooperation was also about gaining a 'door' which was always open to the outside world and always welcoming, to bring people from the wider community to the activities and resources of the NLO. Jelena was convinced that cooperation with *Prostorija* was a good choice. She argued:

> It opens our space to the outside, to the street—this one, one with many passersby—Futoška .... It simply welcomes all types of people, there is no selection, there is no 'what is that?' [as compared to a lesbian organisation] .... What I want to say is that different types of people enter a bookshop. I think strategically it is good for the [entire] venue.[17]

[16]Interview #2, Jelena, one of the leaders of Novi Sad Lesbian Organisation, *MaTerra Mesto*, 26 February 2014.
[17]Interview #2, Jelena, one of the leaders of Novi Sad Lesbian Organisation, *MaTerra Mesto*, 26 February 2014.

ACTIVIST CITIZENSHIP IN SOUTHEAST EUROPE

While the café attracted mostly people who knew very well where they were going (a venue co-run by an activist lesbian organisation), the bookshop did serve as an entry point for people not connected in any way with the world of activism. Having entered, they would typically first browse the books in the first room (occupied exclusively by *Prostorija*), then notice the café and the fact that the place was a cultural centre offering exhibitions and events, and then find their way to the second room of books, where books sold by *Prostorija* were mingled with those of the Lesbian Reading Room and a collection of leftist and anarchist publications. It is hard to say whether such an encounter with a library full of books on social and political activism (in most cases, an encounter limited to noticing the existence of that library) had any lasting impact on such accidental visitors. One thing is certain, however: the accessibility of this space and its everyday existence made it different from the often over-professionalised, event-centred and, for many people, altogether inaccessible 'NGO world' (Belloni 2001; Grødeland 2006).

Other than being accessible, *MaTerra Mesto* was probably the most visibly socially engaged of the places studied. It hosted a number of exhibitions, presentations, lectures, and evenings of Serbian and Hungarian poetry, as well as providing artistic residencies, like that of the abovementioned German artists who made book-art. As one regular visitor to *MaTerra* told me, it was a place where 'one could come, sit, communicate, set up an organisation, [an] exhibition ... [and it was a] place created to be multicultural and multidisciplinary'.[18] In many respects, *MaTerra* was a counter-space, an 'initially utopian alternative to actually existing "real" space' (Lefebvre 1991 p. 349). It was a space exhibiting a number of distinguishing features: books on the LGBT community were not hidden but readily accessible; shelves full of books in Hungarian testified to the city's multi-ethnic character; people from the neighbourhood could meet seasoned activists; and joint readings of contemporary Serbian and Hungarian poetry took place where everyone spoke their own language and each word, not only the poetry but also comments and discussion, was translated. This space developed its path towards self-sustainability[19] against the belief, widespread among NGO activists, that external funding is necessary for socially engaged work to happen regularly and achieve its goals.[20] It was a space that, like other 'everyday utopias', revealed its own possibility 'against the assumption that anything outside the "normal" is impossible' (Cooper 2014, p. 4) and in effect empowered its visitors to keep planning and engaging in further activism.[21]

[18]Interview #14, anonymous middle-aged Novi Sad activist who regularly visited *MaTerra Mesto*, Novi Sad, 20 June 2014.

[19]*MaTerra Mesto* was established with the help of a small grant which the NLO received from its long-standing partner organisation from Sweden, with the aim of developing into a self-sustainable entity. The place had only existed for five months before the institutions and collectives using it were expelled on the premise of conflicting legal claims to the property that they occupied. Although such a short period was not enough to develop full self-sustainability, *MaTerra* was about 'half-way' to it when it was closed and the gradual development of its turnover suggested it would have developed into a completely self-sustainable entity in the not too distant future (follow up Skype interview with interviewee #2, Jelena, one of the leaders of Novi Sad Lesbian Organisation, *MaTerra Mesto*, 12 May 2016).

[20]I base this observation on my conversations with NGO/charity activists in Poland, Hungary, Serbia, and the UK. When, asked about my research, I explain that I focus on organisations/groups which exist without external funding, this is typically met with a mixture of surprise and scepticism, often manifested in the question 'But, how do they manage?'. Leaders of 'typical NGOs' (Goldstein 2016, p. 142) in particular see applying for project grants as an unfortunate (because of its unpredictability, effort needed to prepare applications, and in their eyes often awkward donor requirements) but still most readily available and reasonable way of fundraising for their organisations.

[21]From just a few informal follow up talks conducted in 2016, I learned that at least one frequent visitor to *MaTerra* had started her own, self-sustainable activist space and that evenings of Hungarian–Serbian poetry which started at *MaTerra* continued to take place regularly in various venues across the city.

ACTIVIST CITIZENSHIP IN SOUTHEAST EUROPE

Beyond books and coffee

Despite all the opportunities relating to combining books and a café/meeting-space with social engagement, this is by no means the only possible form of everyday activism. One example of a not-for-profit initiative in Novi Sad which is neither an NGO nor a typical protest movement—and has nothing to do with either books or coffee—is *Free Team Pokret* (Free Team Movement), a 'group of friends' who organise different types of free initiatives.[22] They give away 'Free Hugs' and organise 'Free Salsa', 'Free Yoga', 'Free Film Screenings', and other free events. Such activities may sound trivial, but it can be argued that most of these events are important to the local community and could potentially attract international donor funding. Free salsa, yoga, dodgeball, and cinema keep young people occupied, away from drugs, alcohol, and other problems; on top of that, such activities facilitate new friendships and 'networks of trust' (Putnam 1992). In addition to organising different types of free activities for the general public, *Free Team Pokret* has also organised small performances and games for children with autism and those suffering from cancer, and they regularly work with children and adults with Down syndrome.[23] However, like Lemi and Roman, who had the potential to make their businesses more profitable but decided not to do so, the people from *Free Team Pokret* have decided not to make it an NGO or look for sponsors, so as not to compromise their principles. They used an argument similar to that of Roman and Lemi: why would they spend their time translating their website into English, looking for sponsors, writing evaluation reports, and other such tasks when they could use that time doing what they want to do? As one of *Free Team Pokret*'s (informal) leaders told me in an interview:

> Many organisations have offices, and there are two–five people in the office every day, but what are they doing? … If nothing comes out, they get paid to be there, you know, come at eight, leave at four, it's a work day. It's not an activity in the same sense as an action on the street. I'm a street person …. We organise but we are not an organisation.[24]

Consequently, they have chosen to organise events with no budget or on very low budgets and, when necessary, earn funds to support them by their own work.

Many of the events organised by *Free Team Pokret* seemed to be about setting an example. Rather than organise seminars or training on living without alcohol, the importance of trust or 'non-violent communication', instead, they would organise a vegetarian meal, not accompanied by alcohol, in a flat where several of them lived, to which they would invite young people whom they had recently met. One such meal which I observed in November 2015 was followed by games. It was an excellent example of an encounter characterised by fun, friendship, and respect, without alcohol or drugs. For *Free Team Pokret*'s new friends, this example, which they themselves had a chance to experience, might have been not less (or maybe actually more) convincing than the leaflets or training they could have received from a professional NGO promoting the same values.

---

[22]Quote from interview #21, anonymous interview with two of *Free Team Pokret*'s informal leaders, Novi Sad, 17 August 2010. For more examples of what could be seen as everyday activism see, for example, Jacobsson (2015), Polanska (2013), Polanska and Chimiak (2016).

[23]'Humanitarni Rad', *Haos Animatori*, 2015, available at: http://www.haosanimatori.com/avanture/#humanitarni-rad, accessed 12 May 2016.

[24]Interview #21, anonymous interview with two of *Free Team Pokret*'s informal leaders, Novi Sad, 17 August 2010.

Fun and play have always been at the centre of *Free Team Pokret* activities. This should not be seen as insignificant and not connected with activism. As Asef Bayat argues:

> Fun, whether foreign and commoditized or indigenous and innocent, can be subversive …. Fun disturbs exclusivist doctrinal authority because, as source of instantaneous fulfilment, it represents a powerful rival archetype, one that stands against discipline, rigid structures, single discourse, and monopoly of truth. It subsists on spontaneity and breaths in the air of flexibility, openness, and critique—the very ethics that clash with the rigid one-dimensional discourse of doctrinal authority. (Bayat 2010, p. 148)

In addition to this everyday activism, *Free Team Pokret* also engages in even more obviously political and activist actions. In December 2011, approximately 100 citizens of Novi Sad, coordinated by a well-organised but not formally registered collective of NGOs, associations, informal groups, and individuals, in what they called 'illegal but legitimate' action, broke into, cleaned, and occupied former army barracks to convert them into *Društveni Centar*—a social and cultural centre. *Free Team Pokret* was at the site with music, from a speaker plugged into a small, petrol-powered electricity generator, and offering free hugs.

Hipster activists?

At this point one may think that the people involved in the work of *Free Team Pokret* or the others mentioned in this essay are 'hipster activists' engaged in a 'comfort-zone activism': that they do things not-for-profit because economic circumstances are not important to them.[25] According to my observations and interviews, the opposite was true: their activism was often at a high personal cost. Some of them would supplement their activist work with another 'real' job (or multiple small jobs), others would simply live on a shoestring. In any case, their work was not informed by a studied indifference to material comfort underpinned by affluence, but rather the readiness to earn less, or at times to not earn at all, in order to engage in what they believed was more important than profit. It was this readiness—far from obvious in a country undergoing an economic transition in which success is often measured in one's ability to become rich—that allows us to see their commitment as radical.

Networks and entanglements

Historically, Central European literary coffeehouses, precursors of today's bookshop-cafés, created, as Steven Beller argues, a '"free-floating" network, of connected "spaces of freedom" that provided the setting, the space of Central European culture, making that space inclusive of many points of view, a pluralistic space, open to the possibilities and varieties of human thought' (Beller 2013, p. 57). In many respects, the bookshop-cafés which I have listed so far created such a 'free floating network' of independent spaces; however, they were not the

---

[25]This argument is related to a similar one, that western Balkan civil societies are a 'middle-class phenomenon' (Grødeland 2006, p. 239) and thus are detached from local communities (Belloni 2001, p. 177; Stubbs 1997, p. 58). In my earlier investigation of civil society, broadly defined, in Novi Sad and Mostar, through quantitative data from over 70 NGOs, associations, informal groups, and movements, I was able to show that in reality different strata of the local population are well represented within the civic sector (Goldstein 2013, pp. 146–89). It is also instructive to ask whether, in twenty-first-century Europe, terms such as 'middle class' or 'hipster' do not encompass too broad a variety of circumstances to remain useful.

only ones of this type. *Radio Café 021*, a space combining a bookshop and a café with an independent local radio station and a foundation, was another. The place was very openly socially engaged. The radio presented itself, first of all, as a place where 'we can do some minimal corrections of the world in which we live'.[26] Here, as in *Serendipiti*, *Lemijeva*, *Knjižara Gradska*, and *MaTerra*, books were carefully chosen and this choice was 'part of a larger project',[27] a project of 'not accepting cultural and political populism'.[28] Two other similar places were *Izba*, not a bookshop but a café-bar with a small art gallery filled with books (not for sale) that were easily accessible to anyone interested, and *NuBlu*, once home of *Prostorija* and now a café-bar run by a *de facto* cooperative of three young women who rent part of the space to a bookshop and organise a full programme of recreational activities.[29]

This 'free-floating network' was very important for activists in Novi Sad. It offered free space for meetings whenever funding for office space ran out; space for events when no funding to rent a place was available or when space was needed quickly and going through the process of applying for grants was out of the question; and many opportunities to network, 'spontaneously' meet other activists, and discuss questions related to politics and social engagement. The importance of this network for a particular organisation can be illustrated through the example of *Ogledalo* (Mirror), an independent activist theatre group. *Ogledalo* is known for approaching questions of discrimination and violence against women, physically impaired, and other oppressed groups through theatre performances, workshops, and festivals and happenings in the city space. The theatre has frequently changed offices and places to rehearse and perform throughout the 20-plus years of its existence. When at one point it lost its office altogether, its meetings moved to *Knjižara Gradska*, *NuBlu*, and some of the other aforementioned sites. When in 2012 it needed a performance space, the group was given the opportunity to use the basement hall of *Izba*. A couple of years later, the leader of the theatre was hired by *Radio 021* to work in the radio's newly established foundation. There she brought in her experience and contacts while gaining a new environment and resources for her activism. Other people engaged in the theatre's work met regularly in *Izba* and in other places within this 'free-floating network'.

This network was not a network in the sense of interconnectedness: even if owners of these different places knew each other, they did not formally cooperate. It was, rather, a network of spaces offering autonomy from both state and international donors (with their own policies, ideas, limitations, and interests), spaces similar to what Hakim Bey (2011) calls 'Temporary Autonomous Zones' (TAZs). According to Bey, a Temporary Autonomous Zone

> is like an uprising which does not engage directly with the State, a guerrilla operation which liberates an area (of land, of time, of imagination) and then dissolves itself to re-form elsewhere/elsewhen [sic], *before* the State can crush it. Because the State is concerned primarily with Simulation rather than substance, the TAZ can 'occupy' these areas clandestinely and carry on its festal purposes for quite a while in relative peace. Perhaps certain small TAZs have lasted whole lifetimes because they went unnoticed .... (Bey 2011, p. 70)

---

[26]'O nama', *Radio 021*, available at: http://www.021.rs/O-nama.html, accessed 25 March 2015.
[27]Interview #16, a manager of *Radio Café 021*, 20 June 2014.
[28]'O nama', *Radio 021*, available at: http://www.021.rs/O-nama.html, accessed 25 March 2015.
[29]While the place had formal management structures required by law, the three women said that they actually took decisions and operated as if the place was a cooperative (interview #10, the three owners of *NuBlu*, 18 June 2014).

ACTIVIST CITIZENSHIP IN SOUTHEAST EUROPE

Through such a lens, *Free Team Pokret* constitutes a TAZ, a type of discreet activist resistance which does not engage directly with the state. It is one which fulfils different needs from bookshop-cafés but is similar in the claims it makes (opposition to consumerism and the commercialisation of public space, concern for the education of future generations, opposition to political and cultural populism). Similarly to bookshop-cafés, it might be facilitating activism, but it is not merely a 'preamble' to a 'more real' activism. It is activism in its own right, different from the more visible activism of NGOs or within protest movements, but not necessarily any lesser for it.

Activist citizens

In March 2016 a construction company demolished the last Armenian gravestone in Novi Sad. An informal group called *Pokret Uličnih Čitača* (Movement of Street Readers) was one of the first groups to protest, which they did by reading Armenian poetry aloud in public where the gravestone once stood. At the forefront of *Pokret Uličnih Čitača* were Lemi, his wife, and some of the readers (Lemi refused to call them 'customers') who came regularly to the bookshop. This illustrates two important characteristics of the (counter) spaces presented in this essay. Firstly, for the engaged individuals, more often than not, they constitute just another type of activism, often practised in parallel to other forms of activism, such as participation in protests and NGO work. Indeed, Roman, the owner of *Serendipiti*, was also a founding member of the Association of Publishers of Vojvodina (established in 2001) and of Centre for New Media (established in 2008). When I asked if he had a plan for if *Serendipiti* went bankrupt, he replied without hesitation that he might engage in the 'promotion of the civic society [*građanskog društva*] and human freedoms, in some other way'.[30] Similarly, Lemi, when asked about his past, replied: 'I have been in the bookstore business already for 25 years. Before that I was, in some other way, stimulating [cultural life in] this city ... through, through ... play' and went on to describe his past activist experience.[31] For people like Lemi or Roman, running their place was not a 'warm up' before real activism, but activism proper, in a form which they believed appropriate.

Secondly, these spaces should not be looked upon as a struggle by only a few engaged owners and managers. Most of these spaces were co-created by a number of people whose joint efforts brought them into being and who often continued to co-create them by employing solidarist forms of management. In some cases, such as that of *MaTerra Mesto* and *NuBlu*, their existence was facilitated by the owner of the venue who agreed to rent it for a very low fee because she or he believed that it was important for such space to exist in the city. Drawing on Isin, we can see such acts as acts of citizenship because 'to act, then, is neither arriving at a scene nor fleeing from it, but actually engaging in its creation. With that creative act the actor also creates herself/himself as the agent responsible for the scene created' (Isin 2008, p. 27). Similarly, all of those people who allow *Free Team Pokret* to use various spaces across the city (in parks, schools, and universities) free of charge, sometimes breaching the formal rules of hiring these spaces, practise their own (activist) citizenship through these acts and become co-responsible for making *Free Team Pokret* the (counter) space that it is. Finally, the customers/readers/participants co-create them and facilitate their existence by choosing these spaces rather than others (which many do very consciously) and by actively engaging in their

[30]Interview #8, Roman, owner of *Serendipiti* bookshop-café, Novi Sad, 18 June 2014.
[31]Interview #6, Lemi (Miljenko), owner of *Lemijeva Knjižara*, Novi Sad, 17 June 2014.

activities. For *MaTerra Mesto*, *Lemijeva*, and *Free Team Pokret*, all of which combined very limited resources with ambitious goals and intensive programmes, activism was part of their everyday existence, powered by 'an interaction between friendship, ideas, and ideals' (Bilić 2011, p. 316), or something that Hirschman (1984) would call 'social energy'.

In this context, we can see activism as something not limited by the lifespan of a particular bookshop-café or another initiative, group, NGO, or movement. For those involved, activism is a lifelong affair for which different initiatives and spaces function as 'sites' of citizenship (Isin 2009, p. 370). Individuals may move from one to another, be involved in several at the same time and take on different roles: that of formal leader, informal facilitator, owner, supporter, or participant. Thus, the lack of sustainability of specific initiatives should not be lamented. Despite being temporal, in their multiplicity they provide an avenue for engagement and, hopefully, change.

Conclusion

This essay has considered forms of activism that are different from both professionalised and often donor-dependent NGOs, and independent, but usually short-lived, protest movements. The forms considered are not networks of the type seen by Stubbs (2012) as generational precursors to NGO and protest-movement activism in the Western Balkans. Rather, these are spaces which exist in parallel to NGOs and movements and constitute an alternative way of performing activist citizenship. What makes these spaces unique are their day-to-day operations shaped by the social activism of people who constitute them. For some of these people (for example, members of *Free Team Pokret*), these activisms form an alternative to NGO work, while for others (for example, Roman, the owner of *Serendipiti*) they complement it. For many, they go hand-in-hand with active engagement in movements when opportunity or need arises. The engaged individuals are activist citizens (Isin 2009): people who want to change their local reality and who, in their 'militant commitment' (Isin 2009, p. 383), move between different available forms of activism or create new ones.

Still, it might be intuitive to think of the bookshop-cafés or 'free' initiatives analysed in this essay as spaces for activism, as a 'preamble' to activism, rather than activism proper. Theories of counter-spaces (Lefebvre 1991) and of everyday utopias (Cooper 2014) help us understand these activisms as spaces (physical or not) which, by creating alternative realities, standing in opposition to commodification of public space and to populism, nationalism, or xenophobia, constitute activism on their own and not merely spaces for other, supposedly more 'real', activism. The (counter) spaces studied were in most cases completely independent of NGOs and movements, but at the same time strongly inter-connected with both. For some of the NGOs and movements and also for individual activists, they provided an infrastructure for activist work and/or for more day-to-day micro-politics or infrapolitics (Scott 1990; Goldfarb 2006) in which the activists engaged. This combination of resources and ethos often translated into real-world actions carried out by NGOs and movements. Everyday activism appeared to be a catalyser for other activisms while at the same time being a form of activism in its own right.[32]

---

[32]It is important to note that this essay assessed a range of, by-and-large, progressive activisms. It is instructive to ask whether it is inevitable that everyday activism is progressive, or whether similar dynamics could (or perhaps already) happen within the sphere of nationalist, xenophobic, and other 'uncivil activisms' (as discussed in Kopecký & Mudde (2012)). Further analytic and empirical research is needed to answer this question.

ACTIVIST CITIZENSHIP IN SOUTHEAST EUROPE

Recognising discreet, hard-to-notice forms of activism like those analysed in this essay might be particularly important in the context of (South) Eastern Europe. As Alla Marchenko noted in her article, 'one of the most common visions of civic engagement in Europe is that countries of the post-Socialist bloc demonstrate a relatively low level of civic engagement' (Marchenko 2016, p. 12). Perhaps the problem lies not only in the civic engagement itself but also in the way we assess it. A focus on the everyday rather than on quantifiable (NGOs) or extraordinary (protest movements) activism could bring new insights to our understanding of activism in the region.

ORCID

Piotr Goldstein **(iD)** http://orcid.org/0000-0002-5068-3263

References

Balibar, É. (2004) *We, the People of Europe?: Reflections on Transnational Citizenship* (Princeton, NJ, Princeton University Press).

Bayat, A. (1997) 'Un-Civil Society: The Politics of the "Informal People"', *Third World Quarterly*, 1, 18.

Bayat, A. (2010) *Life as Politics: How Ordinary People Change the Middle East* (Amsterdam, Amsterdam University Press).

Beller, S. (2013) 'The Jew Belongs in the Coffeehouse: Jews, Central Europe and Modernity', in Ashby, C., Gronberg, T. & Shaw-Miller, S. (eds) *The Viennese Café and Fin-de-siècle Culture* (New York, NY, & Oxford, Berghahn Books).

Belloni, R. (2001) 'Civil Society and Peacebuilding in Bosnia and Herzegovina', *Journal of Peace Research*, 2, 38.

Bey, H. (2011) *TAZ: The Temporary Autonomous Zone* (Seattle, WA, Pacific Publishing Studio).

Bieber, F. & Winterhagen, J. (2006) *Ethnic Violence in Vojvodina: Glitch or Harbinger of Conflicts to Come?*, ECMI Working Paper 27, available at: http://www.ecmi.de/uploads/media/working_paper_27.pdf, accessed 2 April 2013.

Bilić, B. (2011) 'A Concept that is Everything and Nothing: Why Not to Study (post-)Yugoslav Anti-war and Pacifist Contention from a Civil Society Perspective', *Sociologija*, 3, 53.

Bourdieu, P. (1984) *Distinction: A Social Critique of the Judgement of Taste* (Cambridge, MA, Harvard University Press).

Bourdieu, P. & Passeron, J.-C. (1990) *Reproduction in Education, Society and Culture* (2nd edn) (London, Sage).

Carens, J. H. (1986) 'Rights and Duties in an Egalitarian Society', *Political Theory*, 1, 14.

Cooper, D. (2014) *Everyday Utopias: The Conceptual Life of Promising Spaces* (Durham, NC, & London, Duke University Press).

Cvetičanin, P., Nedeljković, J. & Krstić, N. (2012) 'The Cultural Map of Serbia or the Reconstruction of the Field of Cultural Practices in Serbia', in Cvetičanin, P. (ed.) *Social and Cultural Capital in Serbia* (Niš, Centre for Empirical Cultural Studies of South-East Europe).

Deigh, J. (1988) 'On Rights and Responsibilities', *Law and Philosophy*, 2, 7.

Eyal, G., Szelényi, I. & Townsley, E. (1998) *Making Capitalism Without Capitalists* (London & New York, NY, Verso).

Fagan, A. & Sircar, I. (2013) 'Environmental Movement Activism in the Western Balkans: Evidence from Bosnia-Herzegovina', in Jacobsson, K. & Saxonberg, S. (eds).

Fuller, S., Kershaw, P. & Pulkingham, J. (2008) 'Constructing "Active Citizenship": Single Mothers, Welfare, and the Logics of Voluntarism', *Citizenship Studies*, 2, 12.

Goldfarb, J. C. (1980) *The Persistence of Freedom: The Sociological Implications of Polish Student Theater* (Boulder, CO, Westview Press).

Goldfarb, J. C. (2006) *The Politics of Small Things: The Power of the Powerless in Dark Times* (Chicago, IL, University of Chicago Press).

Goldfarb, J. C. (2008) 'The Sociology of Micro-politics: An Examination of a Neglected Field of Political Action in the Middle East and Beyond', *Sociology Compass*, 6, 2.

Goldstein, P. (2011) 'Are NGO Activists in Mostar and Novi Sad All Middle-Class? (And Why Does it Matter?)', in Dranidis, D., Kapoulas, A. & Vivas, A. (eds) *Infusing Research and Knowledge in South-East Europe* (Thessaloniki, South-East European Research Centre).

ACTIVIST CITIZENSHIP IN SOUTHEAST EUROPE

Goldstein, P. (2013) *Building Bridges: NGOs, Associations, Movements, Facebook Groups, and the State of Civil Society in Mostar and Novi Sad*, PhD thesis, University of Manchester.

Goldstein, P. (2015) 'Grassroots Narratives and Practices of Diversity in Mostar and Novi Sad', in Matejskova, T. & Antonsich, M. (eds) *Governing through Diversity: Migration Societies in Post-Multiculturalist Times* (London, Palgrave Macmillan).

Goldstein, P. (2016) 'Everyday Active Citizenship the Balkan Way: Local Civil Society and the Opportunities for "Bridge Building" in Two Post-Yugoslav Cities', in Valentine, G. & Vieten, U. M. (eds) *Cartographies of Differences* (Frankfurt am Main, Peter Lang).

Grødeland, Á. B. (2006) 'Public Perceptions of Non-Governmental Organisations in Serbia, Bosnia & Herzegovina, and Macedonia', *Communist and Post-Communist Studies*, 2, 39.

Helms, E. (2003) 'Women as Agents of Ethnic Reconciliation? Women's NGOs and International Intervention in Postwar Bosnia-Herzegovina', *Women's Studies International Forum*, 1, 26.

Hirschman, A. O. (1984) *Getting Ahead Collectively: Grassroots Experiences in Latin America* (New York, NY, Pergamon Press).

Horvat, S. & Štiks, I. (2012) 'Welcome to the Desert of Transition! Post-Socialism, the European Union and a New Left in the Balkans', *Monthly Review*, 10, 63.

Isin, E. F. (2008) 'Theorizing Acts of Citizenship', in Isin, E. F. & Nielsen, G. M. (eds) *Acts of Citizenship* (London, Palgrave Macmillan).

Isin, E. F. (2009) 'Citizenship in Flux: The Figure of the Activist Citizen', *Subjectivity*, 29.

Jacobsson, K. (ed.) (2015) *Urban Grassroots Movements in Central and Eastern Europe* (London & New York, NY, Routledge).

Jacobsson, K. & Saxonberg, S. (eds) (2013) *Beyond NGO-ization: The Development of Social Movements in Central and Eastern Europe* (Farnham, Ashgate).

Jeffrey, A. (2007) 'The Geopolitical Framing of Localized Struggles: NGOs in Bosnia and Herzegovina', *Development and Change*, 2, 38.

Kearns, A. (1995) 'Active Citizenship and Local Governance: Political and Geographical Dimensions', *Political Geography*, 2, 14.

Kopecký, P. & Mudde, C. (eds) (2012) *Uncivil Society? Contentious Politics in Post-communist Europe* (London, Routledge).

Lefebvre, H. (1991) *The Production of Space* (Oxford & Cambridge, MA, Blackwell).

Mac Ginty, R. (2014) 'Everyday Peace: Bottom-up and Local Agency in Conflict-affected Societies', *Security Dialogue*, 6, 45.

Marchenko, A. (2016) 'Civic Activities in Eastern Europe: Links with Democratic Political Culture', *East European Politics*, 1, 32.

Marinetto, M. (2003) 'Who Wants to be an Active Citizen?: The Politics and Practice of Community Involvement', *Sociology*, 1, 37.

Nussbaum, M. C. (2010) *Not for Profit: Why Democracy Needs Humanities* (Princeton, NJ, Princeton University Press).

Offe, C. (1991) 'Capitalism by Democratic Design? Democratic Theory Facing the Triple Transition in East Central Europe', *Social Research*, 4, 58.

Polanska, D. V. (2013) 'Grassroots Mobilizations Do Occur in Post-socialist Civil Society', *Baltic Worlds*, 6, 2.

Polanska, D. V. & Chimiak, G. (2016) 'Organizing Without Organizations: On Informal Social Activism in Poland', *International Journal of Sociology and Social Policy*, 9/10, 36.

Putnam, R. D. (1992) *Making Democracy Work: Civic Traditions in Modern Italy* (Princeton, NJ, Princeton University Press).

Putnam, R. D. (2000) *Bowling Alone: The Collapse and Revival of American Community* (New York, NY, Simon and Schuster).

Salmenniemi, S. (ed.) (2012) *Rethinking Class in Russia* (Farnham, Ashgate).

Sardelić, J. (2013) '"Communist Zombies": Notes on Active Citizenship in Slovenia', *Citizenship in Southeast Europe*, available at: http://www.citsee.eu/blog/"communist-zombies"-notes-active-citizenship-slovenia, accessed 24 October 2014.

Scott, J. C. (1990) *Domination and the Arts of Resistance: Hidden Transcripts* (New Haven, CT, Yale University Press).

Statistical Office of the Republic of Serbia (2012) '2011 Census of Population, Households and Dwellings in The Republic of Serbia: Ethnicity—Data by Municipalities and Cities', available at: http://media.popis2011. stat.rs/2012/Nacionalna.pripadnost-Ethnicity.pdf, accessed 15 September 2017.

Stevanović, S. (2013) *Arhitektura Novog Sada u periodu 1945–2013: potraga za identitetom*, unpublished Master's Thesis, University of Novi Sad.

Štiks, I. & Horvat, S. (2014) 'The New Balkan Revolts: From Protests to Plenums, and Beyond', *Open Democracy*, available at: https://www.opendemocracy.net/can-europe-make-it/igor-štiks-srećko-horvat/ new-balkan-revolts-from-protests-to-plenums-and-beyond, accessed 24 October 2014.

Štiks, I. & Horvat, S. (2015) 'Radical Politics in the Dessert of Transition', in Horvat, S. & Štiks, I. (eds) *Welcome to the Desert of Post-Socialism* (London & New York, NY, Verso).

Stubbs, P. (1997) 'NGO Work with Forced Migrants in Croatia: Lineages of a Global Middle Class?', *International Peacekeeping*, 4, 4.

Stubbs, P. (2012) 'Networks, Organisations, Movements: Narratives and Shapes of Three Waves of Activism in Croatia', *Polemos: Journal of Interdisciplinary Research on War and Peace*, 30, XV.

Tonkiss, F. (2005) *Space, the City and Social Theory* (Cambridge & Malden, MA, Polity).

The Role of the Feminist Movement Participation during the Winter 2012 Mobilisations in Romania

ALEXANDRA ANA

Abstract

Feminist activism is only at an early stage in Romania, yet feminist activists have been able to mobilise mass street protests over the past few years. By looking at the 2012 mobilisations in Romania, this essay aims to understand how feminist movement participation affected the dynamics of these protest events. It is argued that feminist activists have drawn attention to some of the current difficulties faced by women in bringing to the fore alternative voices and messages and resisting patriarchal modes of mobilisation.

AS A RESPONSE TO THE FINANCIAL AND ECONOMIC CRISIS THAT started in 2008, the Romanian government adopted some of the most stringent austerity measures in Europe (Stoicu 2012). Protests organised by trade unions and civil society actors failed to win popular support or to affect public policies. Grievances and discontent related to perceived social injustices increased during 2010 and 2011 as a result of the high social costs of anti-crisis policies (Tătar 2015). The protests in 2012 occurred after a long period of disillusionment and hostility towards political participation and engagement in the public sphere during the post-communist transition (Tătar 2015; Margarit 2016). Unemployed people, pensioners, civil society organisations, environmental activists, feminists, students, academics and football supporters[1] all took to the streets in January 2012 in different cities in Romania, including its capital, Bucharest, where protests took place in the University Square. These groups were united in their general discontent with the political class and governance (Stoica 2012).

After 1989, Romanian civil society was considered weak, with low potential for political mobilisation. Political alienation (Tătar 2011a) was translated into a diminished sense of civic engagement, a lack of interest in politics, and a mistrust of political elites, as shown by reduced expectations regarding the efficiency of the political class and their accountability

---

The research for this essay was conducted during my MA at Université Libre de Bruxelles.

[1] Football supporters participated from the beginning at the University Square protests to support Raed Arafat. The gendarmerie associated the violence during the first week of protests with football supporters who 'set fire to the flags and, after breaking the windows of a florist, threw pieces of glass towards the gendarmes' ('Romania in a 7-a zi de proteste. VIOLENTE in Piata Universitatii: 5 raniti si 40 de retineri. VIDEO', *stirileprotv.ro*, 19 January 2012, available at: http://stirileprotv.ro/stiri/actualitate/mitingul-usl-si-protestele-de-la-universitate-scot-in-strada-un-numar-mult-mai-mare-de-jandarmi.html, accessed 17 October 2017.

© 2017 University of Glasgow

ACTIVIST CITIZENSHIP IN SOUTHEAST EUROPE

(Tătar 2011b). Moreover, a strong anti-communist backlash crystallised within the public sphere, academia and the mass media. Intellectual understandings of post-communist realities were thus confined within an economic and political liberalist frame (Ban 2015, p. 643).

During the first two decades of post-socialism, in the 1990s and 2000s, rates of participation in elections and other forms of political activity in Romania were amongst the lowest in Eastern Europe. According to World Values Survey (WVS) data, turnout for parliamentary elections steadily decreased, dropping from 86% in 1989 to 41.7% in 2012. The trend continued after 2012, with a 39.5% turnout in the 2016 elections. In 1994, 18% of people surveyed attended a peaceful demonstration, but only 6% did so in 2009. Participation in unofficial strikes[2] also decreased, from 6% in 1994 to 1% in 2009; and the percentage who reported signing a petition decreased from 14% in 1994 to 8% in 2009. More generally, interest in politics during this period was low and declining, according to WVS.[3]

This general disillusionment with politics has been augmented by harsh austerity measures. In 2010, the Boc government, endorsed by President Traian Băsescu, imposed a series of tax increases and major cuts in public sector wages, pensions, and social welfare benefits.[4] Furthermore, at the end of 2011, the government introduced a new law which sought to reform the healthcare system through privatisation, including hospitals, and the deregulation of the health insurance market with reduced state subsidies for health benefits. Raed Arafat, the Under-Secretary of State for Health, vehemently opposed these reforms, fearing that the legislation would greatly undermine public health services. Under pressure from President Băsescu, Arafat tendered his resignation. His departure prompted public indignation and a series of protests in January 2012 (for a detailed chronology of these protests, see Appendix 2). While Băsescu's public criticism of Arafat is widely seen as the catalyst for the winter 2012 protests, the motivations of participants also included low quality of life, abuses by state institutions—especially the gendarmerie,[5] and calls to remove Băsescu (Presadă 2012). Police repression of protesters further impelled citizens to take to the streets. Their initial claims widened in scope and revealed discontent with more fundamental problems faced by Romanian society, from the lack of access to public goods and services, to corruption and the quality of democracy, the environment, gender inequality, and police violence and repression. The winter 2012 mobilisations not only produced actual outcomes in terms of changes to political leadership—Arafat was reinstated and Prime Minister Boc resigned together with the entire government in February—and public goods and services, such as the withdrawal of the law-project aiming

---

[2]Strikes that are not approved by a trade union.

[3]The data come from the World Values Survey 1981–2014 time series. See World Values Survey 1981–2014, available at: http://www.worldvaluessurvey.org, accessed 6 October 2017.

[4]Salaries in the public sector were cut by 25% and pensions by 15%. VAT was increased by 5% and there were additional budget cuts to education, health, and social assistance.

[5]The Association for the Defense of Human Rights in Romania—the Helsinki Committee (APADOR-CH) registered numerous complaints about gendarmes abuses in Bucharest and some of these cases are presented on their website. Abuses concerned people being loaded into police vans and brought to the police station where they were detained. This happened after those who were stopped and searched presented their IDs and could be identified. See, 'De ce o banală identificare se lasă cu privare de libertate?', APADOR-CH, available at: http://www.apador.org/publicatii/proiect/files/de-ce-o-banala-identificare-se-transforma-in-arestare/index.html, accessed 11 October 2017; 'Narcis Iordache: M-am opus amprentării și fotografierii', APADOR-CH, available at: http://www.apador.org/publicatii/proiect/files/narcis-iordache-m-am-opus-amprentarii-si-fotografierii/index. html, accessed 11 October 2017.

ACTIVIST CITIZENSHIP IN SOUTHEAST EUROPE

TABLE 1
KEY PROTEST DEMANDS AND ASSOCIATED SLOGANS

Demand/grievance	Slogan
POLITICAL SYSTEM: dismissal of President Băsescu, Prime Minister Boc, and the government	'Get out, you miserable dog!'
PUBLIC GOODS AND SERVICES: withdrawal of the law aiming to reform healthcare; increased budget for social welfare services	'We want hospitals, not cathedrals'; 'Money for research, not for cathedrals'; 'We want daycare centres and kindergartens not kerbs and other airs and graces'; 'You drank away the culture budget'
CORRUPTION: corruption of political class	'Please, excuse us, we do not produce as much as you are stealing'; 'We don't want governments run by corporations any longer'
ENVIRONMENT: reversing the policies related to the exploitation of the Roşia Montană gold mine	'You took a big bribe for Roşia Montană'; 'We want cyanide for the dictatorship' [NB: the gold mining operation would require tonnes of cyanide]; 'Roşia Montană is not for charity'
VIOLENCE: denouncing police violence against the protestors	'No violence'; 'You have cudgels, we have empty hands'
CALLS FOR MOBILISATION	'Get out of the house, if you care'; 'Another revolution, for the constitution'
CITIZENSHIP	'Indignant citizens demand to be respected'; 'Wake up, Romanian women!'
FEMINISM: denouncing the patriarchal state; demanding rights and equality of opportunity; and demands for childcare infrastructure and social welfare policies	'Our glass is full/ This state is misogynistic'; 'A woman citizen asks for rights and equality of opportunity'

to reform the health care system, but also opened a new cycle of protest. The main protestor demands and examples of corresponding slogans are illustrated in Table 1.

While the diversity of issues and demands was framed in public debates and the media as being a weak point of these mobilisations, revealing incoherence and lack of unity, protesters perceived the variety of claims as complementary, with University Square in Bucharest functioning as a space to share different perspectives. The diverse claims mirrored the diverse participants, including discontented individuals, non-governmental organisation (NGO) activists, anarchists, environmentalists, feminists, football supporters, nationalists, royalists, poor people, the unemployed, and students. While some groups had a particular identity and voice, such as environmentalists, feminists, football supporters, and anti-ACTA activists,[6] others, such as trade unionists and students, were united simply by their general discontent (Presadă 2012). Whilst NGO activists had been involved in small-scale protests since 2000, and trade-union members had participated in labour-related demonstrations, there were others who had never protested before the 2012 University Square mobilisation. Nevertheless, the layout of University Square, which is crossed by a large boulevard, split the protesters into two groups from the beginning (Bulai 2012). One group, composed primarily of young people, students and academics, ecologists, and feminists, protested at the Danube fountain. The other group, comprising older people, along with retired, unemployed, or precariously

---

[6]The signature by the EU and many of its Member States of the Anti-counterfeiting Trade Agreement (ACTA) entailed a wave of protests all over Europe. A protest against ACTA was organised on 11 February in different cities in Romania, including in University Square in Bucharest. The protesters considered that the agreement could affect fundamental rights such as privacy and freedom of expression.

employed workers, protested in front of the National Theatre. Civil society organisations initially engaged with the mobilisations, but soon withdrew their official institutional support, while leaving members free to participate as individual citizens.[7] This change came about due to protesters' concerns that the mobilisations would be 'co-opted' by NGOs or political parties, after discussions during one of the protesters' General Assemblies.[8] The protests were seen as a grassroots movement, an instance of unorganised civil society, to be distinguished from an apathetic organised one, associated with formal NGOs, engaging mostly in transactional activism and having a low capacity for public mobilisation (Tarrow & Petrova 2007). Table 2 summarises the main characteristics of the 2012 protests.

These protests were the first time that feminist activists had made their voice heard within a popular mobilisation in Romania. However, existing studies (Stoica & Mihăilescu 2012; Stoica 2012; Presadă 2012) largely ignored the influence of feminist participation and discourses of justice on the University Square protests. To fill the gap, this study complements existing understandings of the winter 2012 mobilisations in Romania by analysing the role and participation of the feminist movement in affecting the dynamics of mobilisation. Feminism as a movement exists not just separately, but also in interaction with other social movements, and is characterised by a multiplicity of facets, various collective representations, and dynamic boundaries. The aim of this research is to show how feminist movement participation influenced and challenged the dynamics of the 2012 anti-austerity protests in Romania.

Along with the general analytical tools provided by the dynamics of contention approach (DCA), I draw on the theoretical framework advanced by recognition and redistribution theories, namely the 'perspectival dualism' of Nancy Fraser and Axel Honneth (2003), complemented by Myra Marx Ferree and William Gamson's (2003) insights on power relations and empowerment. These theories inform my analysis of how feminist perspectives influenced the understandings of citizenship, particularly Engin Isin's (2009) notion of activist citizenship.

To understand the importance of women's situated knowledge,[9] I draw on the experiences of feminist participants during the winter 2012 mobilisations, in order to acknowledge their involvement, struggles, and understandings of the dynamics of the University Square protests. This research takes a qualitative approach; data were gathered through detailed participant observation between January and March, along with in-depth interviews with 15 feminist

---

[7]One such organisation was *Centrul pentru Dezvoltare Curriculara si Studii de Gen, Filia* (Center for Curricular Development and Gender Studies, Filia), which published a declaration entitled 'Centrul FILIA este present la protestul din Piata Universitatii. De ce?' ('FILIA Centre is present at the University Square Protests. Why?'). After the discussions that took place during the General Assemblies Filia officially withdrew from participating in the protests as an organisation, leaving the possibility for its members to participate individually. More information about the organisational participation of Filia Centre at the 2012 protests can be found in 'Revista presei de gen', *Feminism Romania*, 16–22 January 2012, available at: https://www.feminism-romania.ro/presa/revista-presei/723-revista-revista-presei-16-22-ianuarie-2012-sp-1392421415, accessed 12 October 2017.

[8]During the University Square mobilisations, protesters gathered in General Assemblies, once or twice a week, to discuss their (potential) identity, the guiding principles of the group, and strategies to attract and mobilise people.

[9]Situated knowledge is a concept coined by Donna Haraway (1988) to express the way in which objectivity, as one main principle of positivism, was transformed into feminist objectivity. Feminist objectivity is about limited location and 'situated knowledge', referring to the fact that only a partial perspective promises objective vision (Haraway 1988, p. 583).

TABLE 2

MAIN CHARACTERISTICS OF THE 2012 UNIVERSITY SQUARE PROTESTS

Organisation	There was no pre-existing movement organisations or support from traditional mobilising agents, such as trade unions or civil society organisations, although people involved in these structures participated at the protests.
	While protesters initially displayed their organisational affiliation, in the following days of mobilisations, activists debated and decided to revoke any kind of organisational alliance and to stand up solely as individual citizens.
	After the first two months, when the mobilisations diminished in intensity and protesters started gathering in General Assemblies to organise their efforts, they also decided to form working groups. According to the minutes of the General Assembly from 18 March 2012, seven working groups were created: Politics and policies; New forms of political organisation; Actions and strategies; Communication and PR; University Square Media; Law and legal questions; IT.
Leadership	Officially the University Square protests had no leader. They had a horizontal structure, and even though some higher-profile figures emerged, they mostly represented voices from the University Square mobilisations, not leaders of the protests.
	After Claudiu Crăciun participated in the conference 'The Romanian Democracy: Political Abuse and Citizens' Reaction' organised at the European Parliament on 31 January 2012 related to the Romanian protests, the media tried to portray him as a leader.
Space	The protest space was divided, since Boulevard Magheru crosses University Square. During the first days of mobilisations, the protesters blocked the boulevard while marching.
	Afterwards, protesters, representing distinctly different interests, split into two groups, divided by Boulevard Magheru: the group at the Fountain and the group at the National Theatre with different profiles of protesters.
	Despite the boundary of the Boulevard dividing University Square and the different profiles, each of the two groups pledged solidarity with the other, chanted slogans in support of the other group, and organised small marches across the boulevard to visit the other group.

141

protesters who were either part of NGOs or informal left-wing groups.[10] Some of them were academics. The sample of interviewees was based on three main criteria: self-declared feminist activists who advocated feminist claims during the winter 2012 mobilisations; duration of participation in the protests; and the political groups or organisations to which feminist activists were affiliated or informally networked. Interviews conducted during this research were grounded in feminist standpoint theory, rejecting the supposed neutrality of social sciences that in reality view female informants as objects of the researcher's gaze (De Vault & Gross 2007, p. 178). The interviews were thus encounters between feminist women—the interviewer and interviewees, different in various aspects but also with commonalities, who shared knowledge whilst maintaining a critical and reflexive awareness. Codes of ethics for qualitative research mostly refer to the protection of interviewees' identity by using pseudonyms and changing identifying details, which I have done: the interview data presented in this essay have been anonymised and I use unrelated two-letter signifiers to refer to the interviewees (see Appendix 1). The data collected through participant observation and interviews are complemented with data from the mailing list piata-universitatii@googlegroups.com that was established during the winter 2012 mobilisations to facilitate communication and organisation, the Facebook group of the protests, and relevant blog or newspaper articles.

The essay is organised as follows. The second section provides a brief overview of feminist mobilisation in post-communist Romania. The third section examines the theoretical framework underpinning this research, the dynamics of contention approach and perspectival dualism, complemented by contributions on power and activist citizenship. The fourth section covers the empirical findings, organised in three subsections: redistribution, recognition, and power and empowerment.

Feminist mobilisation in post-communist Romania

Contrary to the expectations of some commentators, the fall of communism in Eastern Europe was not accompanied by the emergence of mass mobilisations in general or the women's movement in particular (Grunberg 2000; Miroiu 2004; Guenther 2011). During democratisation, activism was transactional, professionalised, and lacked potential for broad political mobilisation (Tarrow & Petrova 2007; Cîrstocea 2010). The financial dependency on foreign resources (Gal & Kligman 2003) triggered a premature institutionalisation of social

---

[10]There were approximately 20–30 feminist activists who participated in the winter 2012 mobilisations whose claims were related to gender and sexuality or feminist. Most of them were either informally networked or were affiliated with three feminist groups or organisations, as follows: the Feminist Reading Circle (Cercul de Lecturi Feministe), an anarchist, radical, informal, and non-institutionalised feminist group connected to the Alternative Library Collective; the Front Association, initially a feminist group that built-up and manages the website Feminism Romania (available at: www.feminism-romania.ro) but later became a formal organisation in order to obtain official authorisation for arranging Slutwalk Bucharest in 2011, together with other groups; and the Centre for Curricular Development and Gender Studies, or Filia Centre, a feminist organisation specialising in research and activism and with links to the Masters' programme in Gender Studies at the National School of Political Science and Public Administration (SNSPA). The Filia Centre was 'created in 2000 in order to develop gender studies at academic level, so that they contribute through expertise and epistemic authority to strategies of emancipation in Romanian society'. See: Centrul Filia, available at: http://centrulfilia.ro/istoric/, accessed 5 October 2017.

movements (Della Porta & Diani 1999, p. 246) or the 'NGOisation' of civil society and the women's movement.[11]

In Romania, feminism during the first decade of transition was mainly academic, influenced by liberal feminist theories (Molocea 2015). There was no space for considerations of class, ethnic, and sexual diversity, and there was little capacity for mobilisation (Molocea 2015). Nevertheless, these feminist groups expanded their tactical repertoires over time, particularly during the second decade of post-socialism, as a result of changes in the political context, organisational resources, and personal dynamics. In addition to advocacy or service provision, they began to participate in forms of direct action, such as protests, sit-ins, and occupations (Vlad 2015). The first feminist protest was organised in April 2000, against domestic violence, in response to an article published in *Playboy* entitled 'How to Beat Your Wife Without Leaving Marks'. In 2010, a protest against cuts to childcare benefits took the form of women presenting members of the Boc government with a box of used nappies. Other feminist protests include those organised on 8 March for the International Women's Day (2011, 2012),[12] Slutwalk Bucharest organised in October 2011,[13] the International Day against Violence towards Women organised yearly on 25 November (2011),[14] and the Târgoviște protest in the summer of 2012, organised together with World March of Women.[15]

The January 2012 University Square protests were the first time feminists made their voice heard within a larger popular protest, shouting feminist slogans through megaphones, displaying feminist messages on banners, and participating in protesters' General Assemblies along with other protesters. Until the University Square mobilisations, mass protests in Romania were usually organised by trade unions and rarely represented the intersection of different grievances. Hitherto, academic research has tended to study social movements separately from such organised protests. This approach disguises the processes that create and maintain boundaries between movements and has particular implications for understanding the feminist movement, since its perception as a unitary actor renders invisible participation by women and feminists in other social movements and protests, where their presence is treated

---

[11]'NGOisation' is the process by which external funding contributed to the consolidation of certain organisational forms, such as formalised and professionalised groups (Jacobson & Saxonberg 2013) working on advocacy or service provision (Guenther 2011). This follows Tarrow and Petrova's (2007) notion of the presence of a transactional activism characterising post-communist countries.

[12]For details of the 2012 protest, see: 'De 8 martie luptam', Feminism romania, available at: https://www.feminism-romania.ro/presa/stiri/766-de-8-martie-luptam, accessed 12 October 2017. For the 2011 mobilisation see, 'Vrem reprezentare, nu doar flori si martisoare!', Garbo, available at: http://www.garbo.ro/articol/Social/7229/Vrem-reprezentare-nu-doar-flori-si-martisoare.html, accessed 12 October 2017.

[13]For details of Slut Walk Bucharest see, 'Marsul Panaramelor/SlutWalk Bucuresti', Feminism Romania, available at: https://www.feminism-romania.ro/presa/stiri/608-marsul-panaramelor, accessed 12 October 2017.

[14]For details about the protest see, 'Protest, vineri, 25 noiembrie, stop violentei asupra femeilor', Feminism Romania, available at: https://www.feminism-romania.ro/presa/editoriale/662-protest-vieneri-25-noiembrie-stop-violentei-asupra-femeilor, accessed 12 October 2017.

[15]The feminist protest in Târgoviște was organised on 11 August 2012 as one of the actions organised during the Camp of Young Feminists of Europe of World March of Women that took place in Moroieni, Romania. The declaration of the group denounced a migration system that allows some people to move freely and imprisons others in their territories, poverty resulting from the capitalist, racist, imperialist, and patriarchal system, and the poverty and violence that affect mostly certain women, such as Roma women, women belonging to cultural minorities, young women, lesbians, trans and queers, elder women, and many more. The declaration can be found on the blog Young Feminist Camp, available at: https://youngfeministcamp.wordpress.com/2012/08, accessed 5 October 2017.

as an exception, rather than as a regular characteristic of their activism (Ferree & Roth 1998, p. 626). To fill the gap, this research addresses the role of the feminist participation during the winter 2012 protests in University Square in influencing the dynamics of the mobilisations.

Extending social movement theory: redistribution, recognition, and empowerment

The predominant classical social movement approaches include political opportunities (Meyer 2002; Kriesi 2004; Campbell 2005), resource mobilisation (Jenkins 1983; Zald 1991), collective action frames (Snow 2004; Snow & Corrigall-Brown 2005),[16] and repertoires of contention (Tilly 1995; Taylor & Van Dyke 2004; Taylor & Rupp 2005; Tarrow 2011). Criticising these approaches to social movements for treating such movements as static, McAdam *et al.* (2001) developed the DCA by redefining core concepts to capture the relational features of contention and advance a dynamic, encompassing model of the mobilisation process. In order to have a real impact on individuals as prospective challengers, political opportunities and threats must be seen as subject to attribution, rather than to objective structural factors and must meet two *sine qua non* criteria: namely, they must be visible to potential challengers; and be perceived by those challengers as an opportunity/threat (McAdam *et al.* 2001, p. 43). Rather than concentrating on already existing structures, as resource mobilisation theory does, DCA shows that challengers are more likely to have organisational deficits rather than resources, and focuses instead on how existing resources are appropriated and used for mobilisation purposes (McAdam *et al.* 2001, p. 44). Framing is seen as developing dynamically from the interaction between contenders, adversaries, the state, third parties, and the media with increased attention to innovative repertoires of action (McAdam *et al.* 2001, p. 44).

Although informed by a structuralist tradition, DCA addresses social interactions, relationships, and communication not solely in structural, rational consciousness, or cultural terms, but more 'as active sites of creation and change' (McAdam *et al.* 2001, p. 22), considering negotiation either in a general manner, or particularly regarding identities as part of the dynamic of contention processes (McAdam *et al.* 2001, p. 22). It captures the dynamic interaction between actors and identity and connects their transformations during contentious actions with the altered trajectory and outcomes of the mobilisation process. Rather than explaining regularities through standard sequences within trajectories of contention, DCA finds that regularities actually lie within the mechanisms that affect actors' formation, mobilisation, or elimination and those adjusting the strategies adopted and the alliances established.

Although DCA provides a good foundation from which to explore social movements in a dynamic way, it is necessary to further refine the theoretical framework to incorporate appeals to social justice and to apply a feminist optic to the University Square protests. Struggles and claims based on social justice are divided between redistribution, aiming at a just share of resources and welfare, and recognition of marginalised groups and people (Fraser &

---

[16]Collective action frames are 'action-oriented sets of beliefs and meanings that inspire and legitimate the activities and campaigns of a social movement organization' (Benford & Snow 2000, p. 614). Oppressive frames refer to those action-oriented ideas and understandings used by social movements that are based on beliefs that help maintain and reproduce racism, sexism, classism, homophobia, transphobia and ableism, and that objectify and devaluate the subjectivity of those who are subjugated within these systems of injustice. An intersectional resistance to oppressive frames responds to complex configurations of social inequalities such as the interrelation and interaction between interlocking systems of oppression.

Honneth 2003, p. 7). To enquire about the cultural replacing the material or identity replacing class is inadequate, since it confines recognition to identity politics and ignores the dynamic relationship between redistribution claims and challenges to misrecognition (Hobson 2003, p. 1). Equitable distribution of economic resources and access to social goods are associated with the end of subordination related to race, ethnicity, gender, sexuality, or citizenship.

The fall of communism, free market ideology, and the ascendancy of identity politics played an important role in downgrading redistribution claims, especially in CEE, but also in other parts of the world where demands for recognition are increasingly predominant (Hobson 2003, p. 8). Redistribution and recognition claims are frequently analysed separately. Within feminist movements, redistribution claims as a corrective to masculine domination are disconnected from those for recognition of gender difference as a reciprocal relation between equal but separate subjects (men and women). This illustrates a wider trend of dissociating cultural politics from social politics, or the politics of difference from the politics of equality (Hobson 2003, p. 8). To address this artificial distinction, 'perspectival dualism' perceives redistribution and recognition as two interconnected dimensions of justice. In order to clarify how recognition and redistribution have been construed as antithetical, Fraser and Honneth reconstruct the folk paradigms of justice, defined as 'sets of linked assumptions about the causes of and the remedies for injustice' that inform contemporary struggles and social movements (Fraser & Honneth 2003, p. 11). To avoid obscuring either the identity forms of economic injustice, or the recognition dimension of class struggles, rather than aligning redistribution with class politics or recognition with identity politics, they should be approached as two different components of social justice in every social movement (Fraser & Honneth 2003, pp. 11–2). Different forms of subordination contribute concomitantly to class and status subordination in contemporary capitalist societies becoming entwined and manifested transversely across social movements (Fraser & Honneth 2003, p. 48).

While class structure refers to the institutionalisation of economic mechanisms that 'systematically deny some of its [society] members the means and opportunities they need in order to participate on a par with others in social life', the hierarchical status order represents the 'institutionalisation of patterns of cultural value that pervasively deny some members the recognition to fully participate as partners in social interaction' (Fraser & Honneth 2003, p. 49). Social welfare creates and ranks various subject positions or stigmatises and devalues certain recipients, so redistribution claims affect recognition (Fraser & Honneth 2003, pp. 64–5). Proposals to remedy androcentric evaluative patterns that have economic effects on the targeted beneficiaries show the potential effects of recognition on distribution (Fraser & Honneth 2003, p. 65). To foster parity of participation and the achievement of social justice, social movements claim both 'recognition' for categories of personhood and 'redistribution' of material resources (Gal 2003, p. 93).

Acknowledging that injustices and struggles over power include moments of recognition or redistribution, but are not reducible to them, Ferree and Gamson (2003, p. 35) complement the 'perspectival dualism' model with the dimension of power. Starting from feminist critiques of conventional stratification models,[17] they integrate power analysed both as autonomy, reflecting the individual level of self-determination, and as authority, referring to actual participation in decisions at the societal level. Personal autonomy and collective authority reveal relational attributes of power as the determinants of the relations between the community and individuals (Ferree & Gamson 2003, pp. 36–7). Power struggles have implications for both redistribution and recognition, as the empowerment of women—a central goal of much feminist organising—occurs in close interaction with women's race and class (Ferree & Martin 1995, p. 23).

Framing problems collectively rather than individually gives a sense of 'we-ness'. Within the feminist movement, this translates into solidarity among women, a feeling of connection, the power to act collectively, and a sense of empowerment (Ferree *et al.* 2002). Empowerment can be fostered through citizenship, but citizenship can also enforce the domination of one group over another (Isin & Turner 2002). An institution that 'governs *who* are citizens (insiders) and non-citizens as their others (strangers, outsiders) and abjects (aliens) and *how* these actors are to govern themselves and each other through a body politic' (Isin 2012, p. 150), citizenship contributes to domination and empowerment separately or simultaneously (Isin 2009, p. 369). Becoming a citizen means either to adopt insider modes and forms of conduct or to challenge them through identification, differentiation, or recognition (Isin 2009, p. 369). What constitutes the proper modes and forms of conduct to perform citizenship represent the object of struggles between 'citizens, subjects and abjects through claims to citizenship as justice' (Isin 2012, p. 151).

The distinction between 'active' and 'activist' citizens shows how the two essential and irreducible dimensions of justice—redistribution and recognition—are interrelated. Acts of citizenship can foster empowerment. While active citizens act out of 'already existing scripts' such as paying taxes or voting, activist citizens create and perform the scene and the scripts (Isin 2009, p. 381), challenging the law that misrecognises them and disrupting already established societal arrangements in their pursuit of justice. One example would be claims to justice by *sans-papiers* when they do not have the capacity, legally, to make such claims (Isin 2009, p. 382).

The theoretical framework presented above, which draws on the interrelated concepts of redistribution, recognition, and empowerment, will be used in the following sections to provide a gender-sensitive analysis of the 2012 University Square protests, highlighting the role of feminist activists and their contribution.

Redistribution

As political opportunities go beyond objective structural factors, the proposed liberalisation of the emergency medical system that triggered the 2012 mobilisations in Romania should be understood in the wider context of austerity measures promoted by the Boc government during the economic crisis. The gendered consequences of the austerity measures have been

---

[17]Such critiques distinguish between economic stratification and general social stratification and emphasise the need to widen the perspective on stratification by including, along with the dimension of inequality expressed in terms of differential access to and control over economic resources, the dimensions of autonomy, understood as freedom to make life choices and freedom of movement and power in the sense of participation in decisions concerning the specific group (Ferree & Hall 1996).

examined previously (Băluță 2011 p. 124; Barry 2014; Rafferty 2014).[18] The restructuring of the National Agency for Equal Opportunities between Men and Women (ANES)[19] made it difficult to gender mainstream the public policies implemented during the crisis, and was criticised domestically.[20] Law 118/2010 decreased salaries by 25% in the public sector, which is characterised by a preponderance of women workers and significant gender pay inequalities. Pensions were reduced by 15% and VAT was increased by 5%, disproportionately affecting the purchasing power of the poor. This affected women more, given the feminisation of poverty and the high gender gap in pensions.[21] Social transfers were decreased and the health sector was restructured with many hospitals closing or merging with others, which increased *inter alia* women's informal unpaid care work at home (Băluță 2011).

One interviewee from the Alternative Library[22] collective in Bucharest explained that she saw the Raed Arafat issue as integral to the austerity measures and difficulties that people had faced for many years, which were exacerbated during the crisis. This had encouraged her to engage in the mobilisations as a critique of the neoliberal system, the state, the political class, and the supra-structures and entities such as the EU and its institutions 'playing' with peoples' lives.[23] Many interviewees emphasised the austerity measures as a reason for their participation in the protests. This was reported both by the Romanian and international press; for example, CNN reported police repression and brutality towards protesters mobilised against 'austerity measures and poor living standards' (Ciobanu 2012).

Maldistribution was also a motivation behind feminist participation. Accounts vary between those feminists positing that redistribution claims prevailed and those maintaining that recognition demands predominated. Nevertheless, many slogans were related to demands for equitable distribution, such as: 'we want day care and kindergartens not kerbs and other

---

[18]'The Price of Austerity—The Impact on Women's Rights and Gender Equality in Europe', European Women's Lobby (EWL), 15 November 2012, available at: http://www.womenlobby.org/EWL-publishes-report-on-impact-of-the-austerity-measures-on-women-s-rights-and, accessed 3 September 2017.

[19]The National Agency for Equal Opportunities between Men and Women (*Agentia National+a pentru Egalitatea de Sanse intre Femei si Barbati*—ANES) was disbanded through a government emergency ordinance No. 68 on 30 June 2010. See, 'OUG 682010 privind unele masuri de reorganizare a MMFPS', Ministry of Labour, Family and Social Protection by the Romanian Government, Official Journal No. 446, 1 July 2010, available at: http://www.mmuncii.ro/pub/imagemanager/images/file/Domenii/Egalitate%20de%20sanse/OUG%2068-2010%20privind%20unele%20masuri%20de%20reorganizare%20a%20MMFPS.pdf, accessed 12 October 2017.

[20]A total of 19 NGOs and five academics from across the country signed a letter of protest related to the abolition of ANES. The letter was submitted to the Prime Minister and the Minister of Labour. Moreover, five female Romanian MEPs appealed to the European Commission regarding the 'abusive decision' taken by the Romanian government to disband the institutional frame for gender equality, child rights, and the rights of persons with disabilities (Sarbu 2010).

[21]In 2009 in Romania the gender gap in pensions was 32%. The gender pay gap in the public sector was 12.3% and 4.6% in the private sector. See, 'The Gender Gap in Pensions in the EU', Directorate-General For Justice, European Commission, 2013 available at: http://ec.europa.eu/justice/gender-equality/files/documents/130530_pensions_en.pdf, accessed 7 October 2017. The gender gap in pensions in 2010 was 32% and in 2012, 31%, according to 'Gender Gap in Pensions in the EU. Research Note to the Latvian Presidency', European Institute for Gender Equality, 2015, available at: http://www.eige.europa.eu, accessed 7 October 2017.

[22]The Alternative Library is the initiative of an informal group with the aim of sharing information and serving as a venue for discussion on initiating social change. The website of the Alternative Library and additional information about the group can be found on the blog 'Biblioteca Alternativa', available at: https://biblioteca-alternativa.noblogs.org/despre-biblioteca/, accessed 5 October 2017.

[23]RI, member of the Feminist Reading Circle, Bucharest, 10 April 2013.

airs and graces',[24] or 'we want hospitals not churches'. The latter slogan targeted government hospital closures, a measure that increased women's burden of caring for family dependents. These slogans were adopted by other protesters. As one member of the Front Association explained, they were demands with which everybody could empathise, and not necessarily from a feminist perspective. Those who were shouting them might have traditional views about gender roles, yet regard care-related slogans as legitimate and relevant to themselves.[25]

One interviewee, from the Filia Centre, emphasised that while participating in the mobilisations, her plan was to gender the anti-austerity slogans by highlighting how austerity measures affected men and women differently. Her goal was to make the feminisation of poverty visible in the context of austerity measures. The general reaction she received from other protesters was that 'everybody is poor' and 'everybody has a problem'. This should be understood in the context in which many protesters had lost their jobs or suffered salary cuts, and consequently the message about the feminisation of poverty was not perceived as valid by the other protesters.[26] By contrast, gendering other types of slogans such as 'Ale, ale, ale ale ale, indignant citizens want to be respected' ('Ale, ale, ale ale ale, cetățeni indignați vor să fie respectați') had greater resonance among the protesters.[27]

Gendered redistribution claims made by feminists affected the collective frames in terms of justice, contributing to their creation and re-creation by opposing resistance to the heteronormative patriarchal frame, or at least by interrogating the dominant discursive field. The 2012 mobilisations involved different actors from social movements. Although the general frame was built upon a democratic discursive perspective, several competing frames were evident during the protests.

To understand feminist resistance processes within protest dynamics, frame resonance[28] becomes important, since it reflects the cultural understandings of potential supporters and their location in the current political context (Snow & Corrigall-Brown 2005, p. 232). Feminist protesters found it difficult to accommodate racist, heteronormative and neoliberal frames reflecting a patriarchal, racist and capitalist society. When frames are not culturally and politically resonant, they are likely to remain invisible and be silenced. As part of the everyday struggle during the mobilisations, feminist frames were constantly resisted and challenged. One interviewee from the Alternative Library explained that she felt constantly under siege within the group of protesters, which she ascribed to her position as 'a woman, young, without social legitimacy, but also because [I am] a feminist and [I have] a radical perspective'.[29]

The dilemmas protesters have regarding the means of expressing discontent and preserving solidarity reveal impasses about how to give course to grievances and advance political action and show the complexity of both the occurrence and dynamics of mobilisation (Williams 2004, p. 94). During the mobilisations, different ideological perspectives and ways of practising

---

[24]This slogan makes reference to the fact that the government always finds financial resources to restore kerbs, for example, that are already in a good condition, but they do not allocate money for much needed services such as kindergartens whose number has dramatically decreased after the 1990s.

[25]IC, member of the Front Association, Bucharest, 30 April 2013.

[26]ER, Filia Centre, Bucharest, 14 April 2013.

[27]In its gendered version, this slogan became 'Ale, ale, ale ale ale, cetățene indignate, vor să fie respectate' ('indignant female citizens want to be respected').

[28]Frame resonance refers to the '"fit" between frames and audiences' previous beliefs, worldviews, and life experiences' (Williams 2004, p. 105). Thus, whatever frames social movement actors use, they must 'resonate' if audiences are to respond (Williams 2004).

[29]CL, member of the Feminist Reading Circle and Alternative Library collective, Bucharest, 16 April 2013.

feminism affected how activists developed their claims. Two main perspectives regarding the economic system and redistribution claims appeared. One concerned the need for a coherent and consolidated welfare system within a democracy, with a moderate critique of neoliberal policies. The other incorporated maldistribution and economic injustices within a wider anti-system, anti-colonial and anti-capitalist framework. These feminist positions were associated with various groups of protesters and alliances were created based on this ideological proximity. The moderate feminist protesters favouring incremental change within a democratic framework were associated with the group around Claudiu Crăciun, one of the informal leaders of the mobilisations who espoused a European democratic agenda.[30] The radical feminist challengers were associated with the Alternative Library and the Common Space,[31] which produced alternative discourses. A member of the latter group explains that she was aware of different ideological positions from the Slutwalk Bucharest protest.[32] Though she stood in solidarity with more moderate feminists, she protested with the Alternative Library group advocating feminism integrated into an anti-authoritarian, communitarian, and anti-colonial perspective.[33] By contrast, another feminist displaying a banner reading 'I love democracy', a popular slogan during the protests, stated that she disagreed ideologically with a message that put sexism, homophobia, and capitalism on an equal footing, explaining that she 'wouldn't blame capitalism that much', but rather people who do not inform themselves or pay attention to capitalism's negative impact.[34]

During the 2012 demonstrations in University Square some feminists also employed specific tactical repertoires such as 'guerrilla actions' (for example, organising into small groups to distribute flyers about the effects of austerity measures). They raised awareness among women regarding political participation and rights, explained why it was crucial to join the mobilisations, and convinced some women to participate. The discussions facilitated the understanding of the status of frame resonance and the discursive articulation between women as protesters and claim-makers, and women as audience and potential challengers.

Feminist activists deployed redistribution messages within the framework of the gendered impact of the financial and economic crisis, proposing competing frames, alternative to the general ones already displayed in the University Square and ensuring that their claims reached an audience both of potential supporters and already mobilised protesters. When the University Square protest was consolidated through General Assemblies, working groups and discussions on the protest group's identity, the feminist strategy was to socialise mobilised people with

---

[30]Claudiu Crăciun is a lecturer at the National School of Political Studies and Public Administration and ex co-president of the Green Movement–Democratic Agrarians party (*Mișcarea Verzilor–Democrați Agrarieni*) in Romania. He was one of the most vocal and visible figures during the University Square mobilisations in 2012 and was identified as a leader by the mainstream media (Mungiu-Pippidi 2012).

[31]The Alternative Library appeared at the initiative of an informal group, with the aim of sharing a series of materials meant to contribute to the development of critical thinking towards the world and the society in which we live, while also serving as a site for discussion on initiating social change. It is organised according to the principle of participation and non-hierarchy. It represents an autonomous, non-profit project, based on the voluntary contribution of those who want these kinds of spaces to exist, develop, and remain independent of European or any institutional funding. See the section 'About the Library', Alternative Library, available at: https://biblioteca-alternativa.noblogs.org, accessed 12 October 2017.

[32]Slutwalk Bucharest was organised on 6 October 2011, as the Romanian version of the transnational movement of the same name. Women and feminist activists called for an end to rape culture and blaming victims of sexual aggression. Participants held carnations in their mouths as part of their tactical repertoire.

[33]CL, member of the Feminist Reading Circle and Alternative Library collective, Bucharest, 16 April 2013.

[34]BE, Bucharest, 22 April 2013.

feminist principles of justice.[35] Yet, as noted above, while some messages and slogans gained the attention of protestors and were taken up, others proved more difficult to accommodate.

Recognition

During the University Square mobilisations, protesters gathered in General Assemblies to discuss their (potential) identity, the guiding principles of the group, and strategies to attract and mobilise people. Feminist activists found themselves in a difficult position during General Assembly negotiations, due to their continuous resistance against a patriarchal way of organising or intolerant oppressive frames.

Despite tensions regarding the acceptance of differences, the fact that feminist activists recognised themselves as part of the same movement and acted in solidarity affected the process of building a collective identity, in the case of the general group and during the mobilisations. As a group sharing feminist principles, making feminist claims, and shouting feminist slogans, they built alliances with women of all ages who responded to their message and broke what they called 'a traditional dynamic' of protest mobilisations in which men would have organised among themselves, taken decisions about actions and strategies, while delegating responsibilities to women if they felt it was appropriate.[36]

Interviewees who had participated in other generalist protests prior to University Square noticed the significant difference made by having a feminist group deploying its particular claims within the more general mobilisations.[37] At the beginning of the protests, feminist slogans were not shouted and women did not have access to the megaphone. By the time they ended, however, protesters accepted their slogans and gendered messages shouted through the megaphone. This persistent expression of the feminist identity and the constant presence of feminists in the University Square affected the framings of justice and helped to deconstruct stereotypes related to women, feminists, and feminism. In seeking 'to integrate as much feminism as possible'[38] within the group of protesters, the feminists thus contributed to the destabilisation of the general discourse by providing alternative messages.[39]

In drawing boundaries and defining who was a 'real' protester, time became a crucial variable challenging both the relationships within the group of feminists and between them and other protesters. Daily participation in the mobilisations was considered proof of solidarity. The more time a person was committing to the protests and to the General Assembly, the more s/he was perceived as an insider. One interviewee recalled that:

> After the first day at the protests, I don't know what happened, but I stayed there until March. Almost three months. And I remember during my first cold when I stayed few days at home, I organically felt the absence of the University Square … and I was asking myself to what extent the protest actions are rational and how much emotional.[40]

[35]ER, Filia Centre, Bucharest, 14 April 2013.
[36]ER, Filia Centre, Bucharest, 14 April 2013.
[37]ER, Filia Centre, Bucharest, 14 April 2013; RI, member of the Feminist Reading Circle, Bucharest, 10 April 2013.
[38]ER, Filia Centre, Bucharest, 14 April 2013.
[39]TS, member of the Feminist Reading Circle, Bucharest, 14 April 2013.
[40]RI, member of the Feminist Reading Circle, Bucharest, 10 April 2013.

Despite the gendering of slogans during the protests, however, many feminists felt they were merely being tolerated rather than achieving genuine recognition. One member of the Alternative Library explained that only a specific type of feminism was actually accepted. Nonetheless, this interviewee believed that feminist participation allowed voices to be heard that were not only male, as is the case during most political struggles when the multitude of women's experiences and voices are overlooked.[41]

Challenging status subordination at the micro and intragroup levels became one of the main goals for feminist protesters. One interviewee said that because she did not believe in the power of slogans such as 'Down with Băsescu', she tried acquainting the other protesters with the principles of justice promoted by feminism. By contesting 'unacceptable' attitudes, slogans, or repertoires of action such as episodes of racist violence towards Roma protesters or the display of fascist symbols, feminist protesters destabilised the general dynamics. As one respondent explained, she knew that she did not have the authority to send someone home, but when one of the protesters started distributing anti-abortion leaflets, she confronted the person, not caring whether she had the authority.[42] Many feminists emphasised that it was a constant struggle to react against sexist, homophobic, racist, or nationalist attitudes voiced by various protesters in University Square. This was most clearly emphasised after the protesters finally disbanded, and feminists were accused of destroying the mobilisations.[43]

Particularly illuminating in this regard was an event organised by patriotic and nationalist protesters to celebrate Romania's union with Bessarabia. In the General Assemblies and online, strong disagreements emerged regarding racism and reproductive rights and the organisation of this particular patriotic event. Clashes ensued after feminist activists, along with other protesters, held a counter-protest, carrying banners reading 'Nationalism gives birth to monsters'. During the next General Assembly, feminist protesters questioned racist and sexist attitudes expressed during the 'Bessarabia' event and on the online platform. Some of them pressured other participants to make their position clear on these contentious issues, and difficult conflictual discussions took place about a set of principles that would guide the protest group: promoting non-discrimination and a firm rejection of extremism, that is, xenophobic, racist, misogynistic, and homophobic attitudes.[44] The 'Bessarabia' event organisers opposed these principles and revealed themselves to have extreme rightwing, nationalist views. Feminists and other protesters subsequently withdrew from the group and from the mobilisations.

By forcing the uncomfortable discussion regarding the participation of extreme-right and nationalist adherents, feminists precipitated the disintegration of the protest group, by persuading other protesters to take a clear position on this issue. One interviewee stated that the main resistance to the inclusion of nationalist elements during the protests came from feminist activists or those with a feminist orientation.[45] She noted that nationalist protesters objected to feminist perspectives, since feminists were challenging discourses and practices

---

[41]RI, member of the Feminist Reading Circle, Bucharest, 10 April 2013.

[42]ER, Filia Centre, Bucharest, 14 April 2013.

[43]Discussions on the online platform of the University Square protesters, piata-universitatii@googlegroups. com, after the group broke apart.

[44]ER, Filia Centre, Bucharest, 14 April 2013.

[45]CL, member of the Feminist Reading Circle and Alternative Library collective, Bucharest, 16 April 2013.

embedded in patriarchal, heterosexist, and capitalist structures that reinforced unequal power relations and statuses.[46]

The feminists involved in the broader movement behind mobilisations were diverse in many respects: women were part of different organisations; their discourses varied from moderate to radical, from a Marxist, (neo-)Marxist, anti-capitalist, anti-authoritarian, and anti-colonial to a democratic, liberal, and neoliberal one; they had different experiences as women, feminists, and other social positions. While most of the activists were young educated women, they had different political activist careers. Some were part of radical left and anarchist collectives, while others were engaged in institutional politics, or worked in NGOs as employees or volunteers. On the other hand, some came from non-activist backgrounds: students, university professors, and private-sector employees.

In line with the primary theme of this volume, citizenship was framed by some feminist protesters as a basis for claiming rights and recognition in terms of participating on par with others in social life. Citizenship, however, was a debated concept and some activists saw it as limiting and excluding. Some feminists understood citizenship as an unambiguous encompassing concept allowing women to participate, make claims, and stand up for their rights. Their messages were directed towards parity in political participation, representation, and rights for women as 'full citizens'.[47] Many feminist protesters were motivated to join the mobilisation to express their citizenship in an active manner. Their claims to citizenship-related rights were drawn from a discourse framed in terms of numbers and financial contributions to the state. That is, women represent half of the Romanian population and pay taxes. Other feminist activists did not embrace this citizenship approach, although they acknowledged how it was deployed strategically to mobilise protesters. One activist explained that, when talking about democracy, citizenship, and participation, there may sometimes be a place and a need for a more conventional perspective on citizenship framed in terms of representation and financial contributions to the state, but she did not identify with this approach and described it as 'less comminatory, more superficial, and something that in no way alters the substance of the political system and the way it works'.[48] With regard to the framing of gender justice through citizenship by feminists in University Square, another activist remarked that she understood how, strategically, one could appeal to rights and cultivate laws, but in the long run, it was not a position that she embraced or with which she identified. Nevertheless, she stood in solidarity with other feminist activists and shouted their citizenship-related slogans.[49]

Ethnicity became an issue related to citizenship, sparking debates among the feminists when the slogan 'Deşteaptă-te românco!' ('Wake up, Romanian Woman!') appeared during the mobilisations. The message is a reference to the Romanian national hymn—'Deşteaptă-te, române!' ('Wake up, Romanian [man]!'), a patriotic poem, written and published during 1948 Revolution. As one feminist summarised:

---

[46]Although all the feminists were contesting patriarchal relations, not many addressed heterosexism and heteronormativity. For example, AN was one of the few interviewees who clearly emphasised heterosexism as a generalised attitude at least in some specific groups with extreme-right links. Also, the view of capitalism as an oppressive system was mostly held by the feminists associated with the Feminist Lecture Group, the Alternative Library, and Common Space, and was not ideologically supported by other feminists.

[47]DA, member of the Filia Centre, Bucharest, 15 April 2013.

[48]TS, member of the Feminist Reading Circle, Bucharest, 14 April 2013.

[49]CL, member of the Feminist Reading Circle and Alternative Library collective, Bucharest, 16 April 2013.

ACTIVIST CITIZENSHIP IN SOUTHEAST EUROPE

'Wake up Romanian woman' was a message that was intended to be subversive or ironic; however, it was clearly a nationalistic message addressed only to Romanian women. Because in this country there are no Roma women, no Hungarian women, and it is just the Romanian women who need to wake up [ironically]. Even so, apart from the fact that I believe it is very nationalistic, it also seems condescending when you address this message to Romanian women (plural), but you actually use the expression Romanian woman (singular) which is clearly about identity and not about a group of persons. I find it problematic and uncritical.[50]

Thus, some feminist activists in University Square framed women as taxpayers and as ethnic Romanians to justify inclusive representation and participation. Others considered it problematic to frame rights for women in these terms because it dismissed those women not privileged enough to have an income from which to pay taxes, women belonging to minorities, and undocumented women.[51]

The research shows that there was tension amongst feminist activists participating in the 2012 University Square protests with respect to their understandings of the concept of citizenship. While some of them understood citizenship to mean that women had rights as taxpayers and as half of the population and were therefore entitled to participate on par with men in social and political life, others rejected this more conventional understanding of citizenship, reflecting the rupture from 'active' to 'activist' citizenship described in Isin's work.

Overall, many feminist activists felt mostly tolerated during mobilisations, not fully recognised. Feminist positions that were less threatening were more likely to be incorporated into the framing of the protests. When more radical feminist positions became evident during discussions about racism and abortion, the feminists were no longer acknowledged and were seen as causing the polarisation of the group and its disintegration. This underlines how the feminist position was portrayed as threatening for a group that was trying to marginalise it,[52] and supports existing studies that show how a gendered division of labour is present even in the most progressive movements (Falquet 2005; Fillieule 2009, p. 63). Engagement in collective action is thus confined within a gendered system that differentiates and creates hierarchies among militant positions within social movements (Roux *et al.* 2005, p. 5).

Power and leadership

The University Square protests in 2012 were not based on pre-existing movement organisation or structures. The mobilisations did not have an official leader, although different figures became *de facto* spokespeople. After the group of protesters split between those protesting in front of the National Theatre and those protesting at the fountain, Claudiu Crăciun took the role of informal leader in the latter group. On 31 January 2012, Crăciun also made an intervention at the conference 'The Romanian Democracy: Political Abuse and Citizens' Reaction' organised by the European Parliament in response to the Romanian protests. Subsequent to this, the media tried to portray him as a leader.[53]

[50]RM, Bucharest, 25 April 2013.
[51]There are still many Roma families and Roma women who do not have documents in Romania and who cannot exercise any representation-related rights nor access redistribution rights, including basic healthcare.
[52]CL, member of the Feminist Reading Circle and Alternative Library collective, Bucharest, 16 April 2013.
[53]'Petru Zoltan. Claudiu Crăciun, liderul din Piața Universității: "Traian Băsescu ține prizonieră o întreagă societate"', *jurnalul.ro*, 24 July 2012, available at: http://jurnalul.ro/special-jurnalul/interviuri/claudiu-craciun-liderul-din-piata-universitatii-traian-basescu-tine-prizoniera-o-intreaga-societate-619124.html, accessed 8 October 2017.

The feminist group protested at the University Square fountain. Their position towards Crăciun as an informal leader is relevant in terms of how they negotiated the space, the messages, and their voices during the mobilisations. Two moments are of crucial importance. One concerns the daily protests in the University Square, on the fountain side. The other relates to the General Assemblies, constituted after the protests had diminished in intensity (though continuing on a daily basis).

During the first weeks of the daily protests, feminist activists made efforts to voice their claims and to introduce feminist slogans or to gender some of the existing demands, indicating the gendered consequences of the austerity measures undertaken by the government. Initially, other protesters disregarded or opposed their demands, something which the interviewees attributed to the prevailing patriarchal modes of organisation encountered during previous popular protests.[54]

Some feminists insisted that the appearance of a male leader, Crăciun, during the winter 2012 mobilisations, merely reflected the patriarchal character of Romanian society.[55] Others, however, considered Crăciun as a progressive who favoured feminist slogans and messages that would not be visible otherwise. They saw the informal leadership of Crăciun as potentially advantageous, considering him well-organised, reliable, and open-minded.[56] While acknowledging this, one activist from the Alternative Library collective made sure that other voices were heard and alternative messages circulated. In her radical left group, she was encouraged to take the megaphone and add anti-authoritarian or alternative messages to Crăciun's slogans about democracy and Europe, and he gave her space to do so. Nevertheless, she felt that as a young woman she did not have the same recognition from the movement as an autonomous political subject. This resulted in a certain obtuseness concerning her leadership role, which undermined her capacity to campaign to raise public awareness of the feminist agenda.[57] On the other hand, the lack of recognition of women protesters also sometimes worked to the feminists' advantage, since women were rarely stopped and checked by the police.[58]

As feminist messages and slogans were integrated into the general framework of protester grievances, a transfer of authority gradually took place from Crăciun to Oana Baluță, a feminist protester and then president of the Filia Centre. According to one activist, Crăciun knew that he was recognised as an informal leader and from this position he delegated authority to women. For her it was a situation of tokenisation, since not everybody was recognised to the same extent within the protest space.[59] This transfer of authority and position was problematic for some challengers for whom a successful feminist approach implies recognition by everybody as an autonomous political subject based on intersectional solidarities, not just on feminism or anti-capitalism but also along multiple axes of oppression.[60] Movements can be open to

---

[54]ER, Filia Centre, Bucharest, 14 April 2013.

[55]RO, feminist activist, Front Association, Bucharest, 10 April 2013.

[56]CL, member of the Feminist Reading Circle and Alternative Library collective, Bucharest, 16 April 2013; ER, Filia Centre, Bucharest, 14 April 2013.

[57]CL, member of the Feminist Reading Circle and Alternative Library collective, Bucharest, 16 April 2013.

[58]CL, member of the Feminist Reading Circle and Alternative Library collective, Bucharest, 16 April 2013; ER, Filia Centre, Bucharest, 14 April 2013; GO, Filia Centre, Bucharest, 23 April 2013; TS, member of the Feminist Reading Circle, Bucharest, 14 April 2013; RI, member of the Feminist Reading Circle, Bucharest, 10 April 2013; IC, member of the Front Association, Bucharest, 30 April 2013.

[59]IC, member of the Front Association, Bucharest, 30 April 2013.

[60]CL, member of the Feminist Reading Circle and Alternative Library collective, Bucharest, 16 April 2013.

ACTIVIST CITIZENSHIP IN SOUTHEAST EUROPE

feminism and gender equality without radically transforming the gender relationships inside the movement, where it is not just the feminist discourse that is being instrumentalised, but women activists themselves (Roux *et al.* 2005, p. 11).

During a General Assembly that took place in February, a few feminist protesters took the floor to problematise the fact that women's voices and claims were not sufficiently heard. They pointed out that men did all the talking and questioned their capacity to represent everybody and to talk about women's needs. They called for more women to be heard and their demands to be considered. They did not want to be relegated to the background through compromise. However, they were silenced both by men and women, including feminist colleagues.[61] Thus, the different ideological positions and individual or organisational strategic choices of feminist activists did not allow for a cohesive group to form that could promote women's interests through a common agenda. According to an activist from the Filia Centre, intragroup hierarchies and differences in social power and material resources, as well as the short period of mobilisation and the limited experience of feminist activists, explained the lack of desire to build a common feminist agenda during the protests:

> At one point we talked far less about a feminist common agenda although we were a few voices that proposed this .... We often sat and talked often among ourselves, even people who were not from the same feminist organisation, about how to make common strategies at least to bring the discussions closer to a feminist type of interaction. And that was successful, but in a limited way. But a common agenda, the issue was not even raised, primarily because—and this is important to stress—there were many of us, feminists and non-feminists, who did not want an agenda under any circumstances because there were heated discussions about the legitimacy of the group that defines the agenda.[62]

The informal leadership of Crăciun facilitated the process of bringing together generalist and feminist claims.[63] Some feminist protesters had an affinity with his political views and supported his approach, while others were more sceptical. Nevertheless, when the group of protesters participating in the General Assemblies disbanded at the end of the mobilisations, Crăciun tried to reconcile the feminist position with the nationalist, patriotic one, and feminist activists saw this 'soft' approach as problematically adjusting and altering frames in an attempt to artificially maintain coherence within the movement. This illustrates the dilemma for leaders in contemporary movements, who must find a balance between conflicting objectives, strategic alliances, and opportunities. It also shows the difficulty of advancing the claims of women at popular protests without organising a common agenda as women with claims that could be put forward during mobilisations.

Conclusions

Informed by standpoint feminism, this essay explains the role of the feminist movement's participation during the winter 2012 University Square mobilisations in Romania. While DCA allows for a better understanding of the protest events, the 'perspectival dualism' model on recognition and redistribution, Ferree's account of empowerment, and Isin's concept of activist citizenship provide a more nuanced lens through which to examine the way feminist

---

[61]NA, member of the Front Association, 19 April 2013.
[62]ER, Filia Centre, Bucharest, 14 April 2013.
[63]GO, Filia Centre, Bucharest, 23 April 2013.

framing influenced the framings of justice during the mobilisations. The data gathered provide empirical evidence of how feminist participation influenced and challenged the dynamics of these mobilisations, highlighting some of the current difficulties that women are facing and contributing to the visibility of alternative voices and messages.

Although the emergence and trajectory of the street protests was related to austerity measures and maldistribution, feminist claims also addressed the issue of recognition, supporting Fraser's observation that justice requires a struggle for both redistribution and recognition, neither being sufficient on its own. Feminist activists not only upheld their right to protest and to participate in the mobilisations, but also rendered visible their participation as a group. The data show that redistribution claims were more easily adopted by the other protesters and accommodated with the general frame and demands of the mobilisations. Regarding recognition, there was a simple insistence on the feminist presence in the University Square, but at the same time, many feminists had the feeling that they were mostly tolerated rather than truly recognised, and moreover, that only a specific type of feminism was accepted and promoted—that of the active (not activist) Romanian woman citizen who had the right as a taxpayer to participate.

Feminists who participated in other general protests in Romania before University Square in 2012 explained the difference made by the presence of a feminist group advancing feminist claims by deploying feminist messages and slogans. Feminist slogans were not heard from the beginning and women did not have access to the megaphone at the start of the mobilisations. By the end of the protests, the crowd accepted them and protesters were gendering the messages shouted at the megaphone. The persistent expression of a feminist identity and feminists' constant presence during the mobilisations changed the way feminism was perceived. Feminist participants were visible during the protests and made their voice heard, deconstructing some of the stereotypes related to feminist activists and feminism in general.

A significant finding of the research is that the eventual schism amongst the University Square protesters occurred largely because of feminist resistance to the group's accommodation of nationalist discourses. Generally, feminist participation at the protests contributed to a certain degree to the destabilisation of the general discourse through interventions and resistance in the face of persistent nationalist discourse. However, when these positions radicalised during the discussions about racism and abortion, they were no longer accepted. This contributed to the polarisation of the group and was blamed for its disintegration, showing the fact that the feminist position was threatening for a group that was trying to marginalise it. The disturbing and polarising effects of feminist interventions during the protests support the existing research that shows how even within progressive movements, a sexual division of labour reveals contradictions between the promoted ideals of radical transformation and the maintenance of patriarchal elements that impede a real transformation (Falquet 2005).

The research also shows that feminists were a diverse group, ranging from those with a moderate stance to those with a more radical one, from a democratic and citizenship-oriented discourse to an anti-authoritarian, anti-capitalist, (anti-) and (de)-colonialist one. Differences in ideology and in the amount of time spent participating in the protests contributed to the women holding different views about their involvement as feminists.

Regarding power relationships and empowerment, the research revealed their complexity in the context of the protests. Gender, ethnicity, age and other social factors affected how power relations were established, their structural basis, the way they developed, and how the feminist participants experienced them during the winter 2012 mobilisations in Romania. Some feminists considered it problematic that a male leader spoke in the name of women, supporting existing research that documents the monopoly of speech by men during mixed-sex political meetings (Roux *et al*. 2005). While some interviewees emphasised the problem of the transfer of authority from the male leader Claudiu Crăciun to a feminist being seen as tokenism, others argued that he enabled feminist voices to be heard. Feminists generally agreed upon and problematised the fact that even if women made their voices and claims heard, not everybody was able to do so, and that only a specific kind of feminism was mostly advanced and accepted. During the 2012 mobilisations, struggles for power within the leadership arena, within the feminist group, and in relations with the authorities affected the framing process as well as the development of the protest events.

At the most basic level, many feminist activists participating at the University Square protests expressed certainty that if mobilisations happened again, feminist voices would not be ignored. Feminism's visibility and its constant resistance against a patriarchal way of organising, and against nationalist and extreme-right discourses rife with racism, sexism and homophobia, were the most common aspects highlighted by the feminists in terms of outcomes during the research. Although feminist activists recognised each other as part of a wider, more abstract feminist movement, they did not feel themselves to be a cohesive and united group with a common feminist agenda.

The growing literature on post-crisis in Southeast Europe and prevailing accounts of the Romanian protests fail to intersectionally account for the claims, frames, group composition, and organisational forms of movements' mobilisations. This is because protest events are generally organised across specific lines and themes, rarely envisaging the intersection of different claims and actors within popular manifestations, which in Romania were—until the University Square mobilisations—traditionally organised by trade unions. This division also applies within the academic field, where social movements are generally studied separately. The focus on separate social movements disguises the processes that create and maintain boundaries between movements and has particular implications for understanding the feminist movement, since its perception as a unitary actor renders invisible female and feminist participation within other movements and protest events, their presence in those cases being seen as an exception rather than a regular characteristic of their activism. Interrogating this division, the present research has untangled the role of feminist participation during the anti-austerity mobilisations in Romania. Particularly, it shows how feminist movement participation influenced and challenged the dynamics of the winter 2012 protests. This study has made a contribution towards a gendered understanding of the anti-austerity protests in Romania by using Fraser and Ferree's framework, which could also be applied to reveal features of similar events in Bosnia & Hercegovina, Croatia, and other countries in the region.

ACTIVIST CITIZENSHIP IN SOUTHEAST EUROPE

References

Băluță, O. (ed.) (2011) *Impactul Crizei Economice asupra Femeilor* (Bucharest, Maiko).

Ban, C. (2015) 'Beyond Anticommunism: The Fragility of Class Analysis in Romania', *East European Politics and Societies and Cultures*, 29, 3.

Barry, U. (2014) 'Gender Perspective on the Economic Crisis: Ireland in an EU Context', *Gender, Sexuality & Feminism*, 1, 2.

Benford, R. D. & Snow, D. A. (2000) 'Framing Processes and Social Movements: An Overview and Assessment', *Annual Review of Sociology*, 26.

Bulai, A. (2012) 'Lumile diferite ale protestelor din Piata Universitatii 2012 si "ambasadorii" 'lor: constructia dramaturgica a cadrelor de protest', in Stoica, C. A. & Mihailescu, V. (eds) *Iarna vrajbei noastre: protestele din Romania, ianuarie-februarie 2012* (Bucharest, Paideia).

Campbell, J. L. (2005) 'Where Do We Stand? Common Mechanisms in Organizations and Social Movements Research', in Davis, G. F., McAdam, D., Scott, W. R. & Zald, M. N. (eds) *Social Movements and Organization Theory* (Cambridge, Cambridge University Press).

Ciobanu, L. (2012) 'Police Clashes with Protesters in Romania', *CNN*, 15 January, available at: http://edition.cnn.com/2012/01/14/world/europe/romania-protests/index.html?eref=rss_latest, accessed 3 September 2017.

Cîrstocea, I. (2010) 'Du «genre» critique au «genre» neutre: effets de circulation', in Marques-Pereira, B., Meier, P. & Paternotte, D. (eds) *Au-delà et en deçà de l'état: Le genre entre dynamiques transnationales et multi-niveaux* (Louvain-La-Neuve, Bruylant Academia).

De Vault, M. L. & Gross, G. (2007) 'Feminist Interviewing. Experience, Talk and Knowledge', in Hesse-Biber, S. N. (ed.) *Handbook of Feminist Research, Theory and Praxis* (Thousand Oaks, CA, Sage Publications).

Della Porta, D. (2013) 'Repertoires of Contention', in Snow, D. A., Della Porta, D., Klandermans, B. & McAdam, D. (eds) *The Wiley-Blackwell Encyclopaedia of Social and Political Movements* (Malden, MA, Wiley).

Della Porta, D. & Diani, M. (1999) *Social Movements. An Introduction* (Oxford, Blackwell Publishing).

Falquet, J. (2005) 'Trois questions aux mouvements sociaux «progressistes ». Apports de la théorie féministe à l'analyse des mouvements sociaux', *Nouvelles Questions Féministes*, 24, 3.

Ferree, M. M. & Gamson, W. A. (2003) 'The Gendering of Governance and the Governance of Gender, Abortion Politics in Germany and the USA', in Hobson, B. (ed.) *Recognition Struggles and Social Movements. Contested Identities, Agency and Power* (Cambridge, Cambridge University Press).

Ferree, M. M., Gamson, W. A., Gerhards, J. & Rucht, D. (2002) *Shaping Abortion Discourse. Democracy and the Public Sphere in Germany and the United States* (Cambridge, Cambridge University Press).

Ferree, M. M. & Hall, E. J. (1996) 'Rethinking Stratification from a Feminist Perspective: Gender, Race, and Class in Mainstream Textbooks', *American Sociological Review*, 61, 6.

Ferree, M. M. & Martin, P. Y. (1995) 'Doing the Work of the Feminist Movement: Feminist Organizations', in Ferree, M. M. & Martin, P. Y. (eds) *Feminist Organizations, Harvest of the New Women's Movement* (Philadelphia, PA, Temple University Press).

Ferree, M. M. & Roth, S. (1998) 'Gender, Class, and the Interaction between Social Movements: A Strike of West Berlin Day Care Workers', *Gender and Society*, 12, 6.

Fillieule, O. (2009) 'Travail militant, action collective et rapports de genre', in Fillieule, O. & Roux, P. (eds) *Le sexe du militantisme* (Paris, Presses de Science Po (P.F.N.S.P)).

Fraser, N. & Honneth, A. (2003) *Redistribution or Recognition. A Political-Philosophical Exchange* (London, Verso).

Gal, S. (2003) 'Movements of Feminism: The Circulation of Discourses about Women', in Hobson, B. (ed.) *Recognition Struggles and Social Movements. Contested Identities, Agency and Power* (Cambridge, Cambridge University Press).

Gal, S. & Kligman, G. (2003) *Politicile de gen in perioada postsocialista. Un eseu istoric comparativ* (Iasi, Polirom).

Giulianotti, R. (2002) 'Supporters, Followers, Fans, and Flaneurs: A Taxonomy of Spectator Identities in Football', *Journal of Sport and Social Issues*, 26, 25.

Grunberg, L. (2000) 'Women's NGOs in Romania', in Gal, S. & Kligman, G. (eds) *Reproducing Gender. Politics, Publics, and Everyday Life after Socialism* (Princeton, NJ, Princeton University Press).

Guenther, K. M. (2011) 'The Possibilities and Pitfalls of NGO Feminism: Insights from Postsocialist Eastern Europe', *Signs*, 36, 4.

Haraway, D. (1988) 'Situated Knowledges: The Science Question in Feminism and the Privilege of Partial Perspective', *Feminist Studies*, 14, 3.

Hobson, B. (2003) 'Introduction', in Hobson, B. (ed.) *Recognition Struggles and Social Movements. Contested Identities, Agency and Power* (Cambridge, Cambridge University Press).

Isin, E. F. (2009) 'Citizenship in Flux: The Figure of the Activist Citizen', *Subjectivity*, 29.

ACTIVIST CITIZENSHIP IN SOUTHEAST EUROPE

Isin, E. F. (2012) *Citizens Without Frontiers* (New York, NY, Bloomsbury).

Isin, E. F. & Turner, B. S. (2002) *Handbook of Citizenship Studies* (London, Sage).

Jacobson, K. & Saxonberg, S. (eds) (2013) *Beyond NGO-ization. The Development of Social Movements in Central and Eastern Europe* (Farnham, Ashgate).

Jenkins, C. J. (1983) 'Resource Mobilization Theory and the Study of Social Movements', *Annual Review of Sociology*, 9.

Koopmans, R. & Statham, P. (1999) 'Ethnic and Civic Conceptions of Nationhood and the Differential Success of the Extreme Right in Germany and Italy', in Giugni, M., McAdam, D. & Tilly, C. (eds) *How Social Movements Matter* (Minneapolis, MN, University of Minnesota Press).

Kriesi, H. (2004) 'Political Context and Opportunity', in David, A. S., Soule, S. A. & Kriesi, H. (eds) *The Blackwell Companion to Social Movements* (Malden, MA, Blackwell).

Lipsky, M. (1970) *Protest in City Politics* (Chicago, IL, Rand, McNally & Co).

Margarit, D. (2016) 'Civic Disenchantment and Political Distress: The Case of the Romanian Autumn', *East European Politics*, 32, 1.

McAdam, D., Tarrow, S. & Tilly, C. (2001) *Dynamics of Contention* (Cambridge, Cambridge University Press).

Meyer, D. S. (2002) 'Opportunities and Identities: Bridge-Building in the Study of Social Movements', in Meyer, D. S., Whittier, N. & Robnett, B. (eds) *Social Movements, Identity, Culture and the State* (Oxford, Oxford University Press).

Millward, P. (2011) *The Global Football League. Transnational Networks, Social Movements and Sport in the New Media Age* (Basingstoke, Palgrave Macmillan).

Miroiu, M. (2004) *Drumul catre autonomie* (Iasi, Polirom).

Molocea, A. (2015) '(Re)constructia feminismului romanesc in cadrul miscarii de femei (1990–2000)', in Miroiu, M. (ed.) *Miscari feministe si ecologiste in Romania (1990–2014)* (Bucharest, Miroiu).

Mungiu-Pippidi, A. (2012) 'Cum să-ți speli rufele la Parlamentul European', *România Liberă*, 1 February, available at: http://www.romanialibera.ro/opinii/comentarii/cum-sa-ti-speli-rufele-la–parlamentul-european-252152, accessed 29 April 2016.

Ovidiu, B. (2012) 'RAED ARAFAT SE ÎNTOARCE LA MINISTERUL SĂNĂTĂȚII, după ce s-a întâlnit cu Băsescu. Mesajul medicului pentru protestatari. Se termină protestele', *gandul.info*, 17 January, available at: http://www.gandul.info/stiri/raed-arafat-se-intoarce-la-ministerul-sanatatii-dupa-ce-s-a-intalnit-cu-basescu-mesajul-medicului-pentru-protestatari-se-termina-protestele-9152098, accessed 12 October 2017.

Presadă, F. (2012) 'Case Study on the Romanian Protests, 2012', *The Resource Center for Public Participation CeRe*, September, available at: http://www.ce-re.ro/upload/Romanian_Bucharest_Protests_2012.pdf, accessed 6 October 2017.

Rafferty, A. (2014) 'Gender Equality and the Impact of Recession and Austerity in the UK', *Revue de l'OFCE*, 2, 133.

Roux, P., Perrin, C., Pannatier, G. & Cossy, V. (2005) 'Le militantisme n'échappe pas au patriarcat', *Nouvelles Questions Féministes*, 24, 3.

Sarbu, D. (2010) 'Declaration', 7 July, available at: https://dacianasarbu.wordpress.com/2010/07/07/comisia-europeana-sesizata-privind-desfiintarea-abuziva-a-anes-de-catre-guvernul-boc/, accessed 6 October 2017.

Snow, D. A. (2004) 'Framing Processes, Ideology, and Discursive Fields', in David, A. S., Soule, S. A. & Kriesi, H. (eds) *The Blackwell Companion to Social Movements* (Malden, MA, Blackwell).

Snow, D. & Corrigall-Brown, C. (2005) 'Falling on Deaf Ears: Confronting the Prospect of Non-Resonant Frames', in Croteau, D., Hoynes, W. & Ryan, C. (eds) *Rhyming Hope and History, Activists, Academics and Social Movement Activists* (Minneapolis, MN, University of Minnesota Press).

Stoica, C. (2012) 'Fatetele multiple ale nemultumirii populare: O schita sociologica a protestelor din Piata Universitatii din ianuarie 2012', *Sociologie Romaneasca*, 10, 1.

Stoica, C. A. & Vintilă, M. (2012) *Iarna vrajbei noastre: protestele din România, ianuarie–februarie 2012* (Bucharest, Paideia).

Stoicu, V. (2012) 'Austerity and Structural Reforms in Romania', *International Policy Analysis* (London, Friedrich Ebert Stiftung), available at: http://library.fes.de/pdf-files/id-moe/09310.pdf, accessed 3 September 2012.

Tarrow, S. & Petrova, T. (2007) 'Transactional and Participatory Activism in the Emerging European Polity the Puzzle of East-Central Europe', *Comparative Political Studies*, 40, 1.

Tarrow, S. (1998) *Power in Movements* (Cambridge, Cambridge University Press).

Tarrow, S. (2011) *Power in Movement: Social Movements and Contentious Politics* (Cambridge, Cambridge University Press).

Tătar, M. I. (2011a) *Participare politică și democrație în România după 1989*, PhD thesis, University of Oradea.

Tătar, M. I. (2011b) 'Votez, deci exist? Un studiu longitudinal al participării la vot în alegerile parlamentare din România', *Sociologie Românească*, 9, 3.

Tătar, M. I. (2015) 'Rediscovering Protest: Reflections on the Development and Consequences of the Early 2012 Romanian Protests', *Journal of Identity and Migration*, 9, 2.

Taylor, V. & Rupp, L. J. (2005) 'Crossing Boundaries in Participatory Action Research: Performing Protest with Drag Queens', in Croteau, D., Hoynes, W. & Ryan, C. (eds) *Rhyming Hope and History, Activists, Academics and Social Movement Activists* (Minneapolis, MN, University of Minnesota Press).

Taylor, V. & Van Dyke, N. (2004) '"Get up, Stand up": Tactical Repertoires of Social Movements', in David, A. S., Soule, S. A. & Kriesi, H. (eds) *The Blackwell Companion to Social Movements* (Malden, MA, Blackwell).

Tilly, C. (1986) *The Contentious French* (Cambridge, MA, The Belknap Press of Harvard University Press).

Tilly, C. (1995) 'Contentious Repertoires in Great Britain, 1758–1834', in Traugott, M. (ed.) *Repertoires and Cycles of Collective Action* (Durham, NC, Duke University Press).

Vlad, I. (2015) 'Dezvoltari in miscarea romaneasca de femei dupa 2000', in Miroiu, M. (ed.) *Miscari feministe si ecologiste in Romania (1990–2014)* (Bucharest, Polirom).

Williams, R. H. (2004) 'The Cultural Contexts of Collective Action: Constraints, Opportunities, and the Symbolic Life of Social Movements', in David, A. S., Soule, S. A. & Kriesi, H. (eds) *The Blackwell Companion to Social Movements* (Malden, MA, Blackwell).

Zald, M. N. (1991) 'The Continuing Vitality of Resource Mobilization Theory', in Rucht, D. (ed.) *Research on Social Movements: The State of the Art in Western Europe and the USA* (Boulder, CO, Westview Press).

Appendix 1.   List of interviews

Ref.	Role/place	Date
GO	Filia Centre, Bucharest	23 April 2013
NA	Member of the Front Association, Bucharest	19 April 2013
AN	Bucharest	3 April 2013
TS	Member of the Feminist Reading Circle, Bucharest	14 April 2013
RI	Member of the Feminist Reading Circle, Bucharest	10 April 2013
ER	Filia Centre, Bucharest	14 April 2013
SM	Bucharest	30 April 2013
BE	Bucharest	22 April 2013
RM	Bucharest	25 April 2013
DA	Member of Filia Centre, Bucharest	15 April 2013
CL	Member of the Feminist Reading Circle and Alternative Library collective, Bucharest	16 April 2013
RO	Feminist activist, Front Association, Bucharest	10 April 2013
JA	Member of the Front Association, Bucharest	23 April 2013
IC	Member of the Front Association, Bucharest	30 April 2013
VQ	Bucharest	20 April 2013

Appendix 2

TABLE A1. Chronology of events

- **8 January 2012**
Under-Secretary of State with Health Ministry, Raed Arafat declares that the proposed healthcare law destroys the integrated emergency system, replacing the mission of saving lives by commercial competition.
- **11 January 2012**
Prime Minister Emil Boc accepts the resignation of Raed Arafat as Under-Secretary of State for the Health Ministry.
- **12 January 2012**
In Targu Mureş, protests start when hundreds of people go into the streets in support of Raed Arafat; 1,500 people participated in the protest.*
- **13 January 2012**
Protests spread to other parts of the country. In Bucharest, protesters gather in front of the National Theatre to support Raed Arafat and march towards Cotroceni Palace, where the numbers of protesters increases to 2,000.
- **14–15 January 2012**
Protests (considered by some as 'violent') continue in Bucharest.
13,000 people across the country are involved in the protests.†
- **17 January 2012**
Raed Arafat returns to the Health Ministry.‡
10,000 people across the country protest§
- **18–19 January 2012**
Protests continue and on 19 January coincide with a Social Liberal Union (USL) political rally received with hostility by protesters; around 2,500 people.

- **23 January 2012**
Teodor Baconschi dismissed as foreign affairs minister. He criticises the University Square protesters.
- **24 January 2012**
Senator Iulian Urban resigns from Democratic Liberal Party (PDL) after calling the University Square protesters 'worms'.
- **25 January 2012**
President Traian Băsescu makes a public statement on the protests, stating that he will not resign.
- **6 February 2012**
Prime Minister Emil Boc resigns with the entire government.
- **7 February 2012**
Feminist protestors in University Square form a self-styled 'feminist guerrilla group'.
- **9 February 2012**
A new government takes office with Mihai Razvan Ungureanu, ex-director of the Foreign Intelligence Service, as prime minister.
- **11 February 2012**
Protests continue on University Square; hundreds of people protest at the Fountain against ACTA (Anti-Counterfeiting Trade Agreement).¶
- **15 February 2012**
Feminist guerrilla action at Obor Square. A dozen female protesters hand out flyers and talk to passers-by about why women were participating in the anti-austerity protests.
- **25 February 2012**
Feminist guerrilla action in Cişmigiu Park.

- **3–4 March 2012**
Screening of Vlad Petri's documentary film about the University Square mobilisation and debate about civic involvement.
- **8 March 2012**
International Women's Day protests in University Square.‖
- **18 March 2012**
General Assembly meeting at Boheme Café; approximately 60 people attend.
- **22 March 2012**
Protests against shale gas; more than 4,000 people protest in Bârlad and hundreds in Bucharest.**
- **23 March 2012**
Feminist activist protests in University Square against sexual harassment; a dozen people are still protesting each day at the Fountain.***
- **24 March 2012**
General Assembly at Café Boheme
- **26 March 2012**
Groups Assembly at Café Boheme to discuss communication with external groups and plan two events: the International Day Of Protest (12 May) and Global Ecology Day (5 June).
- **27 March 2012**
A group of protesters organise a demonstration to celebrate 94 years since the union between Bessarabia and Romania. Feminist activists hold a counter-demonstration.

(Continued)

TABLE A1.   (Continued)

• **31 March 2012**	• **3 April 2012**	• **6 May 2012**
Critic Atac⁺ and other left-leaning activists propose the establishment of an agora (a public open space for assembly and political discussion) in University Square, on the theme of poverty; feminist activists associated with the Alternative Library also participate.	General Assembly Café Boheme; around 50 University Square protesters and activists participate.	A march for democracy;ᐃ University Square protesters and activists who previously gathered in General Assemblies organise a citizens' march for solidarity, dignity, equality, and freedom in response to diminishing participation in the mobilisation.

Sources: **'1.000 de oameni au protestat in fata Cotroceniului. Lozincile pro Arafat s-au transformat in injurii la adresa lui Traian Basescu', *hotnews*, available at: http://www.hotnews.ro/stiri-esential-11185750-miting-pentru-sustinerea-lui-raed-arafat-piata-universitatii-protestatarii-cer-demisia-lui-traian-basescu.htm, accessed 12 October 2017.

†'BILANȚUL PROTESTELOR de luni—13.000 de manifestanți în 52 de localități. "Un întreg arsenal", descoperit la protestari din Capitală', *mediafax*, available at: http://www.mediafax.ro/social/bilantul-protestelor-de-luni-13-000-de-manifestanti-in-52-de-localitati-un-intreg-arsenal-descoperit-la-protestatari-din-capitala-9152022, accessed 12 October 2017.

‡Ovidiu (2012).

§'Raed Arafat revine la Ministerul Sănătății în funcția deținută anterior, după discuții cu Traian Băsescu și Emil Boc', *antena3*, available at: https://www.antena3.ro/actualitate/raed-arafat-revine-la-ministerul-sanatatii-in-functia-detinuta-anterior-dupa-discutii-cu-traian-151815.html, accessed 12 October 2017.

¶'Protest anti-ACTA, 11.02.2012', *rezistenta*, available at: http://rezistenta.net/2012/02/protest-anti-acta-11-02-2012.html, accessed 12 October 2017.

||'FOTO Femeile au sărbătorit 8 martie în Piața Universității', *totb*, 9 March 2012, available at: http://totb.ro/foto-femeile-au-sarbatorit-8-martie-in-piata-universitatii/, accessed 12 October 2017; 'Manifestație de 8 martie în București, Piața Universității', *criticatac*, 8 March 2012, available at: http://www.criticatac.ro/14915/manifestaie-de-8-martie-bucureti-piaa-universitii/, accessed 12 October 2017.

***'Protest în Piața Universității. Aprobarea explorării gazelor de șist scoate iar oamenii în stradă', *antena3*, available at: https://www.antena3.ro/romania/protest-in-piata-universitatii-aprobarea-explorarii-gazelor-de-sist-scoate-iar-oamenii-in-strada-161556.html, accessed 12 October 2017.

****'România micilor proteste Trei demonstrații în două zile sau de la marș pașnic la bătăi cu jandarmii', *stiri.tvr*, available at: http://stiri.tvr.ro/romania-micilor-proteste–trei-demonstratii-in-doua-zile-sau-de-la-mars-pasnic-la-batai-cu-jandarmii_12970.html, accessed 12 October 2017.

⁺Critic Atac is a left wing group and platform of political, social, and intellectual critique, available at: http://www.criticatac.ro, accessed 12 October 2017.

ᐃ'The Epoch Times: Noul hobby al românilor: exercițiul democratic', *un mars pentru democratie*, 9 May 2012, available at: http://unmarspentrudemocratie.blogspot.be/, accessed 12 October 2017.

Index

ableism 144n16
action repertoires: 'Baby Revolution' 17; 'Social Uprising' 19–20
active citizenship: *vs.* activist citizenship 11–12; defined 11
activist citizens 132–3; and her 'sites' 120
activist citizenship 84, 97–101; *vs.* active citizenship 11–12; defined 11–12; everyday resistance and 97–101; 'NGO-isation' 1; political subjectivation and 97–101
Aganaktismenoi 47
All-Slovenian People's Uprising Committee (*Odbor Vseslovenske ljudske vstaje*) 51, 54, 57
Alternative Library Collective 142n10, 147–9, 147n22, 151, 153n52, 154
Arab Spring 53, 67
Arafat, Raed 138
Armenian Church 126
Armenian poetry 132
Association of Publishers of Vojvodina 132
autonomy: described 50; and horizontality 50
Azzellini, Dario 49

Babovic, Nebojša 101
'Baby Revolution' 10–11, 16–18; action repertoires 17; actors and organisational models 18; collective action frames 17
Bayat, Asef 125, 130
bebolucija 22
Beller, Steven 130
Beranselo movement: disagreement between people and state 102–4; enacting impossible identification 107–12; performative staging of equality 105–6; political subjectivation of 101–12; relevance of 112–15
Bey, Hakim 131
Blokadna Kuharica (*Occupation Cookbook*) 39
'Bologna Declaration' *see* European Higher Education Area
Bologna Process 33, 36–7
'Bonn Powers' 14
books: as symbol 124–7; as tools 124–7

Borba Za Znanje (*Struggle for Knowledge*) 26, 34, 38, 39
Bosnia & Hercegovina: 'Baby Revolution' 10–11, 16–18; learning and empowerment between 2013 and 2014 22–3; 'prefigurative politics' 12; protests of 2013–2014 12–13; social and political context of 13–16; 'Social Uprising' 11, 18–21
'Bosnian Spring' *see* 'Social Uprising'
Bsescu, Traian 138
Building Act 70

Central European culture 130
Central European literary coffeehouses 130
Centre for Environment (Banja Luka) 81
CHF Montenegro 101
Cimbaljeviæ, Gojko 101
citizenship 11; active *vs.* activist 11–12; ethnic-based 16; performative and prefigurative practices of 21–2; *see also* activist citizenship
City Assembly Initiative (*Iniciativa mestni zbor*) 56
City of Zagreb *see* Zagreb
Civic Declaration 105
civil society organisations 98, 140
'Claiming Rights' 71
classism 144n16
CNN 147
collective action frames: 'Baby Revolution' 17; 'Social Uprising' 20
collective action frames 144n16
collective identification: processes 28–30; and Serbia 35–6; and student activists 35–6
'comfort-zone activism' 130
commercialisation of education 38–9
Committee for Direct Democracy (*Odbor za neposredno demokracijo*) 54–5
Committee for Social Justice and Solidarity (*Odbor za pravièno in solidarno družbo*) 54
communism 142, 145
Cooper, Davina 121
co-optation 50

INDEX

Coordination Committee of Slovenian Culture (*Koordinarcijski odbor kulture Slovenije*) 54
Council of the Local Community of Beranselo 98
counter-spaces 120–1
Crăciun, Claudiu 149n30, 153
Croatia: Building Act 70; Physical Planning Act 70; regional diffusion 39–41; Right to the City (*Pravo na grad*) protest movement 65–85; *see also* Zagreb
Croatian Spring of 1973 26

Dayton Peace Agreement *see* General Framework Agreement for Peace (GFAP)
Declaration on the European Higher Education Area 33
della Porta, Donatella 27, 61
Democratic Party of Socialists (*Demokratska partija socijalista* (DPS)) 94
diffusion: defined 29; of innovative practices 29–30
Direct Democracy Now! (*Neposredna demokracija zdaj!*) 55
Down syndrome 129
Druga Srbija 36

empowerment: for activists in Bosnia & Hercegovina 22–3; acts of citizenship and 146; and mobilisations in Romania 144–6; social movement theory and 144–6; of women 146
equality, performative staging of 105–6
ethnic-based citizenship 16
European Higher Education Area 4
European Parliament 153
European semi-periphery: contesting neoliberal urbanism on 70–1; political economy of protest on 67–70
European Union (EU) 34, 36–7, 96, 147
everyday activism: activist citizen and her 'sites' 120; counter-spaces 120–1; everyday utopias 121; micro-politics/infrapolitics 121–2; theorising 120–2
everyday resistance 97–101
everyday utopias 121
Federation of Bosnia Hercegovina (FBiH) 14–15

feminist mobilisation, in post-communist Romania 142–4
feminist movement participation: mobilisations in Romania, role in 137–57; University Square protests and 143–4
feminist objectivity 140n9
Feminist Reading Circle (Cercul de Lecturi Feministe) 142n10
Ferree, Myra Marx 140
15-M movement 53
15O Movement *see* Occupy Slovenia

Filia Centre 142n10
financial crisis of 2008 53
Flower Square 72–4
former Yugoslavia: Croatian Spring of 1973 26–7; 'new left' in 27; student-led mobilisations in 30–2
framing: and activists 30; defined 30
Fraser, Nancy 140
Free Team Pokret (Free Team Movement) 129–30, 132
Front Association 142n10, 148, 160

Gamson, William 140
General Framework Agreement for Peace (GFAP) 13–14, 22
Ginty, Roger Mac 125
Glas Slobode (*The Voice of Freedom*) 13
Global Day of Action 53
Goldfarb, Jeffrey C. 122
Green Action 81, 86

Handbook for Life in Neoliberal Reality 69
Haraway, Donna 140n9
hipster activists 130
homophobia 144n16
Honneth, Axel 140
horizontality: and autonomy 50; described 47, 49; politics between verticality and 49–52; and self-organisation 50
Horvat, Srećko 39
'How to Beat Your Wife Without Leaving Marks' 143
Hungarian poetry 128

'Independent Culture and Youth in the Development of the City of Zagreb' 71
Indignados 47, 56, 67
infrapolitics 2, 121–2
Initiative for Democratic Socialism (*Iniciativa za demokratièni socializem*—IDS) 48, 55; and 2012–2013 wave of protests 59; emergence of 57–60; establishment as political party 58–9
Institute of Hydrometeorology and Seismology of Montenegro 101
International Monetary Fund (IMF) 34
'Invisible Zagreb' 72
Isin, Engin F. 11–12, 94, 97, 120

Janša, Janez 48, 55
Jedinstveni matični broj građana (Unique Master Citizens Number—JMBG) 16
#JMBG *see* 'Baby Revolution'

Kangler, Franc 54
Knjižara Gradska 126–7, 131
Korsika, Anej 53

INDEX

leadership: and mobilisations in Romania 153–5; and power 153–5
leadership-centred organisation model 18
League of Communists of Montenegro 94
learning process, for activists in Bosnia & Hercegovina 22–3
Lefebvre, Henri 66, 67, 120–1
Lemijeva Knjižara (Lemi's Bookshop) 125, 127
'Let's Not Drown Belgrade' (*Ne davimo Beograd*) 67, 81
LGBT community 128
LGBT rights 127
Ljubljana 52
Ljubljana Stock Exchange 53–4
Lonèar, Jovan 101
Lubej, Uroš 51, 56–7
Luka Berane (Port Berane) 109

Marchenko, Alla 134
'market logic' 34
MaTerra Mesto initiative 127–8
Matica Hrvatska (Croatian Academy of Sciences and Arts) 31
Mesec, Luka 53
micro-politics 121–2
Milošević, Slobodan 31–2, 35–6
Mi Smo Univerza (We Are the University) 41
mobilisation: and social movements 29; student, in Serbia 30–2
Montenegro 95; as 'ecological state' 101n17; 'non-anonymous' nature of society in 95; political agency of citizens in 96; political subjectivity in 115; post-socialist 110; socio-political landscape 115; statehood status and 95
Mouffe, Chantal 61
'movement parties' 61
'movements of crisis' 68
Muzil in Pula (Croatia) 81

Nacionalni forum za prostor (National Forum for Space) 75
National Agency for Equal Opportunities between Men and Women (ANES) 147, 147n19
nationalism 31
NATO 122
'The Neoliberal Frontline: Urban Struggles in Post-Socialist Societies' 69
networks and entanglements 130–2
'new left' 27
New Social Movement 99
'NGO-isation' 1
non-governmental organisations (NGOs) 1, 97, 119, 139; independent cultural 71–8; youth 71–8; *Zelena Akcija* (Green Action—Friends of the Earth Croatia) 72

Novi Sad Lesbian Organisation (NLO) 127
Nussbaum, Martha 127

Occupy Slovenia 53
Occupy Wall Street protest movement 22, 53, 67
Ogledalo (Mirror) 131
Organisation for Economic Co-operation and Development (OECD) 34
'Other Serbia' (*Druga Srbija*) 32
Otpor! (Resistance!) 32, 36

The Park is Ours' (*Park je naš*) protests 67, 81
Parliament of Montenegro 105
Peace Implementation Council 14
people, and state 102–4
People's Party (*Narodna stranka*) 112
performative practices of citizenship 21–2
performative staging of equality 105–6
Peroviæ, Aleksandar 108
Petrovcic, Peter 56–7
Physical Planning Act 70
Plato 123
Playboy 143
Pokreta 15.0 41
Pokret Uliènih Èitaèa (Movement of Street Readers) 132
political subjectivation 99; activist citizenship and 97–101; of the Beranselo movement 101–12; everyday resistance and 97–101; as unintended consequence of activist citizenship 94–115
Positive Slovenia (*Pozitivna Slovenija*) 56
post-Yugoslav everyday activism(s): activist citizens 132–3; beyond books and coffee 129–30; books as tool s and symbol 124–7; (counter) space 127–8; hipster activists 130; networks and entanglements 130–2; not for profit 123–30; place and method 122–3; theorising everyday activism 120–2
power mobilisations, in Romania 153–5
'prefigurative politics' 4, 12
prefigurative practices of citizenship 21–2
Primorske novice (*Littoral News*) 56
Putnam, Robert 120

racism 144n16
Radio Café 021 131
Rancière, Jacques 94, 99
recognition mobilisations, in Romania 144–6, 150–3
recuperation, of factories 12, 12n3
redistribution mobilisations, in Romania 144–50
Red University of Karl Marx 31
regional diffusion: Croatia 39–41; Serbia 39–41
repertoires: defined 28; and social movements 28–9
Republic (Plato) 123

INDEX

Republika Srpska (RS) 14–15
Right to the City (*Pravo na grad*) protest
  movement 65–6, 77, 81–2
Romania: civil society in 137–8; feminist
  mobilisation in post-communist 142–4;
  power and leadership in 153–5; winter 2012
  mobilisations in 137–57; women in 152–3
'The Romanian Democracy: Political Abuse and
  Citizens' Reaction' conference 153

Scott, James C. 122
self-organisation: described 50; and
  horizontality 50
Serbia: commercialisation of education 38–9;
  'hybrid regime' 31; occupation of 2006 33–5;
  regional diffusion 39–41; student activists in
  33–5; student mobilisation in 30–2
Serbian poetry 128
Serendipiti 124–7, 131–2
sexism 144n16
Sitrin, M. A. 12, 49–51
situated knowledge 140n9
Slobodni Filozofski (Free Faculty of Philosophy) 40
Slobodni Indeks (Free Index) 40
Slovenia: activism history 52–4; alter-
  globalisation campaigns 52; and financial
  crisis of 2008 53; Ljubljana 52; 2012–2013
  waves of protest in 48, 54–7
Slutwalk Bucharest 149n32
social action: challenging the 'productivist
  vision' of 82–5
Social Democratic Party (*Socijaldemokratska
  partija Hrvatske*) 71
Social Democrats (*Socialni demokrati*) 56
social movements 28; and mobilisation 29; and
  repertoires 28–9
social movement theory: empowerment
  144–6; extending 144–6; recognition 144–6;
  redistribution 144–6
'Social Uprising' 11, 18–21; action repertoires
  19–20; actors and organisational models 20–1;
  collective action frames 20
Socijalni Front 38
Solidarity (*Solidarnost*) 57
Solidarity movement 122
Sr ð Is Ours initiative 81
state, and people 102–4
student activists: and collective
  identification 35–6; on commercialisation

of education 38–9; on EU membership and
  Serbia 36–8; and Serbia 33–5; *see also*
  activist citizenship
student mobilisation, in Serbia 30–2
Studentski Plenum (Student Plenum) 40
Study for Regional Landfill Site Selection 101–2
Subversive Festival 39
Syntagma Square protests 67

'tactical networking': described 80; Zagreb 78–80
'Temporary Autonomous Zones' (TAZs) 131–2
Tito, Josip Broz 30
Today Is A New Day (*Danes je nov dan*) 55
Tomović, Đorđije 108
Tonkiss, Fran 121
transphobia 144n16
2012 mobilisations in Romania: empowerment
  144–6; extending social movement theory
  144–6; power and leadership 153–5;
  recognition 144–6, 150–3; redistribution
  144–50; role of feminist movement
  participation during 137–57

UK National Union of Students (NUS) 37
United Left 57–60
University of Belgrade 26, 31, 33

Varšavska Street 75–7
verticality: described 47–8; politics between
  horizontality and 49–52
'Victims of Milan Bandic Square' (*Trg žrtava
  Milana Bandica*) 74–5

Workers' and Punks' University (*Delavsko -
  punkerska univerza*) 57
World March of Women 143
World Values Survey (WVS) 138

Yugoslav Wars 27, 31

Zagreb: Flower Square 72–4; independent
  cultural (NGOs) and youth NGOs 71–8;
  'Invisible Zagreb' 72; 'Operation City' 71;
  Right to the City movement in 67–70; tactical
  shapeshifting 78–80; *see also* Croatia
Združena levica 48
Zelena Akcija (Green Action—Friends of the
  Earth Croatia) 72
Žilnik, Želimir 127